Stan Lee
Conversations.

WITHDRAWN

D1446816

Conversations with Comic Artists
M. Thomas Inge, General Editor

Stan Lee
CONVERSATIONS

Edited by
Jeff McLaughlin

University Press of Mississippi
Jackson

www.upress.state.ms.us

The University Press of Mississippi is a member of the Association of
American University Presses.

Copyright © 2007 by University Press of Mississippi
All rights reserved
Manufactured in the United States of America

First Edition 2007
∞

Library of Congress Cataloging-in-Publication Data

Stan Lee : conversations / edited by Jeff McLaughlin. — 1st ed.
    p. cm. — (Conversations with comic artists)
    Includes index.
    ISBN-13: 978-1-57806-984-2 (cloth : alk. paper)
    ISBN-10: 1-57806-984-X (cloth : alk. paper)
    ISBN-13: 978-1-57806-985-9 (pbk. : alk. paper)
    ISBN-10: 1-57806-985-8 (pbk. : alk. paper)   1. Lee, Stan—Interviews.
2. Cartoonists—United States—Interviews.   I. Lee, Stan.
II. McLaughlin, Jeff, 1962—
    PN6727.L39Z46 2007
    741.5092—dc22
        [B]   2007004983
        British Library Cataloging-in-Publication Data available

Contents

Introduction

In the 1960s and 1970s, Stan Lee transformed the superhero comics genre through his creation and co-creation of such psychologically complex and realistically portrayed heroes as Spider-Man, the X-Men, the Incredible Hulk, the Fantastic Four, Dr. Strange, Daredevil, and Iron Man. His development of the Marvel Universe, a fictional shared universe where most of the Marvel Comics stories take place and in which events from one Marvel comic title would have repercussions in others, revolutionized the industry. As a writer and editor, Lee's collaborations with such legendary artists as Jack Kirby and Steve Ditko brought the aesthetics of cinema and avant-garde art to mainstream comics. As publisher of Marvel Comics, he oversaw the infusion of contemporary politics and current affairs into superhero books. He is recognized as having introduced the idea of letters pages to comics, and of giving artists' credits. No single figure can lay claim to the omnipresent influence that Lee has had on American comic books and on popular culture.

As the public face of Marvel Comics, Lee has worked in every capacity available in the comics industry—writer, editor, publisher, promoter, educator, entertainer, and even actor in films based on Marvel Comics titles. But ultimately he is just a logophile, a lover of words. Lee likes words of all shapes and sizes and meanings, the way they sound, the way they look on the page. He grew up in tough times during the Depression, and he tells interviewers frequently that he's just a fellow who wrote for a paycheck and who happened to be pretty good at his job. Somewhat embarrassed by his vocation, he tells his interviewers that he kept his real name (Stanley Lieber) in reserve for when he'd write the Great American Novel.

He's done much more than that: he has shaped a universe of mythic proportion that has seeped into our collective cultural consciousness. What sets Lee apart from his predecessors and his contemporaries is that his superheroes do not overcome their humanity; instead, they personify it. They have angst, marital troubles, bouts of depression, and they worry about making ends meet. His comics aren't just popular diversionary tales but are stories infused with themes that strike chords with the readers.

In a meeting with the Newspaper Comics Council in the spring of 1972, Lee commented upon the fact that his audience readily identified with his characters:

> If the reader can empathize, he finds some relevance in what is being done, whether it is a serious story or humor. If the reader can identify with the characters and the situations (even though they are not situations that he may experience and the characters may be alien to the characters that he lives among), you have a more successful result.
>
> We publish a book called *Thor*, the story of the God of Thunder. It is about gods and goddesses. When I lectured on campuses, I found the students were asking me more about Thor than about any other character. They asked, for instance, how I relate the Norse legends with the Judeo-Christian philosophy. . . . I was just trying to write good guys and bad guys . . . so I began to realize that you can be relevant if you write with some sincerity, if you make the characters seem real and if you make the public believe in what you are writing.
>
> I don't think "relevance" means that you have to have a sequence which deals with the election or drugs. It is fine if you want to do that, that's relevant too, but I think relevance is simply having characters behave like real people within the real world that you are creating for them.

Lee didn't intentionally write comic books with overtly social or political messages. While he may try to work in a particular point of view or an interesting thought (for example, that the so-called "important people" can be replaced—but the average Joe or Jane is irreplaceable), he aims to show and not tell; he would rather dramatize than proselytize. Indeed, he sees being too serious as a great way to kill the commercial success of a project. As a result, Lee's seriousness is rarely in the forefront of his work—or his interviews.

This is not to say that he has suppressed his desire to speak about important issues such as social injustices and human cruelty, but rather that he has done so delicately, and within the context of promoting his company's work. Even though in his famous campus lectures he and his audience apparently spent time discussing the socio-political issues of the day, when pressed about his personal views on controversial subjects, he often deflects the questions and refuses to comment on topics that he sees as out of bounds or irrelevant to the promotion of Marvel Comics.

Nevertheless, the depth to which he'll discuss topics such as the well-known falling-out between himself and Kirby, or his views regarding comics in general, often depends upon the context of the interview. If the article is intended for general readership then he uses his happy-go-lucky persona. If the interview is conducted by someone who is more closely associated with comics, he tends to be more serious and provides more significant details regarding assorted historical, personal, and creative elements of the industry. In interviews from the 1990s to the present, for instance, he often speaks out to comics insiders about how the business seems to have lost its way, relying upon darker writing and artwork and appealing to comics collectors and not general readers.

Depending upon one's preconceptions, one might be disappointed or admire the fact that Lee remains extremely discreet and is usually loath to "name names." From his standpoint, however, it doesn't serve any good purpose to try and name artists whom he would like to work with, since if he mistakenly forgets one, feelings will be hurt. Nor, he feels, does it help to criticize someone who can't respond.

As you will see in the unedited interviews that follow, the public continues to want to know about the comics Lee has created and nurtured and the creative process behind them. So he has gladly taken questions from mainstream entertainment magazines and online comic fanzines. He's responded to college students and to children's questions with equal respect. He's participated in television and radio talk shows and has answered inquiries ranging from the merely curious to the fanatical. He does all this with a sense of aplomb and reverence towards the general public because he is well aware of his privileged role and the responsibility that goes with it. He learned this as a young boy after receiving a reply to a fan letter that he wrote to one of his childhood heroes, Floyd Gibbons—a daring adventurist/newspaper writer. Thus in most interviews you get a sense that Lee is giving the readers what they want.

And what they want most of all is to hear the old stories, so he entertains the same questions over and over again: How do you get your ideas? Who's your favorite character? Do you prefer to write about heroes or villains? How did you get started in comics? How do you feel about the current comics industry? He treats each one as if he had just heard it for the first time.

Sometimes, however, he has to say "Sorry, I really don't remember." At first, this response sounds evasive, but in interviews with Roy Thomas and myself, it becomes clear that Lee really wishes he could remember every moment of the seven decades he has been at his job. In fact, when he is asked what super-powers he would want, his answer is 1) immortality, and 2) a perfect memory. Almost as proof of his desire for recollection, Lee's extensive use of alliteration when naming his characters was developed not only to make the names fun to say (such as "J. Jonah Jameson") but also because they provided Lee with a way to remember all his characters. If he could recall the last name "Banner," he'd know it was "Bruce Banner," "Brant" would be "Betty Brant," "Murdock" would be "Matt Murdock," and so on.

As a high school student Lee was impressed by the uncanny ability of some individuals (notably fellow student John J. McKenna Jr., and one of Lee's teachers, Leon B. Ginsberg) to hold the undivided attention of their audience. Lee has mastered this skill with his sense of humor. A shy, reserved representative who isn't forthcoming about his or his company's work is not going to get much attention. And this would severely affect his ability to promote the product. Comic books are after all just that: a product that has to be pushed. Lee has no romantic notions behind the decisions to keep or cancel a title. Indeed, one has to remember that Spider-Man was introduced in a book that was being cancelled and that the *Fantastic Four* was potentially a tired Stan Lee's last creation.

Lee has always been an advertising man at heart and in practice. His comic book titles were never just "Ironman" or "the Hulk." They were the "Invincible Ironman," the "Incredible Hulk," the "Amazing Spider-Man," the "Uncanny X-Men," and even the *Fantastic Four* was dubbed by Marvel as "The World's Greatest Comic Magazine!" He's not wont to shy away from hyperboles. This zeal carries over to his personal conversations. Lee's excitement at the littlest of things is almost manic. It's also one of the things that he is so well recognized for. The latest work by so and so is "beautiful and magnificent!" but so too were the bacon and eggs that he had for breakfast. Yet, his enthusiasm seems genuine, as witnesses will attest to in these pages. When I spoke to him of how he has brought so much joy to the lives of so many people, young and old, I saw this man, who is so famously "over the top" with his own playful sense of importance, truly humbled and embarrassed.

A glimpse of Lee's toughness as a creative talent and as a business man, demanding in both roles the best in order to put out the best, can be seen throughout this collection. So when it comes time for him to refer to someone or something in public as "just okay," or "there's something wrong going on," it's time to prick up one's ears and take note. In a 1977 panel discussion, he argues against a business model regarding the fair treatment of artists put forward by fellow panelist Harvey Kurtzman; this might seem ironic given his later lawsuit against Marvel to receive his fair share of the profits of his characters. On a 1972 panel discussion at Vanderbilt University, Lee respectfully disagrees with Kirby on the ability of comics to deal with serious issues.

Lee's criticisms rarely come in the form of petty disagreements or negative personal judgments of the participants involved. He speaks of his extreme disappointment with both the claim of sole creatorship of Spider-Man made by Jack Kirby and Kirby's portrayal of Lee as being fragile. Unfortunately, Lee mistakenly suggests in a later interview that Marvel was happy to give Kirby his artwork back. Whether this is due to his notorious bad memory is not clear. Lee is a constant star, however, when it comes to his admiration for Jack Kirby as an artist.

Whether they work for DC or Marvel (or other comic book companies), he knows how hard the job is for comic book artists, and how rare a talent each of them possesses. And he respects them for it, since he himself demanded the very best from each of them. Instead, he saves his best biting comments for the competition—not only because they were fighting for the same dollar but because the "competition" is a corporation, an abstract entity that can't have hurt feelings. He speaks of how as a consultant on different television shows based on Marvel characters, his suggestions were ignored. He bristles ever so slightly at the mention of the "Golden Age" of comics since he doesn't think that early era deserves that moniker. He is also critical of the quality of comic books before the Marvel Age of the 1960s, even though he recognizes that he himself was one of the best-known writers during the pre-Marvel Age period. In early interviews Lee forcefully defends comics from the critics who see them only as "funny books" and shows how they have intrinsic value as an art form and how they also have value as a means to promote literacy. He's very particular in stressing the *team* aspect in the creative work of all those in the Mighty Marvel bullpen, ensuring that public recognition and credit is given to all those involved. He's a bit hesitant to answer who his favorite character is, but will answer "Spider-Man" if pushed— perhaps only because it's his most successful character or because we just want to hear him say it. But in reality, he is more personally attached to the Silver Surfer. As the most overtly philosophical character in the Marvel universe, the Silver Surfer comments more as a disinterested observer than as a participant.

To that end, this volume includes a philosophically minded poem by Lee, which he considers to be his best unpublished work. Although the poem "God Woke" has been recited before, this is the first-ever publication of it.

Legend. Icon. Consummate professional and compassionate gentleman. The writer whom the world knows as Stan "the Man" Lee is a true lover of words. And for his words, millions love him. Enjoy!

With the exception of silent corrections made throughout, the pieces herein are presented as they originally appeared. As such, there is some repetition, but this allows for Lee's personality and reflections to come through unfiltered.

A project like this that involves tracking down almost forty years of television, radio, and print interviews must recognize the work of many. Not only must I thank the interviewers and publishers who granted me permission to use their materials, but I am also extremely grateful to all those who went out of their way to help me in this quest. And to all those below, thank you!

Adam Glickman, Alan Dulfon, Alastair Mabbott, Amelia Nash, Andre Gailani, Andy Lanset, Angela Meyer, Ann Hinshaw, Barbara Knisely Michelman, Ben Neuhauser, Beverly Railsback, Bill Hahn, Bob Wayne, Carol Platt, Clifford Meth, Cory Langille, Courtney Reedman, Daniel Brendle-Moczuk, Darlene Chan, David Mcdonnell, David Saunders, Denise Gottshalk, Dirk Deppey, Gary Colabuono, Helen Dalrymple, Jackie Baldwin, James Sturm, Jeff Klein, Jenny Robb, Jerry M. Jenkins, John Morrow, Joshua Jacob, Kathryn Fiegen, Keith Phipps, Ken Gale, Laura Emerick, Leonard Pitts Jr., Leonardo De Sá·, Lewis Shiner, Lucy Shelton Caswell, Mary L. Zuzik, Murray Suid, Peter Coogan, Rita

Eisenstein, Roger Ash, Roger Ebert, Sarah Ann Mockbee, Shawn Thompson, Stanford Carpenter, Stephen Perretta, Susan White, Ted Gangi, Ted White, Thomas Morrison, Walter Biggins, Walter Simonson, Wenxian Zhang. I am most indebted to Ginny L. Kilander and John Waggener at the American Heritage Center at the University of Wyoming for their assistance with the Stan Lee archives. All of my travelling—be it to Laramie to visit the American Heritage Center or to Los Angeles to interview Stan Lee—could not have been done without the financial support of the Scholarly Activity Committee at Thompson Rivers University.

JM

Chronology

1922   Stanley Martin Lieber is born on December 28 to parents Jack and Celia in New York City.

1930   Larry Lieber, Stan's younger brother, is born. Larry proves to be an excellent comic book writer and artist in his own right.

1939   Stan graduates from high school.

1940   Stan takes a job at Timely Comics as an assistant to *Captain America* creators Joe Simon and Jack Kirby.

1941   Stan adopts the pen name "Stan Lee" and has his first text published in *Captain America Comics* #3. His first comic script, entitled "Headline Hunter, Foreign Correspondent," appears in *Captain America Comics* #5. Late in the year Martin Goodman, founder of Timely Comics, fires Simon and Kirby for moonlighting. Lee takes over the duties of editor.

1942   Timely tries out humor titles and Lee enlists in the Army. He is assigned to Signal Corps and is stationed in New York, North Carolina, and Indiana.

1945   Lee returns from the war as full-time editor after a stint as an Army playwright, writing "how-to" manuals in the comic book format (with a character called Fiscal Freddie), which increase the ability of servicemen to learn quickly and effectively. At Timely, he ushers in such female-friendly comics as *Tessie the Typist*, *Millie the Model*, and *Nellie the Nurse*.

1947   Stan meets and is smitten by the future Ms. Lee: Joan Clayton Boocock. Joan divorces her husband and then marries Stan literally minutes later by the same judge, on December 5. Timely turns their focus onto crime genre comics.

1949   Timely's western genre comics become successful and are soon followed by war comics. Stan Lee appears—mask and all—on the cover of *Black Rider* #11.

1950   Daughter Joan Celia is born.

1953   Birth of daughter Jan becomes tragic as she passes away three days later.

1954   Frederic Wertham's *Seduction of the Innocent* is published and the ensuing witch hunt almost destroys the industry. The Comics Code is adopted.

1957   Lee and Joe Maneely create the comic strip *Mrs. Lyon's Cubs*. Martin Goodman's company faces a distribution crisis.

1958   Maneely, whom Lee still considers one of the best comic artists of all time, dies at age thirty-two. Lee starts writing more science-fiction and monster genre stories including "Fing Fang Foom."

1959   Jack Kirby comes back to what will soon be renamed Marvel Comics.

1961   Lee puts together photo magazines with humorous captions. The cover of one of the magazines features a smouldering photo of Joan Lee. Stan is bored and is considering quitting the business. His wife convinces him to write something that "he'd want to read." National Comics (now DC) introduces *The Justice League of America*. Martin Goodman asks Lee to come up with a superhero team to compete with the *JLA*. In the winter, *Fantastic Four* #1 is published and the Marvel Age of Comics is born.

1962   After the success of the *Fantastic Four*, Lee teams up again
        with Jack Kirby and the result is the *Incredible Hulk*. Lee's
        words and Steve Ditko's artwork appear in the last issue of
        Amazing Fantasy (#15). The story marks the first appearance
        of Spider-Man; the *Amazing Spider-Man* would become
        Marvel's flagship title. The *Mighty Thor* is born as well.

1963   *Dr. Strange*, *Iron Man*, the *Avengers*, and the *Uncanny X-Men*,
        all appear on the comic book stands. One of the covers for
        Lee's humorous photo magazines is of President Kennedy. The
        issue is pulled after Kennedy is assassinated.

1964   *Daredevil* arrives on the comic book scene.

1965   Lee and Kirby present *Nick Fury, Agent of S.H.I.E.L.D.*
        Perhaps as a counterpoint to this hard-edged character, Lee
        creates the Merry Marvel Marching Society, chapters of
        which start springing up on university campuses around the
        United States. Lee begins his lecture circuit which he will
        continue for fifteen years.

1966   Steve Ditko, artist of Spider-Man, leaves Marvel.

1967   Spider-Man gets his own television cartoon show which runs
        for three years. It's drawn in the Pop Art style of the 1960s.

1968   Lee gives the Kirby-created character Silver Surfer his own
        solo series. Although not a huge success, Lee considers it
        one of his favorite runs. Perfect Film buys Marvel from
        Martin Goodman for around $15 million so long as Stan Lee
        remains part of the company. Lee doesn't receive any bene-
        fits from the deal. Later, Perfect Film would be renamed
        Cadence and they would appoint Lee publisher.

1970   Martin Goodman leaves the company he founded in the
        1930s. Jack Kirby quits.

1971   The infamous *Spider-Man* drug issues (#96–98) appear
        without the Comic Code seal of approval.

1972   A Night with Stan Lee at Carnegie Hall. His wife and daugh-
        ter recite Lee's poem "God Woke." Marvel is selling millions
        of comic books around the world.

1974   Simon and Schuster publish *Origins of Marvel Comics.*

1977   *Amazing Spider-Man* strip appears in newspapers.

1975   Jack Kirby returns. Kirby exits again in 1978 but before he does, he teams up with Lee one last time for the graphic novel *Silver Surfer: The Ultimate Cosmic Experience.*

1978   *The Incredible Hulk*, starring Bill Bixby and Lou Ferrigno, debuts on CBS Television. Dr. Banner's first name Bruce is changed to David. Lee deftly lets comic book fans know that Banner's full name is David Bruce Banner.

1980   Lee moves to Los Angeles to be head of Marvel Productions in Hollywood, an animation company.

1985   The public starts to hear about Jack Kirby's battle with Marvel regarding the return of his original artwork. This, combined with Kirby's claims that he was the sole creator of *Spider-Man* creates a deep schism between the two former partners.

1986   Marvel celebrates its twenty-fifth anniversary.

1993   Director James Cameron sends Lee a treatment for the film *Spider-Man*. Ultimately, however, Sam Raimi would direct a different version.

1994   Jack Kirby dies on February 6. Lee attends the funeral of his legendary partner.

1995   Marvel has a financial crisis that puts it on the brink of extinction.

1998   Lee signs a contract making him Chairman Emeritus for life. New administrators decide to reduce this period to two years and cut his salary in half. After complaining, his salary is raised and the lifelong contract is restored. Lee forms Stan Lee Media with Peter Paul.

1999   Stan Lee Media starts publishing "webisodes" online.

2000   The movie *X-Men* debuts and brings in $54 million in the first weekend. The dot-com boom goes bust and so too does Stan Lee Media. Lee is financially victimized by the shady business practices of his business partner, who is charged with securities fraud.

2001   Stan Lee is invited to re-imagine the origins of DC Comics' top superheroes in a series of one-shot issues.

2002   The movie *Spider-Man* opens and grosses over $110 million in the first weekend. The combined box office gross of *Spider-Man* and its 2004 sequel is over $1.5 billion world-wide. Lee sues Marvel stating that they agreed to pay him 10 percent of any profits from his characters used in films or television.

2003   Lee develops the adult-themed cartoon *Stripperella* for television.

2005   Lee and Marvel settle the *Spider-Man* dispute out of court.

2006   The movie *X-Men 3* grosses over $200 million in its first three weeks of release at the domestic box office. Lee celebrates his sixty-fifth anniversary of active creativity in the business.

Stan Lee
Conversations

A Conversation with the Man behind Marvel Comics: Stan Lee

TED WHITE / 1968

From *Castle of Frankenstein*, no. 12
(1968), pp. 8–13. Reprinted by permission
of Ted White.

Ted: You've been with Marvel since what . . . 1944?
Stan: I'm pretty rotten at dates. But it's been about twenty-five years, twenty-seven years . . . something like that.

Ted: But the new look in Marvel occurred relatively recently. To what do you attribute this?
Stan: Well, I guess it started with the first issue of *Fantastic Four* about five years ago. They were our first real *offbeat* superheroes. They sort of started the trend.

Ted: What led you to do those? Up until then there had been no superheroes for what . . . about five or six years in this company.
Stan: Before I answer . . . would anybody like a sourball?

3

Ted: Thanks. . . .

Stan: What color? I seem to have red, yellow, orange . . . couple of greens.

Ted: I feel very strange conducting an interview with a sourball in my mouth.

Stan: Well, I guess we were looking for something to hook some new readers. Also, I think boredom had a little to do with it. We had been turning out books for about twenty years. Same old type all the time . . . so I figured, let's try something a little more offbeat. Let's try to . . . I think the big policy was to avoid the clichés. For example in the *Fantastic Four*, the first cliché was: all superheroes wore costumes. We soon learned that was a mistake because, much as the readers like offbeat things, there are certain basics that we must have, and apparently super-hero fans do demand costumes as we learned in the subsequent mail.

Ted: They've been after you to change costumes around ever since.

Stan: Yes, in fact, they . . . costumes were nothing that I ever worried much about, but I see that the rabid fans are tremendously interested in the attire of their superheroes. The other cliché that we . . . I think we were probably the first outfit to break . . . was the cliché of all the superheroes being goody-goody and friendly with each other. If they're members of a team, they're all nice and polite, and . . . We had our Fantastic Four argue amongst themselves. They didn't always get along well and so forth. And this seems to have caught on very well.

Ted: Actually, doesn't this go back to company policy back in the days in the forties when the Sub-Mariner and the Human Torch were fighting with each other?

Stan: Well, the only thing is . . . then the Sub-Mariner wasn't that much of a good guy. It was sort of his personality that he would not get along well. They were natural enemies. Fire and water.

Ted: Well, this was pretty unusual. I guess we can say that, in the comics, Marvel pioneered the whole idea of the anti-hero . . . the superhero who isn't really a hero.

Stan: Yes, I think you could say that because I think certainly Sub-Mariner is the first one that I . . . that I can remember. Bill Everett did the first *Sub-Mariner* . . . he was sort of a hero-villain. He was really more hero than villain . . . but he wasn't 100 percent hero in the sense that the heroes are today.

Ted: The readers would see things from his point of view, of course. Now you've got a full-fledged line, and you're doing very little besides the superheroes. Of course, you have branched out a good bit. You've got *Sgt. Fury* which is about 50 percent superhero and about 50 percent non-superhero, depending upon whether you read his adventures in World War II or his adventures today. And the newest thing you're doing is the TV series. Can you tell us a little about that? How much work do the animators do on the original art?

Stan: Well, quite a bit. They use the actual story and art from the magazines. Basically, it's using our still figures, our still pictures, our panels and then animating the panels.

Ted: They go back to your original black and whites?

Stan: Yes. (*Phone buzzer interrupts*) Excuse me. Yeah? . . . Why sure . . . Just one little interruption. Would you mind opening the door? I think it locks automatically, and Sol Brodsky is coming in. Thanks, yeah. He'll be in a minute. (*buzz*) Whoops! (*into phone*) Yeah?, I'll give Sol something, something to look at. (*Sol Brodsky enters stage left and confers with Stan Lee over comics page*)

Sol: Stan, he's supposed to be catching him here on the rebound?

Stan: Or reaching for him.

Sol: Reaching for him . . .

Stan: He doesn't have to be actually catching him . . .

Sol: Now he's flying by this way . . . and the hand like this looks as if he's throwing.

Stan: I thought the hand could just be like that as if it's going to . . .

Sol: Like this . . .

Stan: Sure, just reaching. Any way that will make sense . . . see . . . 'cause here he grabbed him. Instead of it being this way, we'll turn it that way . . . and now he's *reaching* to grab him, see?

Sol: Yeah . . . we just drew it wrong.

Stan: Right. I just want to give you something. I understand Steranko is here. I'll probably be another twenty minutes . . . so possibly he might want to look this over and then I'll talk to him. (*Brodsky exits*).

Ted: We're curious to know the exact procedure you follow when you brainstorm a story . . . especially one that will continue over several issues.

Stan: Well, what we usually do is, with most of the artists, I usually get a rough plot. By a rough plot, I mean as much as I can write in longhand on the side of one sheet of paper . . . who the villain will be, what the problem will be, and so forth. Then I call that artist in, whoever's going to draw the strip. . . . I read it to him . . . what I've written down, these few notes . . . and we discuss it. By the time we're through talking for about twenty minutes, we usually have some plot going.

And we talk it out. Lately, I've had Roy Thomas come in, and he sits and makes notes while we discuss it. Then he types them up which gives us a written synopsis. Originally—I have a little tape recorder—I had tried taping it, but I found that nobody on the staff has time to listen to the tape again. Later . . . so it's just too much of a waste. But this way he makes notes, types it quickly, I get a carbon, the artist, gets a carbon . . . so we don't have to worry that we'll forget what we've said. Then the artist goes home . . . or wherever he goes . . . and he draws the thing out, brings it back, and I put the copy in after he's drawn the story based on the plot I've given him. Now this varies with the different artists. Some artists, of course, need a more detailed plot than others. Some artists, such as Jack Kirby, need no plot at all. I mean I'll just say to Jack, "Let's let the next villain be Dr. Doom". . . or I may not even say that. He may tell me. And then he goes home and does it. He's so good at plots, I'm sure he's a thousand times better than I. He just about makes up the plots for these stories. All I do is a little editing . . . I may tell him that he's gone too far in one direction or another. Of course, occasionally I'll give him a plot, but we're practically both the writers on the things.

Ted: He actually did do a script while you were away on vacation.
Stan: Yes. We had both plotted that out before I left. But he put the copy in on that one. I do a little editing later, But it was his story. Jack is just fantastic. We're lucky. Most of our men are good story men. In fact, they have to be. A fellow who's a good artist, but isn't good at telling a story in this form . . . in continuity form . . . can't really work for us. Unless we get somebody to do the layouts for him and he just follows the layouts. We've done that in the past.

Ted: That's what it means when you have a little note saying "Layouts by Kirby, Art by So-and-So . . . ?
Stan: Yes. Now that isn't always because of the fact that the artist can't do layouts. There are many extenuating circumstances. For example, an

artist who hasn't done a certain strip may have to do it because suddenly the other artist who is going to do it is ill or something. He isn't familiar with the story line, and I don't have time to explain it. Now Jack has been in on most of these things with me. I can call Jack down. I can say, "Jack, make it a twelve-page story, and, roughly, this is the plot." Jack can go home, and the next day he has the whole thing broken down. He gives it to the artist, and the artist just has to worry about drawing his work on the breakdowns. It's a lot easier than me spending a whole day discussing the philosophy of the strip with a new artist. Also there are some fellows who are starting a new strip, who are a little unfamiliar. They'd rather have Jack break it down for them once or twice until they get the feeling of it.

Ted: Of course, Jack has a very good sense of action.
Stan: The greatest. . .

Ted: And his perspective . . . things seem to be coming out at you on the page. It seems to me that his layouts are a lot more dynamic . . . less static than a lot of the other artists who are working on their own.
Stan: Well, we refer to Jack. It started as a gag, calling him Jack "King" Kirby, but actually I mean it. I think that this guy is absolutely . . . in this particular field, he's the master.

Ted: Of course, he's been working with Marvel on and off practically since Marvel started. He did the original *Captain America*, of course but he was doing work back before *Captain America*, back before he had his long collaboration with Joe Simon.
Stan: I don't know anything about that because I wasn't here at the time . . . and I think he had been with another company before Marvel.

Ted: He did *Blue Bolt*.
Stan: Yeah . . . I think that was for Fox. They're now out of business. But Jack . . .

Ted: No, actually that was for Curtis.
Stan: That who it was?

Ted: They had a different name for the company.
Stan: Might have been . . .

Ted: . . . because the *Saturday Evening Post* didn't have anything to do with comic books.

Stan: Yeah, I seem to remember now. You're right. But Jack . . . I'm probably Jack's biggest fan. And, of course, we have many other talented men (*phone buzz*) I think the staff we have now is really pretty terrific. Excuse me. 'Lo? Er . . . listen, ask him if it's urgent. If it isn't I'll get back to him in about a half hour . . . I'm in that conference now. OK? Thanks.

Ted: Getting back to the TV shows, you're using your own original script from the books?

Stan: Actually, they have to be changed to some degree because some of them aren't complete in themselves. And the animation studio has to change the ending or . . . It has to seem as if it's a complete episode.

Ted: How closely do you oversee this?

Stan: Pretty closely. In fact, I have some storyboards here. They give them to me in this form, you see, and I take them home with me and check them.

Ted: Those are photostats of the original panels? Is that it? Then, of course, they're going to work with those from the point of view of the animation.

Stan: Yes. So I . . . I'm actually, I guess you might say, the story editor on the TV series.

Ted: How closely do you feel that their animation has followed the style of the original artist, bearing in mind that so much of an artist's style is in his handling of thickness of line and . . .

Stan: Oh, very closely, they shoot the actual picture and all that they ani- mate is opening the mouths and shutting and opening the eyes and moving the arms and legs . . . but it's the basic drawing that we've got there. I don't see how anything could be more faithful to the original artwork. Now, naturally, they had to make some little changes . . . but, er . . . I've had experience with other people who've taken properties . . . they usually don't even bother with the people whose property they've taken. They just go out on their own. This particular outfit, Grantray Lawrence, they've been an absolute joy to work with. They check with us on everything, and they're tremendously anxious to keep to the spirit of our own strips and stories. I couldn't be more satisfied with what they've been doing. They're trying their best to keep it in the style, for better or for worse, the style that we have in our books.

Ted: Did you ever see *Jonny Quest*?
Stan: Yes.

Ted: What did you think of that? Would you prefer to see that type of animation?
Stan: That type of animation didn't bother me. I think it has a certain charm. In many ways I think I prefer that to full animation which can ruin a human-type character. It's so hard to animate a human being. Technically, I think this is a very interesting . . . way they're doing our show technically . . . I'm delighted with that. I wouldn't have been happy if it were animated like, you know, like *Mickey Mouse* . . . just regular animation.

Ted: Do you feel that the form of animation they're using is in another sense, somehow related to the mass audience concept of camp which has had something to do with Marvel's success with adults?
Stan: I hadn't thought of it that way, but now that you mention it, it very well could be.

Ted: How do you feel about the way in which the Marvel audience breaks down into age groups? Have you made any effort to find out just what percentage is what age group?
Stan: No. I can just guess by the mail we receive, and the people I meet and so forth. I couldn't give you a figure, but I would say we have a . . . a tremendous amount of young adults reading our books. Now whether this is 50 percent of our readership or 10 percent or so, I don't know. But, as far as the mail is concerned, it's about 50 percent of our mail . . . college students, soldiers, . . .

Ted: You've gotten a lot of attention on college campuses . . . I know a lot of the college magazines have devoted space to the Marvel characters.
Stan: And it seems to be growing all the time . . .

Ted: It's nice to see the Marvel shows taking away the lead *Batman* had two years ago.
Stan: That television show is so much the style of our comic magazines that, if we did our comic magazines live, we would almost look as if we were imitating *Batman*.

Ted: Except that you do not present your characters in the light in which ABC presents *Batman*. It's almost as if the producer is asking the audience to join him in sneering at the hero.

Stan: I agree 100 percent. You get the feeling that they're ridiculing or laughing at their own characters. I would love for some of our characters to be done with the kind of budget that *Batman* has. But er . . . I have no idea whether that's in the works or not.

Ted: It would be wonderful to see *Fantastic Four* done that way. Can you think of the special effects of *Human Torch*?

Stan: Yeah. Or I would settle for any of them. For something even simple . . . like *Spider-Man*. I can see *Spider-Man*-making a magnificent show.

Ted: Have you had any nibbles from the movie studios for full-length movies?

Stan: No, not that I know of. Again, I don't know. The front office may have had some . . . It's nothing that I really discuss with them until the thing is definite. But I haven't been told of any. I wouldn't be surprised though.

Ted: Has there been any conflict between your title the *AVENGERS* and the ABC-TV show?

Stan: No. Apparently it didn't mean anything to anybody.

Ted: You were there first in this country.

Stan: Yeah.

Ted: What is your feeling about the way in which . . . er . . . the Marvel Group has grown in terms of circulation? You see any leveling off? Is it still growing?

Stan: It's just incredible. We just seem to be growing at the same steady rate year after year.

Ted: Does it put more pressures on you? Does it take pressures off you?

Stan: Well, the only thing that puts more pressures on us is if we physically produce more titles, and we're not. We're sort of limited to the titles we have now. If your sales increase, the only pressure is one of jubilation. We . . . about five years ago I guess we were selling about 13 million. Now we're selling about 45 million a year . . . and this has been a steady rise over the past five years . . . and there seems to be no end in sight I'm happy to say. I think we're only limited by how many

we can physically print and how many we can physically distribute.
I think we can really sell many more if we can print them and
distribute them.

Ted: Well, you're getting more competition all the time, of course. New
companies keep coming to the superhero field all the time. There are the
Tower people. . . . and Harvey Comics . . . Those are the most flagrant
imitators. How do you feel in general about the imitators?
Stan: I wish they would peddle their papers elsewhere. The flattery
kick—we've gotten over that years ago. We realize that we are rather
popular now. We appreciate it. But the thing that bothers me . . . corny
as it may sound . . . We really are trying to make comics as good as
comics can be made. We're trying to elevate the medium. We're trying
to make them as respectable as possible. We . . . our goal is that
someday an intelligent adult would not be embarrassed to walk down
the street with a comic magazine. I don't know whether we can ever
bring this off, but it's something to shoot for. At any rate, we try to do
this. Now when other companies come out . . . and they try to make
their books seem like our books, as if they're all in the same class, the
same milieu . . . and yet the quality is inferior, the art is inferior, the
writing is inferior, the plotting is inferior. I feel this does nothing but hurt
us. The adults who don't read comics, but who . . . whose youngsters try
to convince them that comics are really pretty good. You know, who
may read ours and like them, say "Why don't you read one? They're
really good." And the people who are uninitiated but who have heard
about comics and might want to pick one up and see what all the talk is
about are very apt to mistakenly pick up one of these imitations, look at
them and say, "Aw, I knew it. That fellow who told me comics are good
is really an idiot. They're as bad as they ever were." In this way I think
we can be hurt by imitators.

Ted: The imitators make themselves look so much like your line that
many readers may think they've gotten hold of a Marvel Comic.
Stan: Exactly. Now . . . silly as this may sound, or hard to believe as it
may sound, I wish our imitators did better books . . . if they put out
books of comparable quality to ours. Now I don't like this to sound as if
I'm an egomaniac, but I think you see what I mean. If . . . if I felt myself
that the art and stories were as good as our books, I would be happier
because I would feel that we're all elevating the field . . . and we're all
going to benefit by it.

Ted: It would put more pressure on you to get even better . . .

Stan: Right. But as it is, at this particular moment, I still think that we are doing the only somewhat significant work in this field. There's the occasional exception.

Ted: You're up against something which is a periodic phenomenon in the comic book industry. Back in the early fifties, the EC group set really high standards. I don't think you've beat them on art yet. Er . . . When *MAD* came out, and it was a sleeper, someone realized, "My God! That thing is selling!" Suddenly, the stands were covered with *MAD* imitations. Whenever someone notices that someone is doing something original that is making money, they'll all jump on the bandwagon. But for some reason none of them bother doing anything which has the quality of the original. It would seem that if someone wants to capture the Marvel audience . . . or enlarge upon it in anyway . . . they should be less concerned with the superficialities . . . such as having "chatty" covers. That's a gimmick they've taken from you, and now you've dropped it. They never attempt the quality of writing you're doing. And you've kept changing your approach, evolving your characters. In *Thor*, for instance, you've gotten into some great mythological conflicts . . . and away from the nonsense with alter egos, the doctor turning into Thor, and . . .

Stan: We've gotten many letters from readers who say, "Hey! We haven't seen Dr. Blake in a while." So we're trying to see how we can get back to that a little bit. Although I will admit I myself would like to just keep him Thor and keep the stories as they're going. It makes it easier and more palatable to me.

Ted: Originally *Thor* was a very schizophrenic thing. You had the *Thor* feature at the front, essentially a standard superhero with his civilian identity and his civilian lovelife problems, and in the back you had your *Tales of Asgard* which was pretty much pure myth reinterpreted in comic form. Now, although you are dealing less with myth in its original sense, you are including all the mythic figures . . . you've gotten into Grecian mythology . . . Pluto and the Underworld. That's marvelous stuff; that's sense of wonder stuff.

Stan: Oh, you're quite right. Quite right. In fact, we don't really have any set plan for anything . . . so you'll always find changes in our books. One day I'll wake up in the morning . . . or Jack will . . . or any of our artists . . . or Roy Thomas . . . or anybody . . . and say, "Hey! Why don't we do thus and such?" We're very lucky that there is nobody clamping down on us and saying, "You have to stay within these prescribed channels." To me, any new idea is worth exploring. Even a bad new idea is better than a good formulized rut you might be in. So I like to change these. As for as the *FF* goes, they are getting a little bit science-fictiony. I would like to give them a different feeling than, let's say, *Spider-Man*, which isn't science-fictiony. I'm very hard pressed to find out how to make *Spider-Man* very different from *Daredevil*. I, sooner or later, will find a way. I would like all of our books to be different from each other . . . to have their own individual style. It's difficult . . . because we still don't have enough artists. Consequently, I have to alternate. One fellow may draw *Hulk* this month. He may have to draw *Daredevil* next month . . . and so forth. We still don't have one artist for one feature except in the case of *Thor* and *Spider-Man* and a few others.

Ted: Why is this?
Stan: We just don't have enough men. So if one man is ill . . . or if one man breaks an arm . . . or anything . . . somebody else has to do his strip. Then the somebody else's strip is now late. Somebody else has to do this. We're continually running into crises of that sort.

Ted: Is there any way out?
Stan: Just getting more artists. We're looking all the time. But this is what we're up against. The reason I mention this about the art is that it's one of the reasons that it's a little difficult also to stay with a definite theory for each book. As you change artists you change your approach, you see. But sooner or later things will level off. Maybe they never will because we're always in a state of flux. But is keeps it exciting.

Ted: Well, our time is up.
Lee: I'm awfully sorry. Nobody enjoys this sort of thing more than I do. I wish we had another ten hours to go through it.

The Dick Cavett Show: An Interview with Stan Lee

DICK CAVETT / 1968

From *The Dick Cavett Show*, ABC, May 30, 1968, transcribed by Jeff McLaughlin. Printed by permission.

Dick Cavett: If you think that comic books are only for children the chances are that you are wrong. My first, er, my next guest is a gentleman named Stan Lee who is editor-in-chief of Marvel Comics. And Stan maintains that at least half of their sales of 60 million comic books a year is to college students. Marvel comics are different—some of their characters Fantastic Four and Spider-Man, Silver Surfer, the Hulk, and other favorites. Marvel comics are an unusual phenomena in our time and I think we should know more about them.

Comedian Pat —— (*impersonating Oliver Hardy*): Well, I do too, Stanley.

Dick (*also impersonating Hardy*): Say, isn't that a swell idea?

Dick: And here is a gentleman who can tell us: Stan Lee.

(*Music and audience applause. The house band is playing "Barney Google."*)

Stan: Well, I can't think of anything worse than having to follow a funny comedian and a pretty girl and talk about comic books.

Dick: We'll let the comic books stand for themselves and you won't be blamed.

Stan: Okay.

Dick: You know a lot of people are startled by that idea—that comic books are read by college students. Not in the sense some people would expect college students would read comic books, but in another sense. What is the best way to tell people what's different about them?

Stan: Well, I'd like to think it's just because they're better than comic books are supposed to be or ever have been. We try to write them well, we try to draw them well; we try to make them as sophisticated as a comic book can be. As a matter of fact, the whole philosophy behind it is to treat them as fairy tales for grown ups and do the kind of stories that we ourselves would want to read if we read comic books.

Dick: I see. And what kind of reaction do you get from this vast horde of readers that you have?

Stan: Just terrific, Dick. We started out just to amuse ourselves. After years of just doing those ordinary comics, we were a little tired of it, and we wanted to do something different, and we never thought it would catch on the way it has. But after we started the first of our so-called "New Wave of Comics," we now have Merry Marvel Marching Societies on just about every campus in the country. And as I think you mentioned before, half of our mail comes from college kids. And I spend so much time speaking at various colleges, I feel like a member of the faculty.

Dick: Except that you haven't had your office broken into.

Stan: Quite.

Dick: They are very well-written. Who does your actual writing?

Stan: Well, I do a great deal of it, and we have one or two other writers also who handle the rest of the stories. It's a very small, well-knit organization. We have a few people turning out most of the books. Actually unlike most other comic magazine companies, the artists do quite a bit of the writing too in a sense. I will discuss a plot with an artist and he will go home and draw the script. Then it comes back and either I or some other writer will put the copy in, so in a sense the artist himself is creating the situations along with the writer. The writer mainly is in on the plot conception and the dialogue. Writing the dialogue and the captions.

Dick: What are the heroes they dig the most?
Stan: Well, I have found, this is the era, the age of the offbeat. Anything that is far out, anything that is different. Consequently, it seems that our most popular heroes are the most wackiest. We have a character called the Hulk who is just a green-skinned monster and the most unlikely type you expect to be a hero.

Pat: Is that the one that Bertrand Russell writes?
Stan: Well, it's very complimentary of you.

Pat: No, you really upgraded them.
Stan: Then we have one called Spider-Man who is considered an anti-hero hero. He gets sinus attacks, he gets acne, and allergy attacks while he's fighting. He has an aunt who is always on the verge of a heart attack. She's very old. Half of our fan mail says "Will you kill off Aunt May already?"

Dick: That's very heartwarming, isn't it?
Stan: Oh yes. And another thing we've done is that most of our books are continued like Peyton Place in pictures. And we never know from month to month who's going to die and who is going to live. It's a whole new thing. If you haven't been reading them for years, you almost can't understand them unless you make a study of it for a while.

Dick: Or get a lot of back issues.
Stan: Hmmm. Which is good because we like to feel that a lot of back issues are being sold too. And it generates a lot of interest. I'd like to have a back issues store.

Dick: Yes sir. (*to Pat*) Were you about to say something before we went to commercial?
Pat: One thing I like about those comic books is that they're easy to turn while you're sucking your thumb with the other hand. (*audience laughs*)
Stan: Can I change seats?

Dick: We'll be back in a moment. Stay with us.

(*Commercial break*)

Dick: Ack! Got caught leafing through my comic book! One segment, this is called *Fantastic Four*, and in the last panel we see . . . is it Silver Surfer?

Stan: No, that's a character called The Watcher. He's sort of an omnipotent character who is out in the galaxy somewhere watching, and he doesn't have very much else to do. And this is one of the characters in the *Fantastic Four*.

Dick: The lady?

Stan: Sue Storm, the Invisible Girl. Who's pregnant at the moment. She's been out of the story for a while. (*some audience laughter*) In fact one of our biggest problems is that she has to give birth in the next issue and we don't know what the offspring should be really. (*Pat bursts out laughing.*)

And we feel a little bit like God ourselves. We have these characters and we can do with them whatever we like and we really want to do really the right thing always. We get letters it should be twins, it should be a boy, it should be a girl. We had a few letters saying "Why don't you let her die in childbirth, you see, and this will make this strip more dramatic."

Pat: Could be a cult.

Stan: You see, young lady, our next . . .

Young Lady guest: Stan, can I ask a question? Are these made in different languages?

Stan: They are translated all over the free world.

Young Lady guest: Like in French. It's easy if you have pictures to go along with.

Stan: They are sold all over the free world in all different languages as a matter of fact. Well, I have to modify it and say the "free world."

Dick: They are used I'm told in writing courses in some places.

Stan: Oh yes, there are a number of colleges where these books and Marvel comics are used in contemporary writing classes. Not as horrible examples I'd like to think.

Dick: But as good ones.

Stan: Yup.

Dick: Do you ever worry about the amount of power you have with that gigantic circulation?

Stan: Well, no, not really. We kind of enjoy it. I would like to think if somebody has to have power over the young people today, any degree of power, it might as well be us. We are very interested in the youth. We are very aware, or try to be aware of what's happening. We're trying to do whatever we can to make things a little better. I think the more power we can get through these stories, and the more moral the tone of these books we can make, the better it is for everybody.

Dick: Do you have disagreements on your staff as to what the tone is that you're taking, or do people ever want to change the course of the philosophy . . .

Stan: Actually the disagreement is only with the details. Like should Sue have a boy or girl. What we are trying to do is . . . there's very little disagreement. For instance that *Thor* magazine that you have there. We had one sequence where he meets some hippies on the street. And this was done a few months ago, quite a while ago, when hippie-dom was perhaps more of a problem than it is today. But we were concerned about all the young people dropping out, and we had him deliver a little lecture in his own ridiculous way of speaking, mentioning that it is far better to plunge in than to drop out. If there are problems, the way to solve them isn't by ignoring them. And at the time the little page was written, it was a good little sermon. Today, fortunately, I don't think it is as necessary. Youth today seem to be so much more activist, which I think is a very healthy thing. This business of dropping out has seemed to have gone by the boards for the most part.

Dick: What does your unfavorable mail say? Does anyone resent the fact that you're trying to slip a pill in on them in any sense?

Stan: No, because really I don't think we say anything that would offend anybody except what a nut would object to. We're almost square in our moralizing. We're for God, country, and motherhood and apple pie, that type of thing. We don't try any devious little things that we slip in, and we slip in very little. Basically we're interested in telling a good story, but we find that the stories we tell which contain any little bits of philosophy or any little bits of satire or commentary on the everyday scene are the ones that get the most favorable mail. And we could knock ourselves out just to do an exciting story—there isn't much reaction there—but let us put in any comment on things as they are and "Bingo!" everybody seems to go for the yarn.

Dick: Are Marvel comics available in every town? Do they actually sell where other comics do?
Stan: Yes. Actually they sell so quickly they seem not to be available. People will think the store doesn't carry them when they are already sold out.

Dick: Have you ever seen a copy of *Mighty Thor*, Pat?
Stan: (*to Pat*) It has two-syllable words, so you might have a little difficulty. (*audience "ooooh"s*)
Pat: Well, here's a one syllable one for you here.

Young Lady guest: What about *Little Lulu*?
Stan: I think she's still around, but that's a different type of strip.
Young Lady guest: Yeah?

Dick: I understand you got a lot of mail on the one panel here where the girl says, "But what can you do against the all-powerful Silver Surfer?" And the other chap says, "The all-powerful is only the one who deserves that name, and His only weapon is love." You don't often see that sort of thing in comic books. Did anyone wonder what you meant by that?
Stan: No, they all seemed to know what we meant, and boy, we were flooded with mail just on that one little panel . . . parents and teachers and people who said it was just great having a little thought like that in a comic book. I think the big thing that we're trying to do—and apparently we're meeting with some success—is that we're taking these two words—"comic books"—which have always been spoken of with such disdain, and in our own way . . . and it's not an easy job of course because most people the minute they hear "comic book" they turn up their noses. We've been trying to give them a little more respect, we try to increase the quality so that, after all, they are part of the media today, like radio and television, they are a method of communication, and there's really no reason why a comic book couldn't be well-written and well-drawn just like anything else. That's what we're trying to do.

Dick: It makes you wonder why no one ever thought of it before. That's a good idea.
    We'll be back after this message and David Steinberg will be here. . . .

Radicalization of the Superheroes

Lawrence Van Gelder and Lindsey Van Gelder / 1970

WNYC Radio interview, October 15,
1970, transcribed by Jeff McLaughlin.
Printed by permission of WNYC Radio.

Lawrence Van Gelder: There was a time about fifteen or twenty years ago when I guess most of the people our age stopped reading comic books, they thought they were too old for them, they thought they had grown uninteresting. But something new is going on today, and you're the man who I think is most responsible for it. Can you tell us what is new and what is surprising in comic books today?

Stan Lee: Well of course none of it is surprising to me since I'm right in the middle of it. I guess the thing you're referring to as "newness" is the so-called relevancy that seems to be in the comic book magazines today. Instead of just a superhero trying to fight a villain who wants to blow up the world, or little green-skinned monsters from Mars, we try to set our

20

stories in the real world. A character like Spider-Man will be involved in a campus protest and things of that sort.

Lawrence Van Gelder: Do you find that this has an impact among young people, that you get a response?

Stan Lee: Well, I would guess we get a response amongst people of every age. Actually we don't knock ourselves out for the so-called "relevancy" in the sense of getting political issues and so forth and dragging them in. We've been trying to do this for the past, I guess, ten years since Marvel Comics started its so-called "New Wave of Comics." We tried to get relevancy before there were these big burning questions that are playing out now, in the sense that instead of superheroes that are obviously cardboard figures, why not treat our superheroes as real people living in a real world. I think that the theme that we've had is that these are like "fairy tales" for grown-ups, but they were to be completely realistic except for the one element of a super power which the superhero possessed, that we would ask our reader to swallow somehow. You had to believe that somebody could climb a sheer wall or that his body could burst into flame or that he was a green-skinned monster. But excepting those sort of ridiculous points which just made for colorful stories, we tried to do everything else as realistically as possible. For example, if a hero had a superhero power, we didn't, ergo, just assume that he'd be lucky in love and have all the money in the world and everything would come his way. We tried to show that nothing really brings total success, and just because you have big muscles, this doesn't necessarily mean you're going to have big triumphs. And we wouldn't have a character in a silly costume walk down the street and have people not notice it, as they had been doing in comics for years before. We'd likely as not have another character in the story say, "Who's that nut in the skin-tight underwear prancing down the street?" and so forth. We felt that we were being relevant even then; we were trying to get people to act the way real people would act given a set of circumstances.

Lawrence Van Gelder: When we talk about relevancy today, I wonder if you can tell us about some of the ideas you've used lately, because it seems to me that they've been drawn right out of the headlines of the newspapers.

Stan Lee: Well, in trying for realism of course, if something is going on today and it's something we're all concerned with, it's really almost impossible to keep it out of a story. Now for example, pollution. We've had ecology stories in *Sub-Mariner*. One of our writers, Roy Thomas, has been doing many stories of that sort with great bearing on problems that concern people today. We've had ecology stories, I guess. . . . In fact we're big in ecology stories today, in *Iron Man* comics, *Daredevil*. . . . The one in *Sub-Mariner* dealt with the so-called surface race, which is ourselves, polluting the seas, and Sub-Mariner, who as everyone knows is the king of Atlantis, he took a dim view about all this. We've had, as I've mentioned, stories about campus riots. We've had Captain America involved in student dissents. We've tried to do more than just involve the characters in these contemporary problems. We try to also show how our characters themselves react to the problems. And well, one thing that I try and do in my own limited way is to show that nothing is really all black and white. Captain America can't—although he's considered an establishment figure really—he's beginning to have second thoughts about the whole thing. He realizes he can't really side with the establishment 100 percent. He realizes that there's a lot of things that are wrong, and it seems that many of these things that are wrong, well, it seems to be no real simple, legal, effortless way to correct them short of extreme measures. By the same token he's always fought for law and order. He's afraid that too much violence will breed too much violence and where do you stop it. And, well, obviously this is really my own philosophy too. I have the toughest problem in the world in taking a definite stand on almost anything, and I have ambivalent feelings about virtually everything, and this is either going to make our stories extremely dull or extremely realistic. I don't know.

Lindsey Van Gelder: Well are these issues calculated because these are what kids care about or are these issues that your artists and writers and you yourself spend time off the job worrying about?
Stan Lee: Oh, I think you have to say that it's what we care about. I mean, after all, we writers and artists and editors are really, well, we were kids not too long ago, a little longer for some like myself. But we live in the same world as our readers, and certainly what our readers are concerned with, we are concerned with. And I think this is another reason that our books are somewhat successful over the past few years. We've never tried to anticipate our audience's desires. We never thought of ourselves as separate and distinct from our audience. We are our audience. And we've always felt that if we can do stories that interest us, stories about themes that interest us, well, they have to interest the public because we're part of the public. So far it's worked out.

Lawrence Van Gelder: In dealing with some of these problems, you take on problems that some people don't think are problems. I mean, they think that always the police are right, that always the establishment is right, always that the government is right. So in a way you are taking a political stance certainly in the eyes of some people who may disagree with you. Does this lead to a lot of critical comment from readers? Do you get mail from certain parts of the country from people saying, "Now look, this is wrong and how can you do it? You poison people's minds."
Stan Lee: We get such a minuscule amount of that type of mail. I'd think we might say that we almost get none. We either have the most broadly-minded, clear-thinking audience in the world, or else the nation isn't in as bad a shape as everybody thinks. Well, that may sound like a very self-serving statement, in other words, "if you like our stories, then the country's in good shape," I didn't mean it to sound that way. But what I mean, we get many letters from people who disagree with some of the points that we have in the books and take issue with us, but they are very rational well-reasoned letters. And as much as I can tell, they seem to be the letters of fairly reasonable people who have an opposing point of view. Well, my god, we have people in our office who have opposing points of view. I was working on a piece, booklet, for Ken Koch, the poet who's new book just came out—plug—and he's on the staff of Columbia, and the two of us were working on a comic book which would hopefully inform the voters as to which congressmen to vote for who might help end the war in Vietnam a little sooner. And we asked one or two of the people in our studio, the bullpen as we call it, to illustrate the book, and a few of them were desperately anxious to do it, and a few of them said, "Oh golly no, I'm no big dove. I wouldn't want to do anything like that." So even in our bullpen we have divergent opinions, which is something of course if you think about it, everybody belongs to a family, and how often in a family is there ever complete concurrence on every issue? And when you try to think of making the whole world harmonious, or getting people who are so totally different and have different interests throughout a nation to agree on any issue, why it's just a staggering concept.

Lindsey Van Gelder: I want to ask you about the age groups of the people who read Marvel. I've noticed that the letters to the editor column read like a, well, sometimes like a SST [Ed. Note: SuperSonic Transport] arguing session. But usually it seems to be older people arguing very cogent political points. What kind of letters do you get from kids, eight, nine, who might not be steeped in this, or are they?

Stan Lee: Younger people arguing cogent points. (*everyone chuckles*) No, actually luckily we still seem to have a lot of young readers. We receive as many letters from the younger readers. Usually we don't print as many so it seems like we have perhaps an overwhelming amount of older readers. I think it's pretty well balanced though. You see, we try to keep our letters page interesting and indicative of the feelings of our readers.

Lindsey Van Gelder: They're great.

Stan Lee: Thank you. But what happens is that most of our younger readers will write letters such as "Gosh! Wow! Your last issue was groovy!" or "Take Stan Lee out and shoot him! That last issue was terrible! We know he can do better!" And that's about the extent of it.

Lindsey Van Gelder: Do they pick up on politics though?

Stan Lee: Not as much as the older readers, no. But they'll say things like "Sub-Mariner's trunks should always be purple, but in one panel they were green." Well, you can only print so many of those kinds of letters. It doesn't make for a real philosophical situation. So for that reason we do print the more interesting letters, which are nine times out of ten from older readers. But to answer your question a little more specifically, I guess I've strayed all around the point. We do get, an unexpected—unexpected, a few years ago—amount of letters from our readers which deal with politics. In fact, I just wrote a Soapbox column for a future bullpen in which I mention a fantastic thing, in *Captain*. . . . Oh, I might preface this by saying selfishly I use the letters to help me edit the magazine. It shows me what the readers want and don't want. And for the most part I try and follow their dictates because they're the ones that buy the books. Well, I've been very frustrated with our *Captain America* magazine. I find it's as if I've been left alone on an ice floe somewhere and I got to shift for myself. I don't know what the readers want because every letter we've gotten for the past three months for *Captain America* has merely dealt with political issues. Nobody's said a word about the stories or the artwork themselves. Now I don't know if people are just reading the magazine just to pick out whatever philosophy or political connotations there might be. I don't know if anyone cares if we have super villains or if there's any action or anything. I put a little notice in the Soapbox asking a few readers to just kinda drop us a line and let us know if they are still reading the book.

Lindsey Van Gelder: How did you get the idea for the women's libera-
tion issue of the *Avengers*?
Stan Lee: Oh, I didn't. That was probably Roy Thomas's idea. He wrote
the thing. But I would imagine it's a question that almost answers itself.
Women's lib is so big now, how can you not have a story or two about it?

Lindsey Van Gelder: Do you think you might let the Black Widow or
Invisible Girl get her own book?
Stan Lee: Well, that won't have as much to do with women's lib as it
does with if the book will sell or not. Actually we put the Black Widow in
her own strip in one of our books.

Lindsey Van Gelder: She's with the Inhumans.
Stan Lee: That's right. It's either an "Amazing" or "Astonishing." I
always get those two mixed up. We're just waiting for some sales figures. I think it will do well. If it does sensationally well, we'll take the two
strips that are appearing in the one book and give them each their own
book of course.

Lawrence Van Gelder: There was a time, and I'd like to go back a little to
the fifties, when every time you picked up a newspaper or listened to a
speech, some psychologist or some congressman was taking on comic
books. That they were too violent, too gory. What's happened since
then? It hurt the industry at that time, and I think it left a lot of people
who are parents themselves with the idea that they didn't want their
kids exposed to it. What governs you now?
Stan Lee: I'm sorry that every question seems to cause a speech on my
part. I'll try to answer simply. We are living in such a fast-changing world
that things that were bad, or . . . well, even women's clothes, if you could
ever see a girl wearing her skirt as high as they've been wearing them in
the mini-skirt age of a year ago, ten years ago it would have been impossible to even conceive of in the street. Now we accept it. I remember the
Beatles' haircut when they first came out and everybody saw the Beatles'
hair, you know. "Wow, how can they go out in public that way?" I just
saw some old pictures of them recently, and they seemed so conservative.
You sort of wondered what all the fuss was about.

Well, the reason I mention that in the age of Dr. Wertham and all the . . .
I shouldn't really say "all"—he was the leading opponent of comics and the
most vocal one. At the time when he was having his big harangue against
comics, people were very concerned about violence and sex and about,

well, I guess anything Dr. Wertham wanted to mention. And he would point out a panel in a book somewhere where a person was being killed, and he would make it sound so terrible, and the fact that he was a psychiatrist, this impressed parents and they began to think, "Golly, what's going on in these comics?"

Today—and this is why I mention it's a quickly changing world—today, and it's certainty not an original thought on my part, it's been said so many times, there's so much real violence in the world that we live in, you just have to pick up a newspaper. I don't think there's anything we could do in a comic book that would even approximate the terrible things that are going on in the world about us. Not that we attempt to. But I think it's been put in its proper perspective now. Comic books are just an entertainment medium. They are certainly written far better, illustrated more beautifully than they were, they are probably written better than your average TV show or grade B movie. Unfortunately most adults aren't aware of this because they don't think to pick up one and read it. They tell an exciting story with more imagery, more imagination, more fantasy and wonder than you can get anywhere else, except in an occasionally good new science-fiction story, and even that won't be quite as imaginative. That will just cover one point usually, whereas a comic book just seems to explore the whole realm of fantasy and wonder, and it's all for fifteen cents, and it's all in pictures. And I think a person would have to be paranoid to start criticizing comics today. I think they are virtually a public service, and they should be subsidized by the government! (everyone laughs)

Lawrence Van Gelder: Looking at the covers of them I think parents will notice that there's a little seal on them "Approved by the Comics Code," "Approved by the Comics Code Authority," and that is something that came in after the massive attacks on comic books in the fifties. Could you tell people a little bit about this code? I think it might set some parents' minds at rest.

Stan Lee: Well, it's headed by Leonard Darvin, a most capable attorney and most conscientious code administrator. And Len Darvin and his staff of experts or censors or critics or observers, I really don't know what to call them, his staff. They read everything that goes into the comics, and they put their seal of approval on every book before it goes to the engraver. Now this is not just a cover-up. It's not just some window dressing to impress people. Oh, we spend a lot of time arguing with the

Code: "Why can't we have a story like this or a theme like this or a picture like this?" And he says "Well, you got to remember it may be okay
for older readers, and I know you have many of them, but we still have a
lot of younger readers, and we have to think of them." And he very often
sets us back on possibly the right path of worrying about the really young
readers. . . . So I think this mentioning of the Code, which I don't always
agree with, as far as any parent being concerned with a young child reading these magazines; I think these magazines are policed as carefully and
possibly more carefully than motion pictures or really anything else a child
will read. I might add that because I am a big fan of children's books. I
know many of the authors and illustrators, and I look at them occasionally. There is far more liberalism as far as giving an author and artist free
reign to do things that might not have been able to have been done a
few years ago for the children's market. There's more liberalism in the
children's books then there are in comic books, and the average parent is
not going to worry about children's books.

You know an interesting thing about my continuing argument with the
Code. I've been wanting for the longest time to have stories that involve
the theme of drug addiction, just as we have ecology and civil rights and
demonstrations and so forth. And this is one thing the Code is very
staunchly against. They think more harm can be done than good if we
even mention drug addiction. My point, of course, is that it's a fact of life.
It's like not mentioning the Sun, if for some reason you don't approve of
the Sun. At any rate, just yesterday I received in the mail—and I can't
wait until they contact the Code—I received something from the government, oh I forget which office, the office of health, education, and welfare or so, and from somebody apparently highly placed with all sorts of
brochures, a lovely letter that I'm going to keep. "Dear Mr. Lee, we
understand that Marvel Comics is very influential among young people
and so forth. We'd consider it a very fine thing if you would mention
drug addiction and do what you can, and here's. . . ." They enclosed a
number of pamphlets to give me background. And I felt, by god, I cannot
wait to call this guy and say "Don't send me the letter, call the Code and
tell them this." Which is what I'm going to do as soon as I get off the mic
here.

Lindsey Van Gelder: Stan Lee, what about sex and comics? I know that
your competitors have story lines having Superman and Batman pretty
well running away from women, and you don't. You've had some pretty

racy implied sex which may have been in my imagination, but it's the last place you can read stories and use your imagination. I wonder how that can be handled within the framework of the Code.

Stan Lee: You scared me for a minute when you said sex and comics and your competitors had Superman and Batman. . . . You finished the sentence pretty quickly. . . . Well, actually as far as we're concerned we try to be reasonable and rational. Where you wouldn't see a girl wear her skirt above the knee years ago, but now you do, there might be situations. . . . For example, I can't see anything wrong if there's a married couple and you want to show them waking up in the morning in a double bed. But we don't concentrate on those things. I don't even know how the Code would feel about it. I don't even recall if we've done that yet. But we certainly have our characters fall in love, have romantic problems. Again, we try to make everything as realistic as possible without offending anyone. Without offending what we'd consider to be any reasonable person. Now, of course, you could have a radio show on "what is a reasonable person?" But we really have so many older readers and younger readers whose parents look at the books also—we've had no letters of complaint. So, as far as sex, I think we're probably handling the thing perfectly fine, and I know the Code has not complained, and I don't think we're doing it in the way you just described like the cowboy who will only kiss his horse. We sort of give the idea that our characters are reasonably normal human beings who won't turn the other way if a pretty girl comes by. We're not selling sex in our stories. Let me put it that way. We don't attempt to play up the sex in anyway. But if a story should call for somebody who is attracted to somebody of the opposite sex or whatever, we try to put it in so that it makes sense.

Lawrence Van Gelder: There was a time, I know, and I think it still goes on, when you go out and do a lot of lecturing on campus. I gather you get ideas from students. I wonder what feelings you get when you talk to them generally about the magazines.

Stan Lee: The same thing seems to happen. We start out talking about the magazines. And they are tremendously interested in the magazines, which is why I do receive so many invitations to lecture at about every college in the free world I guess. But a strange thing occurs. After we've been talking about oh, five or ten minutes about the magazines. Suddenly one student will say "Well, what do you think about Vietnam?" or "What do you think about Angela Davis?" or whatever.

And we're off and running on things that are far more relevant possibly than on whether Spider-Man should marry his girlfriend. And this takes up almost the whole seminar. In fact these things go on for hours. They're totally fascinating. If I've learned anything from the kids on campus, the thing I've learned is that you got to make your comic magazines or your televisions shows or your movies or whatever relate to the real world because unless they do, you have meaningless cardboard characters, and that's not really what people are into today. They want stories that will tell them something about the world they are living in now. If you are clever enough to make those stories entertaining or exciting and to use continuing characters that they want to read more of, I guess that's the ideal solution. But I've never known anything like [the way things are now]. . . . Why, years ago I used to lecture, and the whole lecture was just about the comics. But now it seems every age group, whether they are radicals or whether they are conservatives, they want to know what about today? What about what's happening now?

Vanderbilt University Symposium with Stan Lee, Jack Kirby, and Others

VANDERBILT UNIVERSITY / 1972

Transcript of symposium held April 28–29, 1972, at Vanderbilt University from the archives of Stan Lee. Printed in part in the *Jack Kirby Collector*, vol. 2, no. 5 (May 1995). Reprinted by permission of Stan Lee.

Q: Mr. Lee, who is your best-selling character at Marvel, and who is your favorite character?

Stan Lee: Well, the best-selling one is *Spider-Man*. *Spider-Man* is absolutely amazing. It's been the best-selling one ever since it started. That's been over ten years, and it's never not been the best-selling comic. And I really don't have a favorite. It's like asking a parent who's his favorite child. Whichever one I write at the moment is my favorite at that moment. But I like them all, really.

Q: Mr. Wilson, do you feel your work has been influenced by Charles
Addams?
Gahan Wilson: Who's Charles Addams?

Q: Mr. Berg, if someone had a story for *Mad* and drew up the completed
story with finished artwork and sent it in, would there be a chance of
having it published?
Dave Berg: Not with the art. There is a pretty fixed art staff. But
writers they're always looking for. Type up your script, mail it to
the editor. It will be looked at. They have a staff to look at it. Believe
me, they're always looking for writers. That's the hardest job of all.
Look at it this way: it's harder to write a short letter than a long letter,
and it's harder to write a short story than a novel, and novelists tell me
that the kind of work we do at *Mad* is the hardest work of all. Now does
that make me smarter than them—it makes me stupid for taking the
hardest work in the world. But if you have a script, send it. It will be
looked at.

Q: Who is Charles Addams?
Lee: Charles Addams is the *New Yorker* cartoonist who draws those
macabre cartoons. I gotta mention one thing. I was stationed with
Addams in the army, and you know he always drew this one gal, a sort
of Vampirella type, with the long black hair, the straight, stringy black
hair. Well, I met Charles Addams's then-wife at the time . . . beautiful,
but she looked just like her.
Wilson: One of the great compliments, and seriously, yes I do know who
Charles Addams is, and yes he was a very definite influence, and all that,
you bet! But one of the great things, and I'm very proud of this, is that I
remember when I was a kid there was a recurrent rumor that Charles
Addams was put away annually in a booby hatch. And now I hear the
same rumor applies to me.

Q: Mr. Lee, when will you solve the problems of characters like Spider-Man
and the Hulk?
Lee: Well, if I can help it, never. I'm sure Allen (Saunders) will agree with
me that as long as these characters have their problems we hope that
that holds the audience. I think all of you here are interested in characters who have problems, so maybe I'll never solve them.

Q: Mr. Lee, as a satiric story, how do you think the idea of a "Student Prince", possibly as a loser in a student/college environment, would fare in comics form?

Lee: Well, the funny thing is that anything is a good idea. I would say that would be perfectly fine. When people say, "Where do you get your ideas from?"—not just to me, but to everybody here and in any creative field—I find myself that ideas are just about the easiest thing. The original idea is easy. It's then what do you do with it? Now your "Student Prince"—fine. Maybe I could come up with something great if I used that idea and maybe I'd fall on my face. Maybe Dave could take it and make it a great feature in *Mad*, or Allen could use it in *Mary Worth*, or Gahan in a cartoon. There's no such thing, to me, as a really bad idea or a really good idea. Everything depends on how it's executed. I hope I've evaded your question successfully.

Q: Mr. Lee, why do the monsters always have such terrible dialogue?

Lee: Why didn't I stay home? Well, I don't know. I guess you can have such dialogue if you're being satirical. Maybe the dialogue sort of points out the satire. Anyway, any monster who has dialogue—well, you were being satirical by asking the question, and thank you for giving us a laugh.

Q: Mr. Lee, how do you keep your head straight trying to keep up with so many characters?

Lee: I don't. I have a lot of assistants like Roy Thomas and Gary Friedrich. Every time somebody says to me, "Hey, Stan, what happened to so-and-so," I say, "Hey, Roy, what happened to so-and-so?" Now Roy is the greatest; this man is all memory. If I were to write something, he'd say, "No Stan, you wrote that in issue #12 of the *Hulk*" or something. With guys like that I don't need a memory, and that's lucky for me because I'm afraid I don't have much of one. But our stories aren't all that authentic, as some of you have intimated, and the big thing is that we just keep rolling along and hope that there's enough excitement and enough going on that people won't realize how many boners we're making.

Q: Mr. Saunders, do you write your strip in day-by-day pattern or in a continuous sequence?

Allen Saunders: I am a creature of habit and over the years I've found that the simplest thing to do is to sit down in my little cubbyhole of an office—I can't work at home because there's too much confusion and I might be asked to rake the yard or something—so I come in and decide,

"Well, today might be a good day to write a week of *Steve Roper* or a week of *Mary Worth*" and I write the copy for one week almost always in one day—that's six dailies and a Sunday page. Then these beautiful drawings have to be done, and I go home and sit in front of the television set—I used to do this with radio because you could draw and listen and nothing happened, and I thought when television came in "Why, those days are gone forever." Seems they haven't gone forever at all since there's so little on television that you really want to look at. I can still sit there in front of the television and draw. So I do the entire copy for one strip in the daytime, and put the sketches in that night.

Q: Mr. Lee, do you enjoy seeing the Marvel characters on television, and do the TV shows affect your books in any way?

Lee: Well, from an aesthetic point of view I think it's horrible, because we try to do *Spider-Man* for an older audience, and on television they do it for the six-year-olds. I don't think it helps or hurts. I think that the people who watch it on television don't necessarily buy the books, and the people who buy the books don't necessarily watch it on television. It's a totally different market. And I was very interested in the television series in the beginning. I flew out to the coast, and I discussed these things with Hanna-Barbera and Krantz Films and so forth, until I realized discussing it meant nothing because all they're interested in doing is pleasing the sponsor. Not the network, not us, but the sponsor. But the sponsor is only interested in the four, five, and six-year-olds who will buy the breakfast food or whatever. So it is such a totally different thing that, except for having the names of our characters, there's almost no relationship.

Q: Mr. Lee, approximately what age audience do you try to pattern your comics for?

Lee: We try the impossible. We try to gather everybody together as our audience. But what happened is, in the beginning comics were read by kids from four years old up to about twelve or thirteen, and maybe an occasional serviceman in World War II, and that was about all. But little-by-little, and I'd like to think since the advent of Marvel, we've been upgrading the audience, too the point now where just about every college and university has a core of Marvel fans. There are adults who read them, so it's certainly not unusual to see seventeen, eighteen, or nineteen-year-olds reading Marvel. To answer your question more specifically, what I try to do in writing the stories is to get enough human interest, drama, good characterization, dialogue—as much as we can within the confines of the comic strip format to interest the older reader, and we try to get enough color and action and excitement not to lose the younger reader, and it's very difficult. We're always straddling the fence. If we get too good we lose a lot of the younger readers and we really can't afford to do that; we need those sales. If we cater to the younger readers, we'll lose the older readers, and we certainly don't want to do that. So it's a real ulcer situation.

Q: Mr. Lee, I was looking at the cover of this comic handed to me at the door, and it says "Approved by the Comics Code Authority." I was wondering if that was composed of people in the industry or the Subversive Activities Control Board or what?

Lee: It's like the Motion Picture Authority, really. Years ago there was a psychiatrist named Fredric Wertham who decided that all the ills of the world were caused by comic books. He got a lot of publicity, and he was really hurting the comic book business, and he was about to go after other industries in the media, so we banded together and the publishers appointed a "comic book czar"—not a man in the industry, actually he was a judge at the time. He has since resigned, and there was a woman who was head of many women's organizations who did the job. There is now an attorney who has the job of "comic book czar." Totally independent of the publishers, and we really listen to them. If they find something that's objectionable, they tell us and we change it. But that happens very rarely. In comics, really, the most you can object to is that they might be boring, you might have read the story before, or we might have made a lot of mistakes. But I don't think there's anything for anyone to make a big fuss over.

Q: Mr. Wilson, how closely do you work with Hugh Hefner?

Wilson: Well, that's very interesting. Hef wanted to be a cartoonist; he's a failed cartoonist. He really is. He did cartoons, tried to sell them, failed. Actually, they were awful. He went to great expense to publicize them, went on TV shows, and in early issues of *Playboy* you find several cartoons signed "Hef." But he went on to become a very good editor and realized he was a lousy cartoonist and fired himself. As an editor though he's really the best. No kidding! The best I ever worked with. Lots of times cartoon editors will give you lots of talk, and it really doesn't sharpen the cartoon. But Hefner has a really extraordinary ability to take the particular artist, and his criticisms will be supremely apt for that artist. Beautifully so, I mean he's really good!

Q: Should a cartoonist be ethical?

Berg: On the question of being ethical, *Mad Magazine* was in peril when a mid-western minister wrote an article about *Mad* which eventually turned into a book. It was Rev. Vernon Ellar, and the book was called *The Mad Morality*, where he claimed *Mad* was often better than Biblical ethics. He made the point that we don't think things are evil, we think things are stupid. Now *Mad* was terrified that the "Establishment" was cheering us. One of the things he said, for instance, was that "underneath the pile of garbage that is *Mad Magazine* beats the heart of a rabbi." Now frankly, I don't know who he's talking about, because I'm not a rabbi—a prophet, maybe—but not a rabbi. It really got us uptight.

Q: What restraints do you feel you're working under? Are they political, or social or . . .

Lee: (facetiously): Economic. If something can make money for Marvel Comics, it is good. What's good for Marvel Comics is good for . . . Stan Lee's country . . . But I don't know. As far as what's right and what's wrong, I don't think those things ever really change. I think everybody has a different conception. It seems to me that anything you can do that doesn't hurt anybody else and pleases you—that would seem pretty right to you. My only taboo is something that might be injurious in some way to other people, and if it isn't, I don't care what anybody says, we'll go ahead and do it . . . unless we lose money.

Garry Trudeau: But how do you think such a thing can be determined? I've found that there's a complete double standard as to what's acceptable on the comics page and what's accepted in the rest of the newspaper. There are so many subjects which editors feel should not be found with the comics—that it should be a tranquilizing experience.

Lee: Well, let me tell you a story about the newspapers. This may be a little known fact, but I had a couple of newspaper strips a few years ago, and it was a frightening experience. It was like *Alice in Wonderland*. I had an editor, who shall be nameless, and I remember I did a gag, and I thought it was kind of funny, and the punch line involved a pogo stick. I don't remember what the gag was, but the two words *pogo stick* were part of the punch line. This editor, in his benign wisdom, said to me, "You know, Stan, you're from New York." Well, I didn't think that was so terrible, but what does that have to do with a pogo stick? "Our strip goes all around the country, boy, and there are people who don't know what a pogo stick is. You know in Slow Falls, Iowa, they may not know that. We better appeal to everybody." And he told me to change it to *roller skates*. Now as I said, I don't remember the gag, and you'll have to take my word for it. This gag was not funny in the context of roller skates. You know, it's like the word *pickles* which is funny, and the word *peach* isn't funny. Now *pogo stick* had a funny sound. Anyway, he was the editor, and we changed the words to *roller skates*, and I might add that the strip was eventually dropped by the newspapers, and this is my defense: I was working for an editor who thought that roller skates were better than a pogo stick. But this type of censorship, to me, is almost indecent. Whether the artist is Garry Trudeau or the writer is Allen Saunders or what, you hire somebody, I assume, for the talent they have, and there might be certain taboos. But it seems to me that if a person is doing something creatively, and he feels that's the way it ought to be done, you've gotta let him do it. That way you either don't let him do the strip at all, or let him do it his way. But I think too many strips, too many motion pictures, too many books have failed because at some point they were emasculated by an editor. And because the artist, or the writer, or the musician, or the actor, or whatever is desperate for the job, he compromises, he feels it should be done one way, the editor wants it done another way, and they compromise. I don't think anything good artistically has ever been accomplished that way. And excuse me. I didn't mean to make a speech.

Trudeau: Are there any questions from the audience?

Audience member: Would anybody care to comment on the connection between writing as an art and the art itself?

Lee: I'll make this short. The art of writing is to write the story, and the art of drawing is to draw the pictures. Now some people just write the stories, some people just draw the pictures, and some guys do both. And if anybody can add anything to that . . .

Jack Kirby: I'll grab hold of this. I've worked with writers and artists. I know that the writing helps the art, and the art is supposed to help the writing. Combined, they're supposed to have an impact upon the reader. Some cartoons don't have writing at all, and I suppose you can call that graphic manual art. That's what makes them work. Sometimes the writing will make an adventure strip work. Sometimes, if you get the right man to write the strip, you can get a strip with a lot of impact. So the writer is necessary to the strip because that's been the format all along. Someone has to write the balloons. If you're an extremely talented artist you can write the script yourself; that's been done too. Writing and drawing are both arts, and the combination of both fields can make a very fine product. They're separate arts, but not inseparable. They help each other in the best way possible.

Saunders: I think a badly drawn strip is the hardest thing in the world to sell next to rotten eggs, or something like that.

Audience Member: What do you think of comic books like *Green Lantern/Green Arrow* which use relevance as a theme?

Lee: Is that for me?

Audience Member: That is for you and Mr. Kirby.

Lee: Well, let Jack go first.

Kirby: I feel that doing any story on a very serious situation in a comic book is wrong. Because of the restrictive nature of its own format, a comic book cannot do a definitive analysis of a given issue. It can do it in a general way, it can probably gloss over it or mention it or maybe devote a segment of the story to it, but it cannot give a definitive opinion of the issue. If I thought *Green Lantern* had done anything constructive in that direction, it would be fine. But I thought they couldn't have given the whole story, and possibly left out an important part of the issue. So I felt they were right by doing it, but they missed the point by not doing it in a different format. They should have done a bigger *Green Lantern*, a book of say 200–250 pages. That would tell a really good story on any given issue, and it would have meant something. Because those issues are not entertainment; they're really problems. And I feel a problem should be extremely well-defined. A comic book, as it is now, really labors to put it across. Certainly, those books did a good job, as far as they went. But I feel they should have been given more of a chance to really tell the story. Because that's what you want, if you have a serious issue, you should get the story, every detail. And that's my opinion on the *Green Lantern* book.

Lee: Well, since *Green Lantern* is a competitive magazine of ours, I think the book is already too big. I must disagree; I don't agree with Jack about comic books not being a medium for serious messages. I've always felt that comics are a legitimate art form, really no different from movies, radio, television, novels, plays, what have you. I think that anything you can say in any other medium, you can say in a comic. Years ago, when I was in the army, one of the things I did was write comic books on very serious subjects for training. I taught people how to operate Sherman tanks and how to avoid venereal disease. Very important subjects, but they used the comics format. We were able to get a message across clearly, succinctly, and briefly and very effectively we found through the use of comics. As far as *Green Lantern* is concerned, basically, I think the editors of National Comics and we at Marvel have basic, total disagreement in editorial policy on the way these things should be handled. I do agree when Jack said comics are entertainment; of course they are. Our purpose is to entertain our readers as best we can. I love trying to get messages into the stories. I love trying to moralize, sermonize, but it has to be done in a subtle way, in almost a subliminal way. On the other hand, at National they love the idea of their books being "relevant" now. And my own feeling is a personal feeling—they try to hit the reader over the head with their "relevance." Their covers say, "Hey gang, this is a relevant issue. Look at the guy with the needle in his arm." and they may be right, but it is totally in opposition to the way I feel about these things.

Kirby: May I add just one point. I think that's one thing they did right. And I think that's one thing the other books did right, is the fact that they do show that. I felt that, as long as they did do it, showing the problem as it is, the needle in the arm is the only way to portray the drug, the only way to portray the issue. Because that's essentially what it is. There's no other way to do it. *Green Lantern* from that point of view I think was good. They didn't take any other way around the issue. I felt that they didn't say enough. I wanted to see a bigger *Green Lantern* in a more definitive way to tell the real story of drugs. When the real story is told and people can take a good look at it and see what it's really like, then I think the people who are inclined to slip into that sort of thing will hesitate to do so. So the needle in the arm, I think, is a symbol of what the problem really is, and if it's ugly, let's face it, it's ugly, and we have to show it. And I think they were very honest to do that, and very right to do that.

Audience Member: I was wondering, I have a comic here, and it has these ads on "How to throw a groovy party for under $5" and "How to lose ugly fat." I was wondering if these things were really necessary to be in your comics, for them to go on sale. Do you need these to make it economically possible?

Lee: Let's try to dispose of this quickly. I couldn't agree with you more. Yes, they are necessary in order for the comics to be financially successful, but they evidence a tremendous lack of judgement and discretion on the part of our advertising department. For years the ads in comic books have been a source of great embarrassment to me, and as soon as possible I intend to try to upgrade them. We had one I thought was a horror, and I insisted they remove this ad. I don't know if you remember it. A few months ago, and I didn't know about it until I saw it for the first time in the book that I was reading. It said "You can be taller. Increase your height by three inches." And I went to my then-publisher and I said, "How can you allow a thing like this in the book?" And so we did take the ad out. Unfortunately, it's just one of the things we haven't had too much time to think about. But I agree with you 100 percent.

Jenette Kahn, Stan Lee, and Harvey Kurtzman Discuss Comics

MIKE GOLD / 1976

From *Tales from Texas*, ca. 1977.
Transcribed and edited by Lewis Shiner.
Reprinted by permission of Lewis Shiner.

A discussion conducted by Mike Gold, head of public relations for DC comics Inc., featuring Stan Lee, publisher of Marvel Comics, Jenette Kahn, publisher of DC Comics, and Harvey Kurtzman, freelance humorist, co-creator of Little Annie Fanny, etc. This discussion took place at the Chicago Comicon, August 8, 1976.

Lee: To me it seems that asking why we're still doing the same thing is like asking General Motors, "Say, how come you guys are still making cars? I mean, why don't you do something original?" We're in the business of doing comic books. What else are we going to do? I mean, Harvey, whom I lo—whom I li—whom I've known for a while (*laughter*) is not in the comic book business, so why should he be doing comic books? He could be doing anything he wants to. So long as my job is publisher of Marvel Comics, of course that's what I'll do, and the same with Jenette. As far as not doing new things, it seems to me we might come up with a couple of things we've done in the past few decades, but there's just so much you can do in the comic book business. You're doing comic strips in book form, and that's it. Saying why don't we get into undergrounds is like saying why don't we cut records, or why don't we do this or that—it's a totally different field. It's for different readers, and you can't really treat it that much as a business. The minute you become successful you can't be too radical—all you can do is the best you can within the confines of what your field is.

Kurtzman: To play devil's advocate for a minute, Stan, I'd like to ask a question. Why is it that comics have such a low grade of integrity? By contrast with so-called slick magazines—the larger proportion of magazines that we're all familiar with—and by contrast with the European comics, which we all know are drawn and printed beautifully?

Lee: Boy, I don't know where to begin. That's like saying, "When did you stop beating your wife?" You're—

Kurtzman: (*Interrupting*) I was going to ask that after you finished the first question.

Lee: Yeah, I know—I haven't stopped! I—I don't know which point to take first . . .

Kurtzman: (*Interrupting*) By low I mean if you could quantify on an abstract scale—low pay, low printing process—I'm not trying to say evil, or bad, just low grade.

Lee: I'm afraid to try and answer—you'll interrupt me again. Can I talk?

Kurtzman: Sure, go ahead.

Lee: You're mad because you said I talked too much yesterday—

Kurtzman: (*Interrupting*) What makes you think I'll interrupt?

Lee: —that's what it is. (*pause*)

Kurtzman: Go ahead, Stan.

Lee: Thank you, Harvey. What you said is certainly true about the comics being printed on cheaper paper, and obviously that's so we can charge 30 cents for a copy. It would be the easiest thing in the world of us to have all the integrity of European publishers, and people would be paying $2.98 or $5.00 for every comic book you bought.

Kurtzman: I'll keep interrupting, Stan, because it's fun. Why doesn't *Newsweek* or *Playboy* or *Time* magazine use the same logic.

Lee: Because they don't make money on the sales of their books. They make most of their money off advertising, just like a newspaper. In order to attract national advertising, they have to print on slick paper with color and so forth. Comic book companies like National and Marvel have been trying to change this image and to upgrade it for years, while you were out doing *Annie Fanny* and deserted us. And we—
Kurtzman: (*Interrupting*) I was busy upgrading the image.

Lee: We could never get General Motors, say, to advertise in the *Hulk*. We would love to. It is very unlikely that Xerox or IBM is gonna advertise—at least in the next few months—in *Howard the Duck*. So we have to live with 100 soldiers for a nickel, or whatever it is. Anyhow, I appreciate you wanting an argument. I love you too much to argue. However Jenette doesn't love you that much, so I'll stop hogging this.
Kurtzman: I'd like to hear what Jenette has to say.
Kahn: A lot of what Stan says in true—

Lee: (*Interrupting*) A lot? What about all, like for example?
Kahn: Not possible. But a lot. But comics are, here in America, a mass medium, and that means we have to sell as many comics to as many people as possible for as low a price as possible. Comics, when they began really were the equivalent of television to most people. They brought more than a movie because you could take it home with you. They were what you had in your home that was narrative, that was fantasy, and that was a visual realization of that fantasy. There was a time when *Crime Does Not Pay*, I think, sold 1,300,000 copies of the comic every time it came out. Of course the numbers have been shrinking, but still comics are meant for as many people as possible, and in order to do that you have to have high press runs. To keep the price down, yes, we have printed on cheap paper. It's a whole different marketing approach to print the French comics. They're a different species, really.

In terms of Harvey's second point, about the artists and writers being underpaid, that's true. Why nothing has happened in thirty years to change that I don't know, but something is happening now at National. And things are changing in that direction because that has been the great inequity of the business.

Lee: I am sure that artists and writers in the comic business, and editors, and most of all publishers, are underpaid. I don't think there is a business in the world where the people in it don't think they're underpaid. But there are very few—there are none—artists and writers in our business who are reasonably good, and are employed, who are on relief or walking the breadlines, or anything like that. I think the average salary, the average income of not the top guy, but a reasonably good artist or writer, certainly at Marvel, is about $20,000 a year. All right, he's not going to be a millionaire, but I don't think this is the worst thing in the world. Usually any industry pays as much as it can. People feel comic books make millions and millions of dollars, but there are many years when the companies have literally lost money. Just think of all the comic book companies that have gone out of business. So it's not a case of everybody's pocketing millions and just trampling on the poor artists and writers.

Kurtzman: I'm going to continue to try to play devil's advocate. Later on we'll kiss and make up, right? My impression of the comic book business, historically, is that comic book publishers have never been inspired. There has a never been in the past inspiration on a publishing level. The kind of inspiration that created the Luce empire or the Playboy empire or—

Lee: Or *Howard the Duck*.

Kurtzman: *Howard the Duck* . . . There are exceptions in comics in 1976, and certainly there are exceptions in France, where—

Lee: Harvey, how many copies of *Linus* do they sell, an issue?
Kurtzman: That's not important . . .

Lee: It's everything! Whaddaya mean it's not important?
Kurtzman: What's important to me is the fact of the existence of good comic book publishing in certain portions of the globe. And these magazines are being put out by inspired publishers.

Lee: Yes, I guess you're right, Harvey. It's only the people who are away from the norm, who are doing things on their own who are doing any good. *Annie Fanny* is no good because it's part of the Hefner empire and you've done nothing new for the last fifteen years and why the hell don't you go out and break the mold, and Hefner's just looking to make money, and Alfred Hitchcock when he does a movie is just looking to make money and Fellini, and their movies are no good, and when Kurt Vonnegut writes a book he's just out to make money and the publisher is doing it—
Kurtzman: Stan—can you—

Lee: Harvey, that's the biggest crock I've ever heard in my life! There are inspired comic books. Read some sometimes. If people didn't enjoy today's comic books, we wouldn't have these conventions. You're talking as though we're discussing a field that has nothing good in it and that nobody likes, and why don't we do something good. We'll admit the paper's no good! We wish it could be better. Find a way to give us better paper and charge 30 cents.

Kurtzman: I will admit that on an artistic level comics have been very inspired over the years. There have always been artists willing to break their heads for their art work. There have always been writers who have been inspired. Publishers, in my experience of comic books, were never inspired like the artists were, like the writers were, like sometimes the editors were.

Lee: Harvey, you are belaboring the most ridiculous point in the world! A) You're making it sound as if you wish comics were printed on lovely paper with fantastic printing—

Kurtzman: (*Interrupting*) Don't you?

Lee: Of course we do! And I wish the books were a hundred and fifty pages each! And I wish we had Kurt Vonnegut writing for us, and I mean, My God! We can all say what we wish, but the thing is impossible at the moment.

Kahn: In the beginning it was accountants and businessmen and people who ran the comic companies, and they did not care about what they produced, and they didn't care about their artists or their writers or their material. Times have changed, and Stan, who began as a writer, is now a publisher. I, who began creating magazines on both the art side and on the writing side, am now a publisher, and both of us I think consider ourselves inspired people who care about the medium, who love comics. And I think you'll see the changes coming. It's not what happened before. That's history now. It's what's going to come in the future. I think that's represented by Stan and myself. (*Applause*)

Question: (*from audience*) I think basically the comic book form is the way it is because people like it. I don't think there's a great desire on the part of most consumers to change the basic format of the comic.

Kurtzman: There's never a great desire for anything that hasn't been invented yet. It's when it's invented that all of a sudden there's the desire. You never work on the premise that you never improve things because people are satisfied with the buggy whip. If you're creative and enjoy what a creative society does, which is ever changing. There's always the argument, "why change anything?" I'll go with that argument, if you just want to go on and on in the same way you've been going. There's virtue in that, too. When you seek to develop new forms, and on this globe I've seen exciting new cartoon forms. I know it's been done. It's been done in Europe. Why shouldn't we be developing those areas as well? Is it because we have a perfectly satisfactory form and we can rest on that? I don't think so.

Lee: What makes you think we're not?

Kurtzman: You can go into a Parisian book shop and find on the shelves four or five, six feet of hardcover on the shelves, four or five, six feet of hardcover comic collections. Not the esoteric quasi-underground stuff that's coming from the rebels or the would-be French undergrounders, but collections of strips out of *Pilote* magazine, *Tin-Tin*, and they're just done in a very respectable format. Somebody's buying all that stuff. Tons of it.

Lee: Not really that many, Harvey, and—

Kurtzman: And we have nothing! NOTHING!

Lee: Let me give you an example. Have you seen the *Origins of Marvel Comics*? Now there's comics on slick paper. The damn book, we couldn't produce it for less than seven bucks. So we managed over a period of a year, we sold 25 or 30 or 35 thousand, which is damn good. But we sell that many—more than that—of *Spider-Man*, month after month after month.

Question: Don't you find that the lack of change in comics represents a certain stability?

Kurtzman: Well, I find that I enjoy change, myself. It's a very personal thing. I find that there are people who are very comfortable with stability. Sameness. If you enjoy sameness, then by all means, nothing should change. If you enjoy change, then let's be creative.

Kahn: I think there's a lot in what you're saying. When I say that comics are a mass medium, that's true, and the more you move in the direction that Harvey's speaking of, the smaller you will shrink your audience. But Harvey did mention at one time there's no reason that both can't be done, and that's really the solution. There's no reason why we can't make ventures into the kind of printing that does go on in France. And find that market, which might be separate from the traditional comic reader. Somebody made the remark that it doesn't seem to matter to the comic reader about the quality of the paper—sure you feel bad about it, but it doesn't take away from the fact that the story is good and the artwork is good. That's really what you buy a comic for—the story, and how it looks. I think one of the ways to go is to give you more story and better artwork, and more creative stories.

The whole other question of quality publishing . . . I don't like to call it a low integrity business because integrity implies morals and ethics, but I'd call it low quality in terms of the—

Lee: No! It's not low quality either. It's probably as high a quality business as you could find. I want to mention one thing that I really take exception to, Harvey, and that is when you talk about creativeness. For years people have considered people who labor for money in the art field as hacks, and the people who go out and just do their own thing in a garret somewhere you know, they're the fine artists and they're the creative ones. It's something I don't really agree with, and I'll tell you why. It seems to me that somebody who has to be creative within a structured framework is in a much more difficult position and has to be more creative. Now look at it this way. If we are not creative presently in the comic business, none of you are going to buy our books or be interested. The only way we hold your interest is to be creative, month after month after month so that you enjoy these stories. Despite what Harvey said, if these things don't keep changing you'll be bored sick!

Question: Mr. Kurtzman, you said there weren't any inspired publishers in the past, and I assume you put Bill Gaines in that bag. Would you like to make any comments about that?

Kurtzman: Well . . . Gaines was the beginning of inspiration for me. For my personal experience, and I was careful to say that my view of the lack of inspiration was most intense between the middle forties and fifties. I came on to Bill Gaines in the middle fifties. There was a certain degree of inspiration involved in his line of comics, although it hardly scratched the surface for me. The intention seemed to be there. The comic book business certainly hasn't been a wasteland, there's been inspiration since the middle fifties. The business could use more. The format is still a low grade format. It's the lowest grade format in media. It's capable of being much, much better, and when it gets better it has to happen on a publishing level.

Lee: Anybody can say, "Hey, listen, I got a great idea, we'll make the book bigger and we'll get more pages and we'll make it round!" We used to laugh in our office in our circulation company—one guy, who suddenly got a lot of money and wanted to be a publisher was going to revolutionize the business. He said, "I got an idea for a book that nobody ever though of. I'm going to print it on round paper! It'll be a round book!" And he really wanted to sink hundred of thousands of dollars into this. Well, we showed him the error of his ways. One of the little problems would be it wouldn't stay on the newstand—it would roll off!

Question: Do you think there's any area other than *Howard the Duck* where fantasy and superhero comics can cross over into the realm of humor?

Lee: Sure, but these things are usually, never planned. Nobody at Marvel, certainly not Steve Gerber, said "I'm going to take a superhero or a fantasy adventure story and I'm now going to inject humor and start a new thing." He was writing it and he thought of this great idea for a plot and put it in and it happened. And that's the way things are. It's very possible—maybe probable—that other things like this will be happening in the next few months. But Harvey was talking about inspiration—basically these things are inspiration. As you write a story, as you draw a story, you're never really sure what the end result is going to be. Sometimes you get a result you didn't even expect. A little incidental character that you just threw in for kicks takes off, sets a whole new trend. This is what happened with Howard, and it can always happen again.

Kahn: Stan's right about the planning. For instance, I'm a great Howard the Duck fan, and I sure wish that Howard the Duck was running rampant through the pages of National. But I would never ask a writer to come up with a Howard the Duck for National. You shouldn't look over your shoulder at what the other company is doing thinking, "Howard's hot, we really ought to have a Howard." You just do what comes really, basically from your heart, or from the inspiration you're talking about. What really feels best and right to you. And then you have the best comics.

Meet the Wizard of Biff! Bop! Pow!

MURRAY SUID / 1976

From *Learning*, November 1976,
pp. 82, 85. Reprinted by permission
of Murray Suid.

Suid: Why do kids like comics?
Lee: There are so many reasons. There's the action, the colour, the fantasy, the fairy-tale quality, the element of the unexpected. Comics give kids something they can't get in other forms of media. They don't get it in newspapers or movies or television.

Suid: But doesn't television supply fantasy?
Lee: Not the way a comic book does. The tube is more realistic. Take westerns or crime shows. They may be unreal in the sense that they're romanticized, but everything is very realistically portrayed. When comic artists want something far out, we can draw whatever we dream. We can draw the impossible. Television can't photograph the impossible. So even fantasy-type shows like *The Six Million Dollar Man* are still very down-to-earth.

Suid: You mentioned a "fairy-tale" quality in comics.

Lee: I think of our stories as fairy tales for people who have outgrown conventional fairy tales. Everybody in the world has loved traditional fairy tales as a young person. I think we all have a warm spot in our hearts for the Grimm or the Andersen stories, the Oz books, Br'er Rabbit, things like that. But when you get a little older—as you reach ten, eleven, and twelve—you don't want your friends to see you reading *Cinderella* or *Little Red Riding Hood*.

Then suddenly you discover that comic books have what you've been looking for. Everything is bigger than life. There's an element of magic. There's a tremendous amount of fantasy running through them. Anything goes! And consequently, the reader is really getting the same type of pleasure he had gotten years before when he read *Jack and the Beanstalk*. He gets it in the comics. Where else can he go for that kind of entertainment?

Now I know that TV and movies also entertain kids magnificently. I wouldn't knock either medium, both of which I love as much as I love comics. But with TV and film, the experience is fleeting. You see it once and it's gone. A comic book, on the other hand, is a *book*. And the wonderful thing about a book or a magazine is that it has a permanence. You can read it at your own pace, go back and reread it if you like, and then digest it or luxuriate in it as long as you wish. And the next day, you can read it again. Or if you're not in the mood, you can put it aside and read it a little bit later. You can spend as much time with one panel as you wish. This is a luxury you simply can't enjoy with theater, with TV, and with the movies. This is why comic books—and books in general—weren't wiped out by the advent of television. Actually, the printed media are bigger than ever in recent years. The fact is, something you see fleetingly on the screen can never replace something you can hold in your hands and experience at your own pace.

Suid: You're including comic books and real books in the same category.

Lee: They're both literature. They belong together.

Suid: You think kids read comics the same way they read a regular book?

Lee: I don't just think it. I *know* it. Over the years, we've been swamped with letters from kids discussing the plots and writing style of our stories. There are almost no kids in the world who just look at the pictures. Even the five-and six-year-olds just learning how to read read the words in our comics and write us letters about what they read and how they feel about it.

Suid: Still, don't most people think of reading comics as being something different from reading real books?

Lee: Reading is reading. Someday I'm going on a crusade and I'm going to stump for comic books to be used in schools. Every time I pick up a newspaper and see the statistics on how the quality of reading is declining throughout the country, I want to devote myself to convincing teachers that anything a youngster wants to read has to be beneficial.

Suid: What makes you so sure?

Lee: We can tell from the letters we receive from both kids and parents. I think one of the greatest letters I ever received was from a mother who wrote that her son was valedictorian of his graduating class. She said: "I just want to tell you that he's an honor student, and his father and I want you to know that the three of us have every reason to be proud of him. We do, because we're his parents, and you do, because you've contributed so much to his education." Imagine how I felt!

Every day we get mail from teachers saying that our books are used in a range of courses—from remedial reading to contemporary literature. They even say that the vocabulary in our comics is better than that found in some of the standard junior high readers; the words are more adult. The teachers are just delighted because the kids have advanced their vocabulary by reading comics.

We never reject a word because it might be over the head of the reader. If a story calls for a word like "radiation" or "subliminal," we'll use it because we feel that the young reader will absorb it by osmosis, or he'll look it up. We get letters from kids in disadvantaged neighbor-hoods, written in the vernacular, so to speak, and these kids will throw in a word like "cataclysmic" that they're seen in one of our comics.

Suid: I'm surprised that you give so much attention to the verbal part of such a visual medium.

Lee: I love words—the sound of them, the flavor of them. I love the rhythm of the words in the Bible. I love the way Shakespeare used words—"What ho, Horatio." I try to get that flavor in stories like *Thor*. When I first started writing comic scripts, my colleagues thought I was crazy. I'm a very fast writer, but I might stop and spend ten minutes looking for the right word. I like to think that anything I write will sound good when it's read aloud.

Suid: Do teachers ever tell you that they read your comics aloud in class?
Lee: Very often. Not only in class, but disc jockeys will read them over the radio. Many English professors have told me that they scan as poetry. They ask: "Do you intentionally write dialogue balloons as prose poetry?" And I do try to get a rhythm in the writing. Otherwise, it's too much like a textbook. When you read for entertainment, the words should flow and the rhythm should be right.

Suid: Do you think this is why kids like to read comics?
Lee: One of many reasons. When I have Thor say, "So be it" instead of saying, "OK," the kid reacts positively because he's aware of the dramatic language. He enjoys reading. And that's the point. Enjoyment. Reading a well-written comic book can be the most, beneficial thing in the world. You read them on two levels. If you're already a literate person, you're reading them for enjoyment. If you are not literate, you're reading them for enjoyment but you're also learning how to read.

If our comics were given to every kid from kindergarten up, I would be greatly surprised if the reading ability of students didn't improve 100 percent. Of course, librarians and teachers might not see it this way. If you're an educator or an educational publisher, you've got to think that textbooks are more influential than cheap volume literature, or, as they think of it, "newsstand sensational material." But what they don't see is that comics can be a bridge for alienated kids.

Take ghetto kids, for example. I have gone into areas where there are black kids who are very hostile to whites. And I'm a hero to them. They say, "Hey man, tell me about Spider-Man." They feel comfortable with me. And it is through the comic book that I have reached them.

Suid: Textbook producers often try out their stuff with kids. Do you?
Lee: No. Never. The minute you reduce it to a science, like writing text-books, you've lost something. We don't control vocabulary. We don't field-test. We don't slant our stories. And kids go out and buy our books. How many textbooks would they go out and buy? Of course, the pictures help them enjoy the words. They are the frosting on the cake.

Suid: But don't the pictures act as a crutch, and maybe even stop kids from taking the words seriously?

Lee: Your question reminds me of one thrown at me by a woman in the audience at one of my speaking engagements. She thought it was bad for her daughter to read comics because it would stop her from using her imagination. I asked her if her daughter's imagination would be harmed if she attended a dramatic presentation of a play by Shakespeare. There you have a marriage of words and visuals. Of course it doesn't harm the imagination! I think our comics should be compared to such an experience. I am not a snob and I don't turn up my nose at any form of culture. I consider pop music as beneficial as classical music. I consider comic books as beneficial as the works of Charles Dickens. I wouldn't put myself in the same class as a writer as Charles Dickens. For all I know, I'm better. Of course, not every story in the Marvel comic series ranks with *Oliver Twist*.

Years ago, comics were written by people who weren't really good writers. Now we're trying to make them totally different. We have writers who are former English teachers. Some also write novels. We have the finest artists in the world. There certainly is nothing wrong in telling a story with pictures and dialogue balloons. It's like a play or movies or television—except that you have less space to say your piece so you have to be more concise. Mario Puzo, the author of *The Godfather*, once tried to write a comic-book script for me. A month later he said, 'Stan, forget it, it's too difficult. In the time it would take me to do this I could write a novel.'

Suid: Are you saying that comics ought to be taught like literature?
Lee: They *are* literature. A guy playing a kazoo is playing music, don't you see? And comic books are *books*.

Suid: Do you try to deliver a moral lesson with your stories?
Lee: Some people think I take myself too seriously, but I have to. I've had so much mail over the years from parents and teachers who say, "Do you realize how influential your books are with young people?" Consequently, I have become hypersensitive about keeping out of the books anything that might be harmful. Sure, we're trying to entertain, but while entertaining we don't want to teach any values that might not be good values. We're very careful.

Suid: What about violence? Do you get condemning letters about that?
Lee: Our comics are not violent. Sure, they have a lot of fighting and action. Fistfights. The kind of fistfights we have in our comics is no

different from those in *King Richard the Lion-Hearted* fighting the Crusades. You've got to have conflict. Good vs. Evil. There has to be the giant saying, 'Fe fi fo fum' and chasing Jack. That's not violence. The real violence in the world is bigotry, war, hatred. We have a character named Dr. Doom. He's one of our top villains, always scheming to take over the world. They can't throw him in jail because there is no law against trying to take over the world. If he were a litterbug or a jaywalker, he could be sent to jail. But he can't be arrested for trying to take over the world.

Suid: Comics really teach values then?
Lee: Yes, in a non-preachy way. The minute you start to lecture kids you'll turn them off. The same is true in schools. Students would love school if they were forbidden to go. But because they're forced to go, the teacher has a tremendous problem. The student walks into the class resenting the teacher. What the teacher needs is to know how to communicate. Teacher training should include practice in communication. Teachers have to make the kids want to be in their presence. The most important thing is not to be dull.

Suid: Do you have any advice for teachers about comics?
Lee: Yes. Use them like crazy. Use them all you can.

Suid: How?
Lee: I'll leave that to you.

Suid: So be it.

The *Foom* Interview: Stan Lee

DAVID ANTHONY KRAFT / 1977

From *Foom*, vol. 1, no. 17 (March 1977),
pp. 7–17. ©2006 Marvel Characters, Inc.
Used with permission.

Foom: Well, despite the fact that you're quite well known for the Marvel Age of Comics, your own origin is still shrouded in mystery.
Stan: The Origin of Stan Lee?

Foom: Yeah. I was wondering if you could talk a little bit about where you were born and grew up—and how you were "created."
Stan: I was born of man and woman, in New York City on 98th Street, a little over fifty years ago. And I've lived virtually all my life in New York. First in Manhattan, for most of the time: then, for a little while, I lived in the Bronx. I went to DeWitt Clinton High School, Mosholu Parkway in the Bronx.

I was on the school newspaper and magazine, and I grew to love lecturing when I was in high school, because I used to lecture in classes in order to make some extra money. In those days, they had students who sold subscriptions to the *New York Times* to other students, and they were allowed to go into a class, during a break, and make their speech to the other students, So I did that. I went from class to class: "Hi, I'm Stan, and I'm selling subscriptions to the *Times*, you lucky people."

I must have been a little bit crazy, even then, because I remember they had a school magazine called the *Magpie* in those days, and it was published in a room called the Tower, which had a very high ceiling, and there was no way anybody could ever reach that ceiling. It was not quite a hundred feet high. One day it was being painted, and one of the painters had left the ladder when he went down for lunch, so I climbed up and wrote *Stan Lee Is God* on the ceiling, which was one of the earliest evidences of my overpowering inferiority complex. When the painter came back from lunch he took the ladder and left. So, unless they ever repainted the school, those imperishable words are probably still up there somewhere. I always got a kick out of that.

So much for my depraved childhood.

Foom: When and where did you begin working?
Stan: Well, I used to work while I went to school. That was right after the Depression. My father was a dress cutter. It seems the world wasn't really looking for a lot of dress cutters. It wasn't easy for him to find work—so I was always looking to help out. I would get whatever part-time jobs I could.

While I was in high school. I got a job writing obituaries for a news service, obituaries of living people, of celebrities. When a celebrity dies, the next edition of the paper carries a whole page write-up of his life. They didn't write that right away, it's been in the files. So I was writing obituaries of people who were still alive, and it got very depressing to me—writing about living people in the past tense. And eventually, even though it paid a few dollars, I gave that up.

I got a job writing publicity for the National Tuberculosis Hospital in Denver. I never quite knew what I was supposed to be publicizing, you know—convincing people to get tuberculosis. So they could go to the hospital—or what? I didn't enjoy that, so I gave that up, too.

Then I was a delivery boy, at a little sandwich shop called Jack May's I delivered sandwiches to the offices at Rockefeller Center, and I think

I made more money than any other delivery boy, because I never stopped running.

Foom: You *still* haven't stopped.
Stan: Yeah. It was like having a money machine. I'd get a dime tip in those days each time I delivered a sandwich, so I figured the more sandwiches I delivered, the more dimes I would get. Some days, I'd make $1.50 or so for a few hours work, and to me, in those days, that was sensational.

Then I decided to be an actor. They had something called the W.P.A. Federal Theatre, which was started by Franklin Roosevelt. It was to keep people working and busy. I went to a show and fell in love with one of the girls who was on the stage that night, and I figured the only way to meet her was to join the W.P.A. Federal Theatre. I did, and I met her. We were friends for quite a while; she was great. I was in a few shows and got the acting bug, and I said, "Hey, this is for me." But, you had to act for love—it paid practically nothing. I should have stayed with it, because it was great, but I was too broke. So I had to give it up. And besides, I stopped going with that girl.

Then I got a job as an office boy for the second biggest trouser manufacturer in the world. I hated it, because nobody ever took the time to learn my name. There were about a hundred people in the office, and there was another office boy, too, who had been hired first. I was the second. Whenever they wanted something they'd shout. "Boy!" And we both were supposed to drop whatever we were doing and come running. After a few weeks, I realized I don't like being called "boy." I mean, dammit, I have a name, I was always doing things wrong and getting in trouble, and hating being called "boy."

They had things called cutting tickets, which listed the sizes, shapes, materials, and the prices of different pairs of trousers. They were really sheets of oaktag, about four feet long and a foot-and-a-half high, and they had to be filed in big bins, like coffins. The company was too cheap to buy enough bins, so I always had to squeeze a lot of oaktags into less bins than there was room for, and I was coming home every night with my cuticles all cut from trying to get those oaktags in. And about two days before Christmas, I was fired.

Not only was it a lousy job, but they fired me because business was bad. Well, I got so angry about the way they did it—two days before Christmas—that when I left. I took a couple of those coffins of oaktags

and I turned them all upside down and just scattered them all over
the room. I've never been back, since.

While I was still in high school, there was a *Herald-Tribune* weekly
contest, open to all high school students. The idea was to write an essay
on what you considered to be the biggest news event of the week. I
won it three weeks running and finally the editor called me down to the
Herald-Tribune. He said, "Will you stop entering the contest, and give
someone else a chance?" I thought that was just great. I was very
proud. I said, "O.K., I'll stop entering." You got paid like a two-dollar
prize. I forget what it was, exactly. But then, he said, "What are you
going to do when you become a real person?" And I said, "I want to be
an actor." At that time, I was still with the W.P.A. Federal Theatre. He
said, "Well, why don't you think of being a writer? I don't know how
good you act, but you seem to be pretty good with words." I hadn't
really thought much about it until I heard there was a job open at
Timely Comics and realized they did *Captain America* which I used to
read then I was about sixteen years old. So I ran up there and I got
the job.

My name was Stanley Martin Lieber and I left, well, if someday I'm
going to become a writer or a great actor. I want to use that name for
the really important things. I do—I didn't figure I'd stay very long with a
comic book company. I didn't want to use my real name just on comic
books, so I shortened it to Stan Lee. Of course, what happened is I
stayed here so long that everyone knew me by that name, and it got to
be ridiculous even to bother with the other name. I had problems with
my auto license, passport, and charge accounts at stores, so I finally
changed my name.

I am now officially and legally Stan Lee (although I think someday
I'll change it back to Lieber, just to really confuse my family).

When I started working here, I was about sixteen, and after a little
while, my bosses Jack Kirby and Joe Simon left, and I was all alone.
Then, I was made the editor, because I was the only other guy around,
so I was a sixteen-and-a-half year-old editor.

Sometimes I'd be in the reception room and some guy would come in
and see me sitting there in my dungarees and sweatshirt, and say, "Hey,
kid, where can I find Mr. Lee?" It always embarrassed me, because
I didn't want to say, "I'm Mr. Lee." 'cause then I knew *he'd* be embarrassed, so instead I'd say, "Just a minute, sir, I'll tell him you're here."
Then I'd run out and say to the girl. "Tell him Mr. Lee went for the

day." just to save him the embarrassment of walking in and seeing me. So there are a lot of people I never saw—just because I was so young.

Foom: Yeah, I still have that experience. I'll call someone on the phone and they'll assume they're speaking to a middle-aged executive. Then I'll show up, and they'll figure I'm the messenger boy, and say, "Oh, give this to Mr. Kraft," I don't clue them in: I just say, "Oh, sure."
Stan: It's a funny feeling, isn't it?

Foom: What was it like in the years before Marvel?
Stan: Well, we were more-or-less a big factory. Unfortunately, we weren't really leaders, and I was so young that it never occurred to me to try to change things. In those days, young people weren't really as smart as I think they are today. You had a feeling, you don't tell older people what to do—older people know best. Years ago, nobody twenty years old would dream of saying to a boss that things should be done differently. So, I took it for granted that the way we had always done things was the way they should be done. The scripts were extremely simplistic, and I always thought the artwork was a little better than the stories, in those days, although some of the plots were good. I'd like to think I wrote a few good ones, but basically they were all one-dimensional. The good guys were good guys, the bad guys were bad guys, the stories had happy endings, and that was the end of it.

We did westerns, we did war stories, we did romance stories, we did funny animal stories, we did crime stories, we did monster stories, we did humor stories—there was no type of story that we didn't do, at one time or other. And I wrote all the different types. I'd usually write the first ones, to set the style.

Foom: Wasn't this about the time World War II began?
Stan: Yeah. And shortly after the war started, I said to myself, "What am I doing here, writing comic books?" I was seventeen or eighteen, I don't know. "Gotta get in the army, be a hero like Errol Flynn or John Wayne," so I enlisted. I figured I was good—I'd go to penny arcades and shoot those little guns and win prizes all the time—so I'd probably become a real war hero Instead, they found out the kind of work I had done, and they put me in the Signal Corps, in the film division, writing training films and instructional books.

I wrote movies and books, and drew posters—educational things. I've never illustrated comics here at Marvel—but when I was younger, I drew. I must have drawn a hundred posters for the army, all different kinds I drew them. I painted them, did everything, I loved it. I always wanted to be an artist—which is why I like the comic book business, although I couldn't draw a strip now—I'd have to go back and start studying all over again. I don't have the patience for all the work and the detail. Posters were easy. It was one drawing, and you were finished.

I've always been impatient, which is also why I like comics. I can script a story in one day, or one afternoon. The thought of writing a novel, having to live with it for months, do the plotting and planning—that's like work. Writing a comic isn't. You sit down, you spend a few hours, you get up and it's done.

Anyhow, the army had me write books and films about *nothing* that I knew anything about. For instance, at that time I had never owned, or even held a movie camera, so I got a job writing about the operation, maintenance, and care of the 16 mm Emo movie camera, operated under battle conditions. That was one that I had to write.

I knew how to read, so I would get hold of a training manual, read it, and then I would do a film on it—or I would rewrite the manual in comic book form. I rewrote a lot of training manuals as comics. I wish I had copies of those now. I never thought to save any.

I found out when I was discharged that there were only nine men in the whole United States Army who had my military classification number— I was classified as a playwright. And I was a sergeant, a tough buck-ass sergeant. But I wasn't tough! I was a skinny little curly-haired kid, and I felt so embarrassed about it. Occasionally, I would meet these rough combat guys, they were sergeants and I was a sergeant. So I'd wear the dirtiest, oldest fatigue uniforms I could find. I'd try to muddy up my face, and I'd spit a lot, I tried to look as tough as they were, but I always felt very out of place.

I almost got courtmartialed once. While I was in the army, I was also still writing stories for the company I had appointed somebody to be here while I was in the service. He'd write to me every couple of weeks, saying: "Stan, we've got to have a Captain America story," or "We need a Destroyer story," so I'd stay up one night or on a weekend and write it for him. One day he called and said he wanted me to do a story—it was a real emergency—so I said O.K.

We had mail call the next day, and I asked, "Where's my letter?" The mail clerk said, "I got nothing for you, Sarge." In those days, the mails were very dependable. He said he had nothing for me, so I figured he goofed. This was Saturday, and at lunch hour they locked the mail room and the clerk left. I happened to be walking past and I looked in the window—and, sure enough, there's my letter in one of the slots! The guy had put it in the wrong slot and he hadn't noticed, but I could recognize it.

So I ran to the Officer of the Day and I said. "Hey, you gotta open the mail room for me—I've got an important letter there and I've got to get it. There's a whole company in New York waiting for me to write this story." The guy was reading a magazine and didn't want to be disturbed, so I said. "I'll open the room myself."

I went back to the mail room, took a screw driver, and just unscrewed the lock on the door, opened it up, got my letter, put the lock back, went home, and wrote the story. A few days later, I got a call from the company commander. I was his pet peeve. He thought of me as a wise-guy New Yorker. He said, "Well, Sarge, I got you now. I think you'll go to Leavenworth. You robbed the mail."

I said, "What do you mean. I robbed the mail?" He said. "Did you or did you not break into the mail room?"

"For crying out loud," I said, "there was a letter of mine there, I couldn't find anyone to open the door, so I opened it and took my own letter." He said, "That's a federal offense." This guy meant it, he was all set to court martial me, and I don't know what would have happened.

Well, luckily for me, the colonel, who was the commandant of the post, intervened. I had just written a training manual on finance for him. They were having trouble training finance officers quickly enough, so comes pay day and the men in the foxholes wouldn't get paid. There weren't enough payroll officers around to pay them. It was wreaking hell with the morale in the army. So I took the manual that told them how to fill out the forms, and I rewrote it in comic-book style: we were able to cut the training time in half, because they could learn quicker from this comic book. The colonel from our post got a commendation, because of the book I had written: in fact, he expected to make brigadier general because of it. So when the captain called to complain, and said he wanted to court martial me, the colonel said. "Another word out of you and I'll send you to the South Pole."

But I was always in trouble. I was in love a hundred times. They shipped me to different cities all over the country: every city I'd go to. I'd meet some other gal I thought was terrific. But I always felt a little guilty because I wasn't overseas: I wanted to go to officers training school, because I figured if I became a lieutenant, they'd have to send me overseas. And they wouldn't let me. They said, "We need you to write these films and stuff, and if you become a lieutenant, they'll take you away from us." They tore up my application.

So there I was, a stateside soldier.

Foom: And after the war, you came back to Timely?

Stan: Yeah. There was a time when we had a staff of close to a hundred people, artists and writers. I had three secretaries myself, and I kept them busy. I used to dictate stories in the office. I was a show-off, in my early twenties, as I look back at it. What I would do was dictate two or three stories at a time. I'd quickly dictate a page of one story to one girl, and while she was transcribing it. I'd dictate a page of another story to another girl, and then maybe a third one to a third girl. I had this great feeling of power, that I was keeping three secretaries busy with three stories, and I knew that occasionally people were watching—and I was so proud. We had a big staff, artists, writers, editors, assistant editors, colorists, proofreaders, assistant proofreaders … and I got a kick out of playing to the crowd.

Foom: How did it compare to Marvel today?

Stan: Bigger. We had a bigger staff then we have today. Now we have other things—we have circulation men, people in the licensing and merchandizing departments. We didn't have any of that in those days, we just had artists and editors and writers. It was just the creative part. And I was never involved with anything but the creative part.

I didn't know what an engraver or a printer did I was just concerned with producing material, taking care of the art and the scripts.

We've had so many guys who have gone on to great things. Many of the people at *Mad Magazine* and at *National Lampoon* used to be with us. Al Jaffee used to write *Patsy Walker* and draw it, and he was an assistant editor here, same with Dave Berg. Jack Davis, who's one of the top advertising artists today—he does covers for *Time Magazine*, and for NBC—has done strips for us. Mickey Spillane used to write stories for us. Anyhow, we had our ups and downs.

We used to have bad periods when the comic book business hit rock bottom. I remember once my publisher said to me, "Stan, we have to let the whole staff go. I'm just going to keep you, but I want you to fire everybody." I said, "I can't do it." He said, "You'd better!" and he went off to Florida, while I was given the job of firing more people than I could count. I think that's what I hated most about my job—whenever I had to fire anybody.

I used to put out extra books we didn't even need, just to keep guys working. If there was an artist or a writer who didn't have anything to draw, it was always so easy—you'd add another book. But after a while, you reach the point that you can't keep doing that. And we had our ups and our downs all the time. There were good years, and there were bad years. Strangely enough, with Marvel it's been different. We've never had a bad slump like that.

Foom: Do you think it's inherent in the market that there are ups and downs—or was it just the period?

Stan: The problem was a deeper one. We were never the leaders. Nobody was a leader, we were all just putting out books. We were subject to the trends, nobody created trends, not really. Simon and Kirby came out with romance books when they were working for Crestwood, and they did pretty well for a while. Then everybody started putting out romance books, and that fizzled out. EC came out with their line of books for a while, then they fizzled out. There was a company called Lev Gleason Publications, they were quite big for a few years, until they fizzled out. Nobody really lasted.

I think that Marvel really changed things, because when we went in hot-and-heavy with the superheroes, we stopped following the trends and created our own, and by doing that we changed the whole complexion of the comic book business. We weren't subject to the whims of fortune any more—we were really doing our own thing.

Foom: How did the changes that you must have gone through in those years—especially with the start of Marvel—affect your own thinking, your own attitudes?

Stan: They made me very happy. We were turning out those monster magazines, and then one day my publisher found out that National Comics had a book called the *Justice League* that was selling reasonably well. Better than our monster books, at least. And he said, "Hey, maybe there's still a market for superheroes: why don't you bring out a team

like the *Justice League*. We could call it the *Righteous League* or something." I worked for him and I had to do what he wanted, so I was willing to put out a team of superheroes. But I figured I'll be damned if I'm
just going to copy National.

I said, "We'll do a superhero team, but let's make it different." And
I thought this was the chance to do all the things I would enjoy—to get
characters who acted like real people, to try to be more imaginative, to
make some stories have happy endings and some not, to continue the
stories and set them in the real world.

While I enjoyed doing it, I never thought it was going to catch on the
way it did. I never knew we were starting something new—a new phase
of comics—it was just a kick.

Foom: When did you realize what was going on?
Stan: I think when the fan mail came in. We never used to get fan mail,
then all of a sudden we were inundated with it. And it was wonderful.

Foom: So you changed your whole approach?
Stan: I realized this had always been my approach, but I never had the
sense to do it. I was now writing the way I wanted to write. Up until this
time, I was writing the way I felt the publisher wanted—and it was my
job to please the publisher. So now I forgot about the publisher. I was off
and running: I was going to have fun with my things. It came easy to me,
because it's my own natural style. Even though the other stuff had come
easily, too. I never really enjoyed it. This new style I began to enjoy.

I wasn't trying to write satire. I didn't even feel the stories were that
different; all I knew was that it was fun to make them continued, instead
of each story existing in a world of its own. I got the idea that if they're
going to be living in the real world, the characters might meet each
other once in a while. So we began to let Spider-Man meet the Fantastic
Four in a story, or to have the Hulk passing by while something was happening to Iron Man.

Of course, it was very easy for me to control, since I was writing virtually all of them and could keep track of them. Also, I could keep them
in the style I wanted. I was creating my own universe. Now, of course,
it's a little more difficult, with different people writing the different strips
and ever-changing writers and artists. One of our biggest problems is
keeping the styles intact, keeping the characters true to what they are
and what they should be.

Foom: I notice that in most of the Marvel Comics you came up with, there was never a complete family unit. There was Thor, Loki, and Odin—but no mother; Peter Parker and his Aunt; J. Jonah Jameson and his son. What's the story behind that?

Stan: That's very interesting. I had never thought of that; I think it just never occurred to me. You just have so much room in a story. Also, I think most of the legends are very vague about Odin's wife or wives; the few that I read always mentioned different women, and I could never pin it down. So I thought of him as a widower.

With Spider-Man, part of the concept was he was living with his aunt and uncle, because he was an orphan. His uncle was killed, and then he was the main support of his aunt, so that was the basis of that.

I thought we really had more families involved than other comic books. But it would have become too hard to handle, if I'd had to have entire families—nephews and nieces and in-laws. There just isn't room for it, because with any more incidental family characters, you'd never have time to get into the plot.

Foom: Since you're listed as publisher, maybe you could run down just what a publisher does?

Stan: I don't really do what a publisher does. In fact, publisher is a very vague word. Usually, in this business years ago, the publisher was the fellow who owned the company. My publisher owned the company. But today, no one-man owns Marvel Comics. A conglomerate named Cadence Industries owns Marvel, and they're a public company.

I, as publisher, should be responsible for the business end—for the circulation, financing, distribution, and so forth. But I don't function that way. I work with Jim Galton, who's president of the company, and is involved in management—in contracts, licensing, circulation, financing, and all that sort of thing. I limit myself just to the creative aspects. I'm like an over-all editor and art director.

Also, I apply myself to new projects. I've been instrumental in getting us a relationship with Simon and Schuster, so that now much of our material is being done in book form—and we're going to have more and more. In fact, we're working now on a series of our strips just done in popular paperback format, so you'll be able to buy a library of Marvel Comics, permanently bound. I'm working on television shows for our characters. I'm also working on movies for them.

I meet with the editor and art director, and with as much of the staff as I can—as often as I can—to determine the way things should be.

Basically, a better name than publisher might be creative head of the company. I think it's important to have the title *publisher*, because when I deal with a movie company or with Simon and Schuster or with other outside companies, the word *publisher* sounds so impressive that I can get the attention Marvel needs by being introduced as the publisher. People never react quite as graciously when you're an editor or a writer. People are funny.

What I do mainly is worry about the product we are turning out—about the strips. I make sure we have the best editing, the best writing, the best artwork, and that we're going in the right direction, putting out the right kinds of books. I check the sales figures, of course, and I read the books as much as I can. As I say, I'm really like an over-all executive editor.

Foom: How much say do you have over new projects?
Stan: In life, nobody has total say. President Carter, if he wants to do something big, has to have the approval of Congress. If I want to do a new magazine, I'm the one who's supposed to precipitate these things, but I then have to get the president of the company to okay the budget to make sure. I'm not going to be spending more money than we can afford. He, in turn, has to get the conglomerate, Cadence Industries, to okay his okay. Basically, if there's something I want to do, it'll get done. I also still do some writing. I write Stan's Soapbox, I write the newspaper strips, the *Origins* books, and film treatments.

Foom: Maybe you could talk a little about the newspaper strip?
Stan: For years people have said, why don't you put Spider-Man in the paper, but I wasn't anxious to, because I had a really rotten experience with the newspaper syndicates, years ago.

I did a strip called *Willy Lumpkin*, and another one called *Mrs. Lyon's Cubs*. Now, *Willy Lumpkin* was supposed to be a great strip. Originally, it was about a cop on the beat. I wanted him to be a real hip cop, and he'd meet real people on a New York City beat I had some great gags. It was really going to be the *Doonesbury* of its day, way before *Doonesbury* came out. Political gags, urban crises gags, and stuff like that. I brought it to this newspaper syndicate, and I called it *Barney's Beat*, the name of the cop being Barney. They loved it.

Then, the head of the syndicate said he wanted me to change it to a mailman. He wanted it to be set in a small town and to feature a lovable character that everybody would love. The kind of strip they'd understand in Chillocothe, Ohio. The next thing I knew, it's called *Willy Lumpkin* and it's a bucolic strip, and if there's one thing I'm not comfortable with, it's a bucolic style of writing. I'm not that kind of a writer.

But again, I was young and I thought they knew best. I did the strip, and it lasted about a year. It wasn't that bad, but it wasn't as great as it should have been, Finally, I gave it up.

Virtually the same thing happened with *Mrs. Lyon's Cubs*, which was about the Cub Scouts, Mrs. Lyon being the den mother. I never wanted to do that, but I wanted to sell a newspaper strip. I had tried a few great ideas, but they didn't bite, so one day I said to this cartoonist jokingly. "I'll bet if I did something about Boy Scouts they'd take it, they'd think it was nice and clean and respectable. You could probably call it *Mrs. Lyon's Cubs* and they'd say it was great."

I submitted it, and they took it like that, so I was stuck with a strip I didn't particularly want. I don't know anything about Boy Scouts and even less about cubs! And that strip died.

So I felt the people at syndicates don't know anything.

As Marvel Comics became more and more popular, over the past few years, newspaper syndicates would come to me about doing one of our characters. I didn't want to. "It wouldn't work for you guys," I said; "you ruin everything."

Finally, Marvel became so popular and so big that the syndicate people came to me and said. "Stan, you can do it any way you want: we won't interfere, we won't touch it." Well, this was incredible. Years ago, it was hard to get my foot in the door at a newspaper syndicate, so I figured, okay, I'll give it a try.

I discussed *Spider-Man* with a real nice fellow, Denny Allen of the Register and Tribune Syndicate. I wanted John Romita to draw it, because John and I had played around with one many years—we'd done a few samples, but never did anything with them. The strip just started in newspapers this January, and it's one of the biggest-selling strips to hit the country. It's already in more than two hundred newspapers, in just a month. The syndicate is delighted with it, but it's hard to write, because ever time I turn around I've got another two weeks of it to do. I try to write it on weekends.

I sold another strip, called *The Virtue of Vera Valiant*, which doesn't have anything to do with Marvel. That was a gag, also. I was talking to some syndicate guy who wanted me to do a detective newspaper strip. I said, "How can you sell a detective strip to newspapers today? No detective story can succeed, unless it's either sexy or violent. You can't be sexy or violent in the newspaper." I told him you'd have to do something that's current, something timely. For instance, if you did a takeoff on *Mary Hartman, Mary Hartman*, it would probably succeed. So the next think I know, we're off and running. I try to write *Vera Valiant* on Saturday and *Spider-Man* on Sunday.

Then evenings I've got these books for Simon and Schuster. We're doing one about the super women, which should be finished by now, yet I haven't even begun it. I've got to start that this week. Then I'm doing THE SILVER SURFER with Jack Kirby—a hundred-page original hardcover. I'm excited about that. I hope it turns out to be a great book. I'm also doing *How to Draw for the Comics* with John Buscema. I'm doing an *Encyclopedia of Marvel Comics* with George Olshevsky, which I think is going to be a real fun thing. It's going to be literally an encyclopedia, just of the Marvel Universe. Two big volumes, probably— or maybe one huge book. Anyway, I've got those four to do.

I just had lunch with a guy from Simon and Schuster, and he wants two more *Origins* books, for the next two years.

And then I write a column—a little paragraph, every month or so— for *Celebrity*, the "Publisher's Perspective," and of course I also write the "Soapbox" for the Marvel Bullpen Page. I write advertisements for our other stuff in trade papers, and so forth, and I'm the consulting editor or associate producer of our television and movie projects, so I've got to read all those scripts and give opinions.

Foom: What can you tell us about them?
Stan: We're working on a *Spider-Man* pilot film for CBS—a live-action, prime-time series, like the *Six Million Dollar Man*. The script has already been written by a very good writer, a guy who's written a zillion television shows. I'm working with him as consultant on it, and it'll be on the air by the end of this year, if all goes well. We're working with Universal Pictures on a deal to take four of our characters and do a television series—also live-action. We're also working on a Classics Comics animated show—*Marvel Classics Comics*—which is very exciting. We may do the animation ourselves, we may set up our own little animation

studio. There are probably other things that I'm not remembering at the moment—there's really a lot happening.

Foom: Whatever happened to the movie you were working on with Alain Resnais?

Stan: I never seem to have the time to get to it. In fact, he was here this morning. He just finished his latest movie. *Providence*, and he asked me when we were going to start. I told him I need at least six months to clear up the things I'm doing, so he said he was asked to do a very quick movie in France, and maybe when he's finished, we'll start. Sooner or later, I'm going to have to do this picture with Alain, who's one of my closest and dearest friends.

Foom: Is it anything related to Marvel?

Stan: Totally separate. It's called *The Inmates*, and it has to do with the whole human race, why we're on Earth, and what our relationship is with the rest of the Universe. It poses a theory which I hope is a very original, unusual one. But it's done in human terms, like a regular story: it's not a far-out science-fiction thing. It's very philosophical—but there *is* a lot of science fiction. I think it's a great story. I've written the treatment for it, and I suggested that Alain get another screenwriter to do the screenplay based on my treatment. It'd still be our story: I'd still be involved in it; yet, this way, we wouldn't have to wait. But he keeps saying he wants it to be my script completely—he wants it to be my language. So I'm very flattered, although I don't have the time to do it, right now.

Foom: Over the years, you've done some things outside the comics field: Are there any we haven't covered?

Stan: I used to write radio shows. Unfortunately, I can't mention titles, because I ghosted them under other people's names. I wrote some western radio shows, years ago, and a detective radio show. I ghosted a number of television shows. I ghosted newspaper comic strips. I wrote the *Howdy Doody* newspaper strip, which I was able to put my name on. I did some advertising work. I love writing advertising copy. The one other thing I do is a lot of lecturing. I go to schools all over the country, all the time, and I love it, because it's the closest you can get to being an actor without actually acting.

Foom: And it also keeps you in close touch with the readers.

Stan: Well, that's the most important thing. Actually, I think I learn much more from the people I speak to, than they're learning from me! We have a questions-and-answers section after each lecture, and I learn so much by the questions they ask about what they're interested in and how they feel. It's invaluable.

Foom: What do you think about the Marvel merchandise, which seems to have been burgeoning lately?
Stan: Well, it's very good for us, because it's great income, and the money that we make enables us to pay the artists and writers to put out more books. If you want to know what I think about the items themselves, I really don't have much to do with them, or pay much attention to them. Some of the toys and games and coloring books are great, I'm sure. It's the type of thing that's really very hard to keep up with unless you spend all your time working on it. Basically, the few things that I've seen have been pretty good, though. It's also very nice to know that people like Marvel enough to buy all these various things—so I'm quite happy with it.

Foom: Where do you see Marvel going in the future?
Stan: I have played most of my life by ear, without too much of a master plan. I guess I'm inclined to feel the same way about Marvel. I see nothing but great things for us, but as to specifically where we're going, each day I get a different feeling about it. I think we're going to be big in television and movies. Eventually, I would really love it if we could produce our own motion pictures and TV shows.

I don't know why we couldn't, because to me the media is all very similar—there's not much difference between a newspaper and a magazine, or a movie, a stage play, a show. It's all the same—it's all a part of entertaining and stimulating the public. If you know how to be interesting and how to make people care about what you're saying, doing, or thinking—then what's the difference whether you're doing, it on screen, in print, or in front of a microphone? Since I feel Marvel is pretty good at entertaining the public, I would like us to be doing it in every type of the media.

I think maybe we should publish some more glossy magazines, higher priced—and I don't mean like National is doing, just buck comics—but different *kinds* of magazines.

To me, the most fun you can have is doing new things. I don't know where we'll be three, four, or five years from now, but you can be mighty sure we'll be going in a dozen different directions—and moving faster than ever!
Excelsior!

The Amazing Stan Lee Interview

TIM FAHERTY / 1977

From *Princeton Spectrum*, vol. 2, no. 50
(December 14, 1977). Reprinted by
permission of Tim Faherty.

If you're walking through Manhattan and you suddenly see a bright
flare in the shape of the number "four" shoot into the sky, don't be too
alarmed. It's only the signal for the Fantastic Four. They're good guys.
Besides, they're probably too busy arguing about who should be the
leader of the group to worry about you. The Fantastic Four are Marvel
comic book characters—the spawn of Stan Lee.

From the day in 1961 that *Fantastic Four* number one appeared on
newsstands, the comic book world has never been the same. That was
the beginning of what thousands of people know as "the Marvel Age
of Comics." It was the beginning of a strange new breed of comic book
heroes. Heroes who were fallible and imperfect, who were sometimes
ugly and often cantankerous and antisocial, who were just as likely to

fight each other as they were to fight super-powered villains. Heroes who didn't always win in the end.

And along with the heroes came the Marvel style. The emphasis was on action, which roughly translated to a lot of twenty-page brawls. The comics became a ballet of battered bodies. Characters like Spider-Man, the Hulk, and the Thing never missed an opportunity to be thrown from a building or stepped on by giant monsters. The readers loved it.

In the late sixties, social problems found their way into the comics. Marvel characterization was combined with real problems, like slums, drugs, racism, and prison reform. The new bi-word of the comics was "relevance."

Now, Marvel is the largest comic company in the country, and it's still growing. Comic books are big business. In addition to the books, there are Superhero toys, commercials, personal appearances, and television movies. There is even an animation studio in the works. For many people, there is one name that is held responsible for the growth and development of the present comic book industry, a name that is almost synonymous with Marvel comics—Stan Lee.

Lee came to Marvel in 1939, when he was seventeen. Marvel was then called Timely. Lee was a "staff writer, proofreader, and all-around go-fer." Soon after this, the art director and editor quit, and Lee was asked to fill in. He wrote under the name Stan Lee, saving his real name, Stanley Martin Leiber, for the great American Novel. (A few years ago he changed it legally to Stan Lee). For the next twenty-two years he wrote everything from romance, to western, to monster comics as the industry struggled through the lean years between the "golden age" of the forties and the birth of Lee's Fantastic Four. Since then, Marvel and Lee have been the innovators. And as the comics have changed, so have the readers. Many readers stay with comics through college and beyond. There are huge conventions where comic freaks meet to buy, sell, trade, and discuss the artistic value of comics. There are college courses taught about comics, and there are exhibits of comic art.

Lee has become the Czar of Marvel Comics. He is now publisher. He makes television appearances, lectures at colleges, and has even done a razor blade commercial. (Who says you have to be a ball player to become a success?)

The halls of the Marvel Comics Company are lined with full-color posters of the various Marvel heroes. They are men, supermen, and monsters. One is even a Norse god. Artists and writers busy themselves preparing next month's comics, and "it's not unusual" to see a caped hero walk by.

In his Madison Avenue office, facing the wall of newly released comics, Lee puts his booted feet on the coffee table, lights a cigar, and laughs as he thinks about the origin of Irving Forbush. Lee is a friendly, happy man, who loves to talk—especially about Marvel comics. The strongest impression one receives when talking to him is that he loves his work. It's hard not to be caught up in the enthusiasm he generates when he talks about his characters or a new project he is working on.

He says that comic books are no longer criticized by people who think that they are harmful for children to read. "I think that has almost become a cliché. In all honesty, I haven't heard any (criticism) for ten years, and I haven't read any. Comics are the greatest defense against the encroachment of creeping televisionitis, and creeping illiteracy, which is hitting the younger generations. If not for comic books there are countless thoughts, maybe millions of kids in this country who would never even read."

"I'd like to think that Marvel comics make a kid equate reading with pleasure. Once a kid begins to think of reading as a means of gaining enjoyment and pleasure, he goes on to read other things. . . ."

Marvel was the first comic book company to print letters from its readers. Each comic has its own letters page where fans comment on past issues, make requests for the kinds of stories they would like to see, present scientific explanations of their favorite hero's powers, and carry on debates with other fans. There is at least one instance of a couple who met through a letters page and were later married.

Perhaps more than any other entertainment medium, comic books are directly influenced by their fans. There are no Nielson ratings in the comic book industry, and sales figures determine which books stay or go. But the actual content of the books is determined to a large extent by the letters the fans write.

Lee says that fans had an even greater influence on comics in the early days of the Marvel renaissance. "The first few years, I was writing most, if not all, of the stories. And I was reading all the mail. And it was new to me. We had never had anything quite so successful before. I was very influenced by the mail."

"Today we have so many different writers, and they switch from book to book. It's such a bigger operation than it was then, and the mail is read by so many different people, that it's tough for any one person to get a real sense of what most of the letters are saying. So, we still read the mail, and we're still influenced by it, but I'd say to a slightly lesser degree."

An example of this influence is Irving Forbush. Forbush is the fall-guy of Marvel; sort of an Alfred E. Newman type. In the early days, Lee was writing a humorous comic book called *Snafu*. On the contents page he wrote "Founded by Marvin Forbush, and losted by his brother Irving Forbush." Lee got so many letters asking "Who's Irving Forbush?" that he brought the name up again years later. Again Forbush began getting mail. Soon his name began appearing all over the comic books. He was quoted in the editorials, insulted on the letters page, and even listed along with the artists and writers ("misspellings by Irving Forbush.") Sixteen years after the fan-mail started pouring in about the Fantastic Four, Lee is still thrilled and flattered by all the attention. Of course, being the best-known name in comics has its drawbacks.

"I can't really go to a comic book convention," says Lee. "Because if people recognize me, which they usually do, they'll say, 'Wait a minute, wait a minute. I've got these books I'd like you to autograph,' or 'I've got these stories I want you to read,' or 'This artwork I want you to look at,' or 'Mr. Lee, how do I get a job in comics?' Again, I could never just look at the exhibits, or talk about the things I want to talk about to the people." Now we know why Spider-Man wears a mask.

At the same time, Lee says, "I think anybody who says, 'I hate auto-graph seekers'—that guy is crazy. It just indicates that there are people who have some interest and who think your signature is worth some-thing. I think you've got to be an idiot not to be appreciative of that sort of thing."

Comic books are very popular with college-aged readers, and each year Lee visits campuses with a lecture tour. Marvel heroes are popular subjects for term papers and theses. "I cannot tell you how many letters I get from college kids, and each one I'm sure thinks he's the only one. 'Dear Stan, I'm doing a thesis this term on comics. Would you please send me your opinions of the following twenty things?' Now he's asking for real philosophical opinions and concepts. I hate not doing it. I usually try to answer them real quickly, or sometimes I write back and say, 'Look, rewrite the letter to me and rephrase the question so I can answer true or false, yes or no.'"

When asked if he feels that it's strange that students write academic studies of comic books, Lee says, "I used to think 'What the hell are they so interested in comics for? These are comic strips!' I've come to realize over the past few years that I was wrong and these people who are interested in comics are right. Because basically, why is it any less seemly to be interested in comics than in movies or novels or the ballet or opera or anything else? It's an art form. It's a method of communicating, of entertainment, of telling stories. If Shakespeare and Michelangelo were alive today and if they decided to collaborate on a comic strip, would you or anybody else say, 'Well, why would anyone be interested in that?' Think of what a work of art that would be. It would be more important creatively than most any book or anything else you could think of. Comics are as valid as any other art form. It just depends on who is writing them, who's drawing them, and how good the stories are. I can see, under ideal conditions, a good comic book being more important than a bad movie. Why couldn't I write something significant in the comic book format if I choose to do it and if I had the ability to do it?"

Writing comic books is largely writing dialogues, and the years Lee spent writing a book a day have left their mark. As you can see from the above quotes, Lee often uses dialogue to make a point. When he was writing most of Marvel's comics, Lee says his wife Joan used to make fun of him. "She'd say I was always talking to myself. I'd be doing the dialogue and she'd come in and say, 'What did you say?' And I realized I'm mouthing the words out loud to get the sound of it."

While he was growing up, Lee read everything he could get his hands on. But he says he was most influenced by Shakespeare. "I read Shakespeare when I was eight, nine, and ten. I didn't understand a lot of it in those days, but I loved the words. I loved the rhythms of the words. I think I loved Shakespeare more than anybody. I think he was a better writer than people think he was, and he's supposed to have been the greatest."

Lee speaks the same way about Walt Disney, for whom he has "unbounded admiration" because "he had the ability to make everything he did a quality product."

Lee no longer writes Marvel's comics. As publisher he is more involved in the business end of comic books now, and in several new projects. For instance, Marvel's expansion into primetime television keeps Lee flying back and forth to the coast. Lee serves as consultant to Universal Pictures, who are making TV movies starring the Marvel heroes. Spider-Man and the Hulk have already appeared in the movies, and others are being made about Dr. Strange, the Human Torch, and Captain America. How much control does Lee have over the movies? "Not enough. When we consult, if I say I disagree and they still want to do it, they can do it. I'm just glad they listen to me at all. And I've disagreed with a lot of what they've done."

As an example, Lee described the second episode of the Hulk. "The plot concerns a stepmother who wants to murder her stepdaughter for her inheritance. The Hulk saves the stepdaughter. Now that's a perfectly fine plot for Agatha Christie, or even for The Streets of San Francisco, but I don't feel it's right for the Hulk. So these are the types of things I haven't been able to control. But I'm beginning to make them understand. They're getting better. They're not as bad as we feared they would be, but we hope they'll be better as time goes by."

Lee also hopes that these pilot movies will become series. Things may just work out that way. During the interview, Stan got a call from Universal, telling him that he had to fly to California, because CBS wants five more Spider-Man episodes.

In the future, Marvel may be making its own movies. The newest area of expansion, and one that Lee is very excited about, is animation. "We're planning to buy our own animation studio on the coast, so that we can produce our own movies the way we want to. We might even, if we're successful, someday go into live-action films. We're negotiating now to purchase one, and if all goes well, by the end of the year we might own it. It could happen very quickly."

Lee loves to be busy, so he must be happy these days. He is writing a series of books for Simon and Schuster about the Marvel heroes. His first book, *Origins of Marvel Comics*, sold extremely well and is still selling. It consisted of reprints of early Marvel comics, along with the stories of their background and development written by Lee. This format, a combination of prose and comics, was continued in three other books. The latest of these, *The Superhero Women*, has just been released. In January, a book which Lee says "Every kid in America" will want, will be released. It is coauthored by John Buscema (one of Marvel's most popular artists), and it is called *How to Draw Comics the Marvel Way*.

Lee is working on another book with Jack Kirby. (Kirby is called "the King" by his fans, and has probably drawn more comic books than anyone else.) It will be a novel-length Silver Surfer story that will be marketed as a hardcover book. "It should be reviewed in the book review sections. It's a real story that we think will have great impact."

Marvel is also invading newspapers. Two of its heroes—Spider-Man and Howard the Duck—have daily strips, and a *Conan the Barbarian* strip will begin in January. The *Spider-Man* strip, which Lee writes and art director John Romita draws, has sold to almost four hundred papers in less than a year. It is so popular that when the *Wichita Eagle* cancelled it, readers raised such a protest, they had it reinstated.

In addition, Lee is supposed to be working on a screenplay for his close friend Alain Renais, although he confesses that he hasn't found time to do much on it.

There are also some new developments in the comic books themselves. Following the tremendous success of the *Star Wars* comics, Marvel is putting out several other books in conjunction with movies. Titles include *Close Encounters of the Third Kind, Kingdom of Spiders,* and *Sgt. Pepper's Lonely Hearts Club Band.*

Increased printing cost is the most serious problem facing the comic book industry. "We hope we can hold the line at thirty-five cents for awhile. We're also trying more expensive books for older readers. I want to get into expensive color like *Heavy Metal*. Put out less books, but make them more expensive, more pages, better printing."

Although Marvel is putting out a few longer, more expensive books, most readers want the standard comics they can read in one sitting, according to Archie Goodwin, editor of Marvel Comics.

Goodwin has worked in comics for thirteen years and says, "You have to be a little crazy to work in comics—in a nice way." He has a wide, contagious smile, and looks about half of his forty years.

He says that the trend in present comics is to put the fun back in them. "In the early seventies comics got grim. Now we're trying to get back to comics as something not totally serious."

"Comics have to be action-oriented," says Goodwin, but he doesn't think readers take the violence seriously. "They know it's not real. It's not like a Sam Peckinpah movie."

Aside from being crazy, Goodwin thinks that "one of the greatest values" in the comic industry is the ability to "stay with something and stay fresh."

Stan Lee Replies to Éric Leguèbe

ÉRIC LEGUÈBE / 1978

Jeff McLaughlin. Printed by permission of
Stan Lee.

*(Editor's Note: Stan is tape recording his answers to questions to be
transcribed by his secretary.)*

Okay, Martha, I'm going to try again on this interview. . . . Here we go.
The first question:

A. Spider-Man was born about sixteen years ago when I decided to do a
character who could be like a real human being who suddenly got super-
power. I wanted a character who was terribly realistic. Who got allergy
attacks, ingrown toenails, worry about money, not be successful with
girls. In short, somebody with whom the reader could relate.

B. Spider-Man is specially important in my point of view because he became our very most popular and best-selling character, and he seems to represent and to typify the entire line of Marvel comics.

C. Yes, I've seen the cartoons done for TV that are now being seen in France. But I haven't really worked on them. We merely licensed them to other companies to do. I think they tried to keep the spirit of Spider-Man. Of course, I don't think they did it as well as if we ourselves had done them.

D. I don't understand this question. I'm sorry I can't answer it.

E. I don't really imagine new partners for Spider-Man. I feel a character like Spider-Man has to be a loner, and I don't expect he really ever will have steady partners in the future.

F. One day Spider-Man had been the friendly enemy of Superman because we did a book in partnership with DC Comics called *Spider-Man versus Superman* in which the two of them meet and fight and then become friends. It was just an experiment; we thought it would be an interesting thing to do, but I don't think we'll ever do it again.

G. I think the film done about Spider-Man which has shown in Paris is fairly good, which is based on a television show which was done here in the United States. I don't think it's as good as it really should be, but it's not as bad as it might have been.

H. I think that TV and cinema are parts of the media and methods of communication just as comic books are. Just as ballet is and just as opera is. I think every form of art is a form of communication. They are all different, but they all try to do similar things. I think the spirit of the style of Spider-Man or any character could be captured by TV or the cinema. It very often isn't captured because different people do the movie than have done the book or the comic book or the novel or whatever it is. But to answer the question specifically, yes, I think it is possible for a movie to keep the spirit of a comic book.

(Ed. Note: For some reason Stan starts to identify the questions using numbers instead of letters.)

1. I became an author of comics accidentally, actually. I never really wanted to be in the comic book industry or intended to be. I originally wanted to be an actor, then a lawyer, then an advertising man. But I

heard there was a job open in comics when I was young, thinking it would be a temporary job, but I've stayed ever since.

2. No, I haven't gone to any sort of artist school nor have I studied writing except when I was in high school when I took an English course, just as everybody else did. I guess whatever I know, I've been self-taught.

3. Yes, indeed, I feel admiration for other artists of comics and the so-called fine arts both from today and of the past. It would take me forever to say which ones. I admire the successful commercial artists of today. I admire Jack Davis, I admire Charlie Schulz. I admire Leroy Nieman, Salvador Dali, Picasso. I admire anybody who is good at anything. I don't feel that fine art is more important than commercial art. In some ways I feel it is harder to be a commercial artist than to be a fine artist, but my admiration extends to anybody who does anything well, whether he be an artist or a pianist or an actor or a shoemaker.

4. Yes, I would have to answer the same way. I feel admiration for writers of yesterday and today, and again that goes for so many of the good ones. I admire . . . my favorite writer of all time was Shakespeare. But I was also a fan of Edgar Rice Burroughs, Arthur Conan Doyle, Victor Hugo, Omar Khayyam, or perhaps I should say Edward Fitzgerald who translated him. Kurt Vonnegut, Robert E. Howard. I just enjoy any good writer. No, I don't have a preference for science-fiction authors. Oh, sorry this is question 5.

5. No, I don't have a preference for science-fiction authors. I enjoy them as much as I enjoy any other authors if they are good. I guess my favorites are Ray Bradbury and Arthur Clarke, and I must say I think *Childhood's End* by Arthur Clarke is probably one of the greatest science-fiction stories, maybe one of the greatest stories that one could read.

6. Yes, when I was a young boy I did enjoy comic strips and comic books, and I enjoyed, well, again, I enjoyed them all, the ones that nobody would even remember today. I enjoyed one called *Red Barry*, one called *Skippy*—he was one of my favorites by Percy Crosby. I liked *The Phantom*. I liked Tim Tyler's *Luck*. I just liked them all. The humorous ones, the serious ones. I liked *Mandrake the Magician*. As far as why— it's hard to know why you like anything, they just gave me enjoyment.

Oh, Martha, by the way, in question five: "Do I have a preference for science-fiction authors?" I'd like you to also mention Harlan Ellison as one of my favorites. By the way, I sure hope that this is coming out okay. I'll shoot myself if this doesn't work. Okay, Question 7.

7. No, today, I don't have a chance to read comic books. I'm so busy traveling and writing my own material and doing the millions of other things I seem to do, so to answer the question, I don't have time. I certainly wish I did have time, but what I do is thumb through the books quickly, I look at the drawings, I try to read a sentence here and there so that I can stay familiar to some degree with what's being done. As far as which ones, certainly I try to read mostly Marvels, but I try to look through the competition to see what's happening.

8. Of course I admit the influence of science-fiction writers. I admit the influence of all writers. I feel that everybody is influenced by everything he reads, or sees, or hears. Anything that touches us has to influence us.

9. I really don't understand the question, I really don't know what he means by "is my work with Marvel part of the space-opera" so I can't answer that question.

10. My method for the construction of the script consists of discussing the story with the artist and having the artist do the pencilled art on his own, drawing whatever he wants so long as it tells the story we've discussed. I would then put in the dialogue and the captions and indicate where the dialogue balloons are to be placed and where the captions go, and then the script goes to the inker—it's lettered of course. Then I have it proofread and that's it. I proofread it myself if it's my own story.

(Ed. Note: Stan starts reading out the next three questions he's being asked.)

11. How long does it take me?
I used to do one complete comic in a day on an average.

12. Do you have a special pace for the writing of a story to another one? I'm not sure I understand the question, but actually I don't remember that I used to write one story differently than another. They all took me the same length of time, and none were really any more difficult or more easier than the others were. To me one story is like another. Maybe the ones that used archaic dialogue may have been a little slower. For example, it might have taken me a little longer to write the dialogue for Thor or the Silver Surfer or Dr. Strange than somebody who spoke totally in a modern idiom.

13. Do I usually go from a hero to another one?

Yes, I never had any problem. The minute I finished one story, I would write another story. It never bothered me to go from one hero to another. It never bothered me to go from a science fiction to a western or to a Millie the Model or to a horror story or to a detective story or to a humor story. No, it didn't bother me at all.

14. The super villains are almost as important as the superheroes—a good super villain can make the story interesting, and a weak super villain makes the story very dull. I can't say what the balance is. There are some super villains, like Dr. Doom, who are probably more popular than some of the second-rate superheroes. Then by the same token, I don't think there's any super villain as popular as Spider-Man or the Hulk. So you can't really answer that question. Or I can't.

15. Probably if I had a bit of tenderness for my superheroes, it would be for Spider-Man because he's the most successful, and also for the Silver Surfer, whom I've always been very partial to. But basically I like them pretty all the same. As far as my stories, the only way I could mention which is my favorite story or stories is to go back and reread most of them, because I've forgotten most of them, because I've written so many.

16. Occasionally I may reread a story over again. I don't have the time to do it. The few times I have, I'm always amazed at how good it seems to be. I never realized that we were writing that good so many years ago. I sort of wish some of the stories today were done in the same style.

17. I thought I had answered this already. No, I don't have time to read comics today.

18. The perfect balance between balloons and drawings is when a drawing is very interesting, I try to keep the balloons small. When the drawing is dull, I try to use a lot of balloons and sound effects and anything else on the panel to liven it up a bit. It depends on what you think of the drawings.

19. No, I don't control the colors. That's one thing I never paid attention to.

20. My method of working with the authors and artists is to try and be as friendly as possible, be as fair as possible, and get the most work out of them as possible. Let them work as much as possible in their own style. Tell them the type of results I want, but not how to obtain them.

21. How do I explain the evolution of my heroes? . . . uuhh, I can't answer that now, I'd have to write a whole book to explain that. It's just too difficult a question.

22. I really don't know what he means by "How did I create Russian superheroes?" I didn't know we had any Russian superheroes. We aren't going out of the way to create Russian superheroes. I'm afraid that question doesn't make that much sense to me.

23. No, I don't do any special research in science, history, social, or evolution for my stories. I never really had any time. That's one of the reasons why when I would mention a scientific device, I would make up a name for it, like a "super gamma ray gun," only because I don't know what a super gamma ray gun is, and I'm sure nobody else does. I never had the time to worry about being technically accurate—it was just more important to get the stories done quickly.

24. Of course I believe that comic books are a special kind of literature, just as novels are, just as plays are. The point of view of drawing as an independent art . . . of course they are an independent art. Comics are a very specific and unique art form, which the more one studies them the more one can appreciate them.

25. It's easier to assume control as far as going with the relationship between Spider-Man, Captain America, Iron Man, and so forth when I wrote all the stories myself, but now that we have so many writers it's very difficult. It's just up to the editor to do as best as he can.

26. I guess the reason for the American and international success of our superheroes is the fact that they have so many humanistic qualities that people all over the world are able to relate to them, because they're really similar to real people, and real people are pretty much the same all over the world.

27. Again, it's hard to understand the question, "[What's] the difference between a classical hero and a superhero?" because many of the classic heroes were superheroes and many of today's superheroes like Spider-Man and the Hulk I'm sure may become classical heroes. I don't know what the difference is. Anything that lasts is a classic and that's all, and if our superheroes last, they'll become superheroes.

28. As far as the difference between the creation of the daily strips and the comic books, yes, there is a difference. The comics books are easier

to write because you have more panels for dialogue. The story keeps flowing steadily. The daily strips you only have three or four panels. The first panel has to summarize what happened before, the last panel has to be a sort of cliff-hanger. So you only have one or two panels in-between to move the story. It's really much more difficult to do a newspaper strip than a regular comic book story.

(Ed. Note: Questions 29 and 30 are missing from the recording. We only get the last line of Stan's reply to what question 30 was about.)

30. Maybe science-fantasy stories will be in the future what western stories were in the past.

31. Are we living in a new golden age of comic books?
Yes, I'd like to think so. And I'd like to think of it as the new Marvel Age of Comics.

32. The present phenomena of nostalgia for comic books of yesterday has been caused by people loving today's comics so much and getting interested in comics and wanting to learn what comics used to be like. You only love things in the past when you care about them in the present. If you don't love today's movies you won't be interested in old-time movies. I think the whole thing is a tribute to the comics of today.

33. Okay, I'm sorry, but again I can't understand the question. How do I assume the formation of my writers and artists? I don't know what that means.

34. How do I feel about the merchandising of our superheroes—the buttons, t-shirts, stickers, gadgets—and are they part of the glory of the star? Well, I don't know if they are part of a glory of a star, but they are good business, and the money helps us to make us rich enough to pay better rates to our artists and writers. I think there's nothing wrong with our merchandising, I think it helps to publicize our characters. Again, it's only done because people like our characters. When you like something, you want to wear a t-shirt with its picture on it. You enjoy wearing little jewelry that represents the character, you enjoy reading it in other forms, playing games based upon it. I think it's a very good thing that we have a lot of merchandising.

35. Of course there are some artists that I work with more easily than others, but I don't like to mention that. I don't like to mention favorites

or things I like the least—it's not fair to the others. I will say, though, that the quality that I ask first of an artist is that he be a good artist. That he be a good artist and draw the kind of stories that people will want to read. He doesn't have to be a person I like, he doesn't have to be any special age or nationality or sex or anything. The most important qualification is that he be a good comic strip artist. First and foremost.

An Interview with Stan Lee

LEONARD PITTS, JR. / 1981

Previously unpublished. Printed by
permission of Leonard Pitts, Jr.

Pitts: You came to Marvel in 1939. Why?

Lee: I needed a job. I had just graduated high school and I was looking
in the papers at the want ads and I saw an ad for a comic book company
that needed somebody to help out—somebody with writing ability to
also be a go-fer. I figure I must've been the only guy who answered
the ad, because I got the job.

Pitts: How did you know you had writing ability?

Lee: Oh, I had done a lot of writing in high school. There was a newspaper then called the *New York Herald Tribune*, and they had an essay
contest for high school students called the Biggest News of the Week
contest. You had to write a 500-word article about what you thought
was the biggest news event of the week. I entered it for three weeks

running and I won it for the three weeks. The editor called and asked me to stop entering the contest and give someone else a chance.

Then he said, "What do you want to be, when you become a person?" And I said, "I'd like to be an actor," because at that time that's what I thought I wanted. He said "Don't be crazy. You ought to be a writer." And I previously had a job writing for a hospital—writing publicity releases. That was spare-time stuff while I was in high school. I got a job for one of the news services; I wrote obituaries of famous people who were still alive, so that when they die, the obituary is all ready to put in the paper. But I quit because I got very depressed writing about living people in the past tense.

Pitts: What did you find when you got to Timely Comics?
Lee: I found a very small staff. It was just me and a few other people, and we only were publishing about three or four magazines a month. I did a little of everything. I went down and got people their lunches and I filled the inkwells and I did some proofreading and I did some copywriting. Little by little, I began to write stories.

The fella who had been the editor, he quit after a while, and there was nobody around to replace him, so the publisher asked me if I could hold the job down temporarily until he got somebody else. At that time, I was seventeen, and I guess he didn't figure a seventeen-year-old was qualified to be the editor. I said, "Sure. I can do it." He gave me a chance at it, and I think he forgot all about me, because he never hired anybody else, so I stayed there ever since.

Pitts: I get the impression that he didn't have a lot of time to pay attention to the comics anyway. Didn't he have other things he was publishing?
Lee: He had other magazines, but he paid quite a bit of attention to the comics, too. He was much more involved in the early days than later on.

Pitts: Okay, so for the next twenty or thirty years you were there turning out monster stories—
Lee: Well, I did everything. We worked according to whatever the trend was. If there was a trend for cowboy books, we did two dozen cowboy titles. When romance books came in, we did two dozen romance books. We were just a volume publisher. Whatever was trendy at the moment, we published. We did teenage books, such as *Millie the Model, Chili and Her Friends* . . . on and on. We did *Kid Colt, Two Gun Kid*—my

publisher loved the name Kid—the *Western Kid*, *Ringo Kid*, *Rawhide Kid*, *Black Rider*, *Apache Kid*. We did fantasy books—*Strange Tales*, *Astonishing Tales*, *Journey Into Unknown Worlds*, *Uncanny Tales*, *Adventures Into Terror*. We did war stories—*Combat Kelly*, *Combat Casey*, *Battlefield*, *Battlefront*, *Battleground*, *Combat*. We did romance—*My Love*, *Your Love*, *His Love*, *Her Love*. And those are just a few examples, the tip of the iceberg. Just whatever was a name, we threw in and did the books. None of them were particularly good, none of them were particularly bad. They were just production jobs.

Pitts: But, you weren't getting your creative jollies at this juncture.
Lee: No, I was just doing what my publisher asked me to do. Being young, I enjoyed the feeling of importance of being editor and art director and head writer. It never occurred to me that what I was doing wasn't all that great. I mean, it was adequate. We were making money, but nothing that anybody could really brag about.

Pitts: I know you've been asked this next question a million times, but I hope you won't mind making it a million and one: what was the event that changed it all around?
Lee: Well, as far as I can remember, I was about to quit. I was really bored with what I was doing. This was about 1960. And my wife said, "Before you leave, just once why don't you try to put out the kind of books you yourself would like to do?" So I did.

Martin Goodman, my publisher at the time, told me that he had heard that DC Comics had a book called the *Justice League* or the *Justice Society*. I can't remember—one of those. And it was selling rather well. He said, "Why don't we also put out a book with a team of superheroes?" So I said okay, but I decided to do it differently for once. That was when I came up with the idea of the *Fantastic Four*. I decided to try to make them real personalities and let them react like real people would react to the real world. Jack Kirby drew it and contributed many ideas, too, of course, and it really succeeded far beyond anybody's expectations.

I always thought that was the way comics should be done. And then we came out with—I forget the order of them. I think the next was the *Hulk*, then *Spider-Man*, *Dr. Strange*, *Thor*, *Daredevil*, *Iron Man*, *Sgt. Fury*, the *Avengers*, the *X-Men*. It was like I was on a roll. I couldn't do anything wrong. I don't know that the ideas were so good. I think it was more the style. I think the readers related to that style of writing and storytelling. I think we could've been doing anything. It could've been Superman, Batman, and the Flash, but if we were doing them in our new style, they would've been big hits.

Pitts: When you say style, are you talking about the actual mechanics of the writing?

Lee: The mechanics of the writing is all pretty much the same. The style being, trying to humanize the characters as much as possible. The big formula, if you want to think of it as a formula, was just saying to myself, suppose a real, flesh and blood human had thus and such a super power? What would his life be like anyway? What would happen to him in the real world.

Like Iron Man: okay, so he's got this suit of armor and he can fly and he's very strong, but won't he still have to worry about union trouble at his factory? And won't he still have to worry about women problems, girls who are running after him and so forth, and his weak heart and all the problem he has?

Maybe what I'm saying is: I tried to concentrate more on the characters' personal lives, and not just make the story a case of hero sees a crime being committed, hero goes after the criminal, hero fights him and catches him in the end, which had pretty much been the formula up till then.

Pitts: Would you say, in a nutshell, that the key to the early success of your work was that it gave more respect to the readers' intellect?

Lee: Oh, absolutely, because suddenly we found we were getting older readers. Older readers who had never read comics before were picking them up and enjoying them and were staying with us. There were a lot of other things. We were trying to get more story content also. We used continued stories, which gave us more room. Instead of telling a whole epic in twenty pages, we had a hundred pages, because the stories went on, issue after issue. We could get more subplots, we could get more plot development, more character delineation, we could flesh the stories out and make them like little motion pictures. Even the vocabulary: we would use whatever words were necessary for a situation. We didn't say to ourselves, "This word will be too difficult for the young kids."

We tried to have the people talk like real people. We tried to write the stories as though we were screenwriters, writing screenplays or television shows. The whole idea was to make the stories as adult as possible and still keep them enjoyable and understandable for young kids.

Pitts: If I had walked into the Marvel offices at that point there in the sixties, what would I have found?

Lee: I think you'd have found a small group of guys working like crazy, harassed and hectic—but happy, enjoying what they were doing and very excited about what we were doing. It was something new. We were creating new characters, a new mythology, and the public was reacting favorably to them.

We felt rather proud of what we were doing. We even started putting credits in the books, which had never really been done in comics before. I started writing a column, "Stan's Soapbox," and made up this "Bullpen Bulletins" page. We tried to bring the readers into the whole Marvel world with us so they weren't just fans. They were friends. I tried to talk to the readers as if I was sitting right with them and they were sharing the excitement with me. Tried to keep everything informal and friendly and exciting.

Pitts: You also seemed to enjoy creating, for want of a better phrase, a bunker mentality in which here was little tiny Marvel taking potshots at this huge giant, DC. It was the underdog syndrome.

Lee: That was the case. We were definitely the underdogs. DC was the giant in the field when it came to superheroes. They had I don't know how many superhero titles. We only had the *Fantastic Four* when we started, but we kept adding. DC was owned by Warner Brothers and they were big and wealthy. We were the little outfit, and we were very excited about the fact that we were suddenly starting to compete with DC and people were noticing us. It was a great feeling.

Pitts: In rubbing shoulders with your fellow professionals, did you get the feeling they saw you guys at Marvel as a contender?

Lee: I never really thought of it that way. I was friends with most of the staff at DC and when we got together, we just kidded around and talked. I didn't think of it in those terms.

Pitts: Let's put it this way: was there an event or a time when you suddenly realized that Marvel would, as you liked to put it back then, take over the world?

Lee: I don't know when that time was, but I began to get a sense of that as time went on. I could tell by the fan mail. I could tell by the reception I got when I went to comic book conventions. I would be there with members of the DC staff and all the questions were directed at me from the fans in the audience. All the interest seemed to be for Marvel. And little by little, yeah . . . you'd have to be blind not to realize that Marvel was where the excitement was in those days. I'd like to think it still is.

Pitts: You got a letter once from a woman who thanked you for helping her to raise her son so well. I'm sure that's not the only letter of that type you've received. How does it feel to have helped raise a generation of kids?

Lee: Very good. Wonderful. You're right, I've gotten many letters like that and I treasured them and I cannot tell you how gratified they made me feel, how warm they made me feel. You know, when you're a writer, you sit at a typewriter alone and you're batting out a lot of words and you have no idea if anybody's reading them or if anybody cares. I guess everybody likes to feel that what he does has some meaning to somebody.

I used to liken it to a disc jockey who has a late-night show somewhere and he sits in a little room by himself talking into a microphone. He kind of hopes somebody, somewhere is listening, but how does he ever know? And suddenly, you start getting this mail, all this feedback. I got letters from kids who said, "Stan, I'm having a Bar Mitzvah. I'd love it if you'd come. My father says he'll pay your fare." I got a letter from a kid saying, "I had to deliver a valedictorian address. I just graduated and for the subject of my address, I used a speech you had the Silver Surfer make in issue # so and so" . . . or, "My mother said, how come my English grades are improving so and I told her I'd been reading Marvel Comics and she didn't believe me." Sure, it was wonderful receiving mail like that.

Pitts: I'd be remiss if I didn't tell you that I interviewed Kirby for this book and frankly, I didn't know what I was letting myself in for. He's a very bitter man. Very angry. There were a lot of things he said about you that I would like you to have the opportunity to respond to, if you're of a mind to.

Lee: Okay.

Pitts: Let's start with the picture he paints of his contribution to Marvel. As he put it, "I saved Marvel's ass." He says when he walked in for his first meeting with you, you had your head down on the desk crying because Marvel was to be closed. You were in despair, an emotional wreck, and he came and told you, "Look, we can do this, we can do that, and we can revolutionize comics."

Lee: Well, that's his remembrance. I don't think there's ever been a time when I've had my head on the desk crying. You're meeting me now, I don't think I come across as an emotional wreck. I really don't know what he's alluding to at all.

Pitts: Also, he says every character that's credited as a Stan Lee character is a Jack Kirby character, including Spider-Man, which he says he passed to you and you passed to Ditko.

Lee: (SIGH) Jack has his own perception of these things, and I think I understand the way he feels. It's really a semantic difference of opinion, because it depends what you mean by "creating" something. For example, the first book we did was *Fantastic Four*. I came up with the idea of the Fantastic Four. I wrote it down. I still have the outline I wrote—the whole idea for the story. And I called Jack and I said, "I'd like you to draw this. Here's the outline, these are the characters I want," and so forth. Jack then took it and drew it. Now, Jack did create the characters in the sense that he drew them. I didn't draw them. I wrote them. He created the way they look.

Jack also contributed quite a lot as the series went on in ideas, in plot. Jack is wonderful at story. He's very imaginative. He's the most talented guy in the business as far as I'm concerned, as far as imagination goes. He contributed a great deal. We worked as partners, but the creation of the characters, it seems to me . . . like with the Hulk: I said to him one day, "I want to do a hero who will be a monster. I think that would be great. I want to get a combination of the Frankenstein monster and Jekyll and Hyde. I'd like you to draw it, Jack, and this is what I'd like it to be." And then we would discuss it, and I'm sure Jack contributed a few ideas, too. But it seems to be that the person who says, "I have this idea for a character," that's the person who created it. I could've given it to anybody to draw. Jack was the best. I gave them to Jack.

I have never tried to deny Jack's great contribution in all of these, but for him to say he created them all . . . He's not the one who came to me and said, "Let's do the *Fantastic Four* or let's do the *Hulk*. I came to him and said it. I said, "I want to do a god. Let's do the god of thunder— Thor. Nobody has ever done Norse mythology before. They've done Roman gods and Greek gods. I want to play with Norse mythology, and I think the idea of Thor would be very dramatic." So, if that doesn't give me the right to say I created it, I don't know what does.

As far as *Spider-Man* is concerned, I came up with the idea of Spider-Man. I wanted a character who could crawl on walls. The name "Spider-Man" was mine. I called Jack and I said, "Jack, I'd like you to draw this differently than you draw your other characters," because Jack drew characters very heroically. They were all big and noble looking. I said, "I'd like you to make Spider-Man kind of an average guy. Almost nerdy. He's guy who wears glasses, he's not strong, he's bookworm, he's not that popular with girls.

Jack came back a little while later and brought me two or three pages and I looked at them and they were nicely drawn, but it wasn't what I wanted. The character looked more like Captain America than the way I wanted Spider-Man to look. I said, "Let's forget it, Jack. I don't think this one is for you." Jack had enough other books to do. It didn't matter. I gave it to Steve Ditko. Now, how Jack can say he created it, I don't know. There's only one thing . . . and I don't know, my memory isn't that good: Jack, when he gave me the pages, he had probably drawn a picture of Spider-Man. Ditko may have taken Kirby's costume and when he did the strip, he may have drawn the costume Jack had done. I do not know for a fact whether Ditko made up his own costume or took Jack's. If Jack wants to say he created the Spider-Man costume, he may have. I don't know. If he wants to say he created the Thor costume, the Fantastic Four costumes, whatever else he did, fine. But I don't think that's the same as saying, "I created this book or this concept or this idea."

Pitts: Jack claims that he did the writing you got all the credit for, and he also said he left Marvel that first time because he felt he was creating in you the kind of character he didn't want to create. Can you tell me what he's talking about?

Lee: No, I really don't know what he's talking about. But I don't know much of what Jack is talking about these days. I mean, when I listen to these things he says, I just feel I'm listening to the mouthings of a very bitter man who I feel quite sorry for. I don't know what his problem is, really.

As far as him doing the stories, Jack never felt that the script itself, the dialogue I wrote, was part of the story. Very often, Jack would make up the plots. We would discuss a story before it was done, and I'd say, "Let's bring Dr. Doom back. Let's let him capture Reed Richards or do this and that." Jack would say okay, and I left most of the details to Jack.

It's quite true, a lot of the stories—the plotting of them—he created.
I would give him a couple of words and he did the rest. I've never taken
that away from him. He was wonderful at that.

Then he would bring me the drawings. I would put in all the dialogue
and all the captions. I have a feeling that Jack considers that relatively
unimportant. You know, "Anybody can put the dialogue in." I would
like to feel that the style I gave the stories by putting the dialogue in was
quite important. After all, the manner of speech is really what gives the
characters their personality. As a matter of fact, when Jack left Marvel,
his stories never read the same again, the ones he did without me. They
may have been better or worse, but they were never the same. The stories I wrote with Jack had a certain style, and I think they are greatly
responsible for Marvel's success. I think it is a shame that Jack didn't stay
with us. I think he and I could've still done great things together. I have
absolutely no idea why he is so bitter.

Pitts: Let's move on to happier ground and talk a little more in-depth
about the creation of some of your better-known characters. We can go
back to the FF and, if you would, talk about the creation of the individual characters as opposed to the team.
Lee: Well, with the Fantastic Four, I knew we wanted to create a team.
So the next problem was to figure out who should comprise the team.
I figured we have to have one leader. And for a name, I thought he
would modestly call himself Mr. Fantastic. I got a kick out of that.
I figured I'd make him the world's greatest scientist, but unlike some
other books, because he is a great scientist, I tried to write him as
though he was just a little bit stuffy—without too much of a sense of
humor, even though he's a hero. He's always pontificating and explaining things to give the other characters, like the Thing and the Torch a
chance to say, "Boy, he'll never use a word of two syllables when a fifty-
syllable word will do," and he kind of bores the others with his long-
winded explanations.

Then I decided that it would be fun to have a heroine who's not just
the "girl," but who's actually engaged to him. So, we started off the
series with Sue Storm, who was his fiancée. Then, for the obligatory
teenager, I figured, "Why not let him be Sue Storm's younger brother so
he could be the hero's brother-in-law after he married Sue. Because, in
superhero comics or in any comics prior to this, you never had in-laws or
relatives. They were always perfect strangers.

I needed a fourth guy and I figured his power would be the power of strength. I've always liked the injection of tragedy, and I figured, what if he's not only incredibly powerful, but the thing that gives him his power also turns him into a semi-monster. To keep it simple and offbeat, I decided to call him the Thing. The one that was totally unoriginal, of course, was the Human Torch, because we'd had a character like the Torch many years ago. I thought we'd give Johnny Storm, the kid brother of Sue, the same power but we'd change him by making him a teenager. The original Torch was an android as I remember. And also, I attempted to give him a personality that would be unique to Johnny Storm.

The one thing I always tried to concentrate on was the dialogue . . . the way they talked. I tried to have Johnny talk differently than the others—more the way a youngster would. And I tried to have Ben talk like a real tough, surly, angry guy, but yet the reader had to know he had a heart of gold underneath. Ben, of course, was the only one who couldn't become normal at will the way the other three could. So he was always bitter about that.

I knew without any doubt that Ben, the Thing, would be the most popular character, and he was. He was the most unique. People always like characters who seem very powerful but yet, you know they are very gentle underneath and you know they would help you if you needed it. It's almost like having your own genie on your shoulder.

Pitts: With Dr. Doom, you created the runaway most popular villain in comics and easily the most complex. How?
Lee: There again, I wanted to make him a scientist also, because I felt he had to be able to compete with Reed Richards. I thought it would be fun if they had been classmates in school together. The one quality I tried to give him was a quality of . . . well, he's regal. He's not just the average villain who wants to commit crimes and make money. Doom has all the money he needs. What he wants is to take over the world—to run the world. And I tried to write it as though maybe Doom could. Maybe he could do a better job than is being done now. He might be thought of as a benevolent despot.

In fact, in later stories and in my newspaper comic strip when I've featured him, I've had him saying things like, "I may rule with an iron hand, but there's no crime in Latveria"—which is his country—"there's no poverty and no unemployment and there aren't many prisoners in

jail." Of course, that was because he had most of them silenced. I also
tried to give him a strong sense of honor. I seem to remember I wrote
some stories where Doom would say, "If you do thus and such, I'll set
you free." Sue would say, "How can we trust him?" And Reed would
say, "Dr. Doom, for all his faults, has his own code of honor." In his way,
he was the most noble of all the bad men. I loved the idea of him being
a king, the idea he could come to America and be safe from arrest
because he had diplomatic immunity.

I didn't want him to be that hateful. I thought it would be fun to
have a villain you could kind of relate to, in a way. I think one of my
favorite stories was when Reed fought Dr. Doom and Doom won.
At the end of the story, Doom was very happy because he'd finally
defeated the Fantastic Four, but it turned out that Reed had hypnotized
him or something. Doom hadn't really won, but Reed felt that's the one
way to get him off his back forever. If he thinks he's won, he'll never
bother them again.

Pitts: Okay . . . Galactus.

Lee: He was a semi-god. He, uh . . . I never was too sure exactly
what he was. Or how big he was. Jack drew him different heights
many times. He was very much the same as Dr. Doom, except more so.
I remember I would have Galactus say, "I don't want to hurt anybody,
I don't want to kill anybody, but I must survive. It doesn't bother you
humans if you step on a anthill and kill thousands of ants. You don't
particularly want to kill them, but you can't help walking along. That's
the way it is with me. I don't want to harm anybody, but Galactus
must survive."

Pitts: The Hulk.

Lee: With the Hulk, I just wanted to create a lovable monster—almost
like the Thing, but more so. I had always loved Dr. Jekyll and Mr. Hyde,
and I had always loved the Frankenstein monster. I always felt the
Frankenstein monster was really the good guy. I'm talking about the
movie, not Mary Shelley's story. In the movie, Frankenstein's monster
didn't really want to hurt anybody. He just wanted to be left alone, and
everybody was hounding him and hunting him . . . those idiot policemen
always chasing him with those torches.

I figured, why don't we create a monster whom the whole human
race is always trying to hunt and destroy, but he's really a good guy.
Then, to give it an extra degree of interest, I figured instead of just a

monster, we'll borrow a concept from Jekyll and Hyde and let it be a man who turns into a monster unwillingly, who must spend his life trying to cure himself of this rather unique affliction.

Pitts: The X-Men.
Lee: They were originally called the Mutants, but my publisher at the time thought that the readers wouldn't know what a mutant was, so I changed it to the X-Men. We're always looking for new superheroes—not so much for new heroes as for new explanations of how they came about, and I was getting tired of radioactive accidents. I felt, why not get some people who were born the way they are, who had mutant powers. So we created the X-Men.

Pitts: Spider-Man.
Lee: I remember, when I was a kid, ten years old, there was a pulp magazine called *The Spider—Master of Men*. And I always thought that title was so dramatic. He was nothing like Spider-Man; he was just a detective who wore a mask, and he went around punching people. He wore a ring with a spider insignia so when he punched somebody it would leave a little mark of a spider on the person. I figured, "Gee, why not call my guy Spider-Man?"

Pitts: Although Spider-Man is arguably the most popular single superhero in comics, legend has it that your publisher, Martin Goodman, took a lot of convincing when you wanted to try the character out.
Lee: He said it was the worst idea he ever heard. He said people hate spiders, and it sounded too much like Superman. The idea of someone sticking to a wall and stuff, he called it grotesque.

Pitts: When you finally talked Goodman into doing Spider-Man, the alter-ego you created for the character was almost the prototypical milquetoast nerd—at least in his earliest incarnation. Where did you get your ideas for the character of Peter Parker?
Lee: More from myself than anybody. In the group, I was always the youngest kid, and I was always the thinnest kid. And, while I was a good athlete—I always played with the other kids; I played baseball, hockey, handball, and everything—because I was the youngest and the thinnest, I was never the captain or the leader and I was always the one getting pushed around. And I figured, kids would relate to a concept like that. After all, most kids have had similar experiences. Turns out I was right.

Pitts: Speaking of Spider-Man characters, Jonah Jameson has to be one of the most inspired supporting players in comics.

Lee: I guess he's my favorite. I don't really know where I got him . . . maybe a combination of everybody I've ever known. The only thing that has always bothered me about Jonah—you can believe it or not—I came up with the idea of the irascible publisher, and Spidey being a freelance photographer; I loved it, and weeks later, I said, "My God! Superman works for an editor, Perry White!" I said, "Oh, how did I get so close?" So, I knocked myself out to make Jonah Jameson as different as possible.

He's much more irascible, he's very reactionary, he thought the last good times we had in America were when Herbert Hoover was president, he hates teenagers, he hated hippies, he hated long hair, he hated guitars. I thought it would be funny to get a guy like that and show he isn't really a villain. He's not a bad guy. He just represents that segment of society that is very arch conservative.

Pitts: The Silver Surfer.

Lee: Silver Surfer really was created by Jack Kirby. After we had decided to do Galactus in a story, when Jack brought the artwork in, I saw there was some funny guy on a flying surfboard. I said, "Who's this?" Jack said, "I figure anybody as important as Galactus ought to have a herald who flies ahead of him and finds planets for him." I loved the idea. I don't remember who made up the name the Silver Surfer—whether it was Jack or me, but I loved the idea, and the drawings were so beautiful, he looked so great that I figured I would try to have him talk differently than any other character—get a quasi-Shakespearean/biblical delivery for him.

Pitts: There was something almost Christ-like about the Surfer. Was that in Jack's original conception?

Lee: No. That was the quality that I gave to him. As he was originally drawn, he was just a powerful guy on a flying surfboard.

Pitts: I remember reading in one of your old columns where you said the Surfer was being quoted in pulpits across the country. How did that affect you? Is there a special place in your heart for him?

Lee: Absolutely. You know, I used to lecture a lot at colleges and very often during the question and answer period, the kids in the audience would say, "Tell us about the Surfer and how he relates to the Judeo-Christian concept of religion. Did you have Jesus Christ in mind?"

They would discuss various quotations from the Surfer. Somehow or other, we seem to have struck a nerve there. People seem to really care about the Surfer.

Pitts: Well, did you have Jesus Christ in mind?
Lee: Maybe subconsciously, I was trying to make the Surfer a pure innocent who is trying to help people and is being misunderstood and persecuted for the very things he is trying to do, which are totally good and unselfish.

Pitts: I've heard it rumored that you passed down the edict at Marvel that no one will write a Surfer series except you.
Lee: I did, and then when I left Marvel physically to move out to the (West) Coast, after a few years there was such a clamor for the Surfer that they're finally putting out some new books, which are being written by someone else. I must say I'm still unhappy about it, but I didn't feel I should make a big fuss about it. I can't insist that nobody else writes it if the world wants more Surfers and I don't have time to do it. But I was always afraid that whoever wrote it wouldn't write him the correct way, because I don't want him treated too much like a normal superhero. Another fear I have is . . . sometimes a writer can try to copy your style too much and it comes across as being too corny.

Pitts: Daredevil.
Lee: There again, we were trying for something different, and I figured, why not a blind superhero? Everybody thought it was a crazy idea, but it really worked. He's one of most popular characters today.

Pitts: Finally, your most recent creation and, in many ways, the most controversial: the She-Hulk.
Lee: Originally, we thought we might be able to sell another version of the Hulk as an animated cartoon, so I was asked to create such a character, and write a good story for it. Someone came up with the name "She-Hulk" and I thought "Why not?" So I did it. But I only created the character and wrote that first issue. I didn't have time for any more.

Personally, left to myself, I wouldn't have done the She-Hulk. Even though she's a good character . . . it smacked to me too much of Superman and Superboy and Superdog and Supersneakers and on and on. I felt one Hulk was all the world really needed.

Pitts: It's been quite a few years since you were actively writing. Have there been any versions of your characters since then that you felt were really excellent—that captured the spirit of what you did and then added something extra to it?

Lee: Oh, sure. It's hard to remember examples. I don't really have time to read the books now, but I would read them a few years ago or at least look through a few of them, and every so often I'd see a story that would make me say, "Gee, that's really terrific." There was one Spider-Man story about a kid who was dying and Spider-Man came and—

Pitts: *The Kid Who Collected Spider-Man.*

Lee: That's it. It was a lovely little story. I thought it was just great. I had seen a few *Daredevils* that I thought were good, I saw some *Fantastic Fours* that I liked.

Pitts: Let's turn it around. Have there been any versions of your characters that you've been especially unhappy with? I remember you saying that you were unhappy with the Gwen Stacy clone story and the whole death of Gwen Stacy in *Spider-Man*.

Lee: Well, the clone, I think, was my suggestion originally. I was so unhappy she was dead I was trying to think of a way to bring her back without claiming it had been an imaginary story or something. Didn't seem to work, though, but I never would have killed Gwen Stacy in the first place. When I gave up the strip, he (Gerry Conway) said, "How should I write it?" I said, "You're the writer now, do whatever you want." I don't feel it's right to try to control something if I'm not there anymore.

I had to go to Europe for a while. When I came back, I found out she had been killed. I said, Sheeesh! I didn't mean kill off all my characters." But it was done. It was irrevocable.

Pitts: Any other examples like that, where something happened with one of your characters that really incensed you?

Lee: Well, there've been a lot of changes in the books since I left. I can't say I've been incensed. I'm confident that Jim Shooter and his staff know what they're doing. Jim's one of the most innovative talents in comics. You can't keep things the same all the time. There are perhaps more changes than I would have made, because I like things that are a little bit more constant and dependable. I would have preferred it if the stories and the plots changed a lot, but if the characters remained more constant. And yet, a lot of the things that have been done at Marvel have been very exciting and very stimulating and provocative, like the *Iron Man* series where Tony Stark becomes an alcoholic. A lot of people have talked about it, been interested in it, cared about it. I think it's great that writers are using their own imaginations and going wherever their own tastes lead them.

I think, by and large, the books and the changes are pretty good.

Pitts: Kirby made an interesting observation that comics are becoming a little too seamy and graphic. Would you go along with that, that there are too many liberties being taken?

Lee: Well, I think there's an effort made to make them more adult and more sophisticated. And of course, the world has changed a lot since I was writing comics. We're living in a different time now. I would not, perhaps, have the stories quite as rough as some of them are. For my own tastes, they're a little too earthy, I think. But I don't know that it's really wrong. It may be that that's what we've come to now in our society. Maybe they're the right kind of stories for this period of time.

Pitts: Why did you stop writing in the first place?

Lee: (PAUSE) I'm not sure. I think I probably just got too busy with my publishing duties. I may also have felt that it was time to step aside and try my hand at other things. Now my work in film keeps me fully occupied. Sure, I guess I sometimes miss comicbook writing, but I still do the *Spider-Man* newspaper strip and I also do an occasional comicbook for Marvel whenever my longtime friend, Jim Galton, Marvel's president, may request me to write some special issue. Jim's one of the greatest guys I know and I'd never turn him down.

Pitts: What are your current duties?

Lee: Right now I'm putting together a number of motion picture projects, both live action and animated, as well as developing some prime-time TV series. I've made my headquarters at Marvel's new animated studio here in Van Nuys, California, where I'm in charge of the creation and development of new projects. I work with the creative staff, as well as with lovely Margaret Loesch, the brilliant president of Marvel Productions.

Y'know, I sometimes get the strangest feeling of déjà vu. It's as though I'm once again reliving those exciting days of the early sixties when we were building Marvel Comics. Suddenly I'm back in harness again, having the time of my life, working with clever, talented artists and writers, creating characters and concepts at a vital, fast-growing studio, developing movie and TV projects, and keeping busier than ever doing all the things I love.

From the Publisher's Perspective: Comments by Stan Lee and Jenette Kahn

M. Thomas Inge / 1985

From *The American Comic Book: An Exhibition at the Ohio State University,* an exhibition catalog edited by Lucy Shelton Caswel, 1985. Reprinted by permission of M. Thomas Inge.

Stan Lee heads the Marvel Comics Group and Jenette Kahn heads National Periodical Publications, known as DC, the two major American comic book publishers.

Q: Some feel that American comic books since 1950 have not matched those published during the previous "golden age." Have more recent comic books been better, worse, or simply different? How so?
Lee: The comic books of today are better. They're better written and better drawn. Those before 1950 were extremely spontaneous, less organized. The artists and the writers were doing whatever they felt

like. After 1950 the audience was larger and the scripts had to be more professional.

Kahn: In 1938, when Superman was first published, his immediate and awesome popularity gave birth, literally, to an entire industry. Hundreds of characters were spawned in those early years, what we now call comics' Golden Age. Among them were the Batman, debuting in 1939, and Wonder Woman, published one year later. Of all the heroes created then, in the industry's headiest period, only these three characters—Superman, Batman, and Wonder Woman—have been published without interruption to the present day.

Yet while these characters have transcended four and half decades, the artwork and scripting of them today is radically different from that which was done in the forties. This applies not just to the primary super-heroes, but to all characters whether old or newly created, whether costumed heroes or science-fiction protagonists.

The Golden Age comics are crude and simplistic by today's standards, but with a raw immediacy within gives them a hard-hitting power that is hard for contemporary comics to replicate. Early creators were energized by the visceral thrill of creating a new art form. They looked everywhere for inspiration to shape their newborn medium. Mary Shelley's *Frankenstein, The Cabinet of Dr. Caligari*—classics both—were only two of the many sources for the Batman. This connection with other art and other forms invigorated the best of the first comic books. It is a connection that has waned as comics, like all maturing art forms, have turned inward.

Although comics have paid a price for this inward-turning, they have also evolved to a level of sophistication which makes them deservedly appealing to a far older audience. The best comics today are now driven by characterization rather than plot. Story-telling is no longer strictly linear but includes flashbacks, cuts, and well-developed sub-plots. The writing itself is less explicit and therefore depends more on the reader's intelligence and participation. The use of language itself, as in Alan Moore's current *Swamp Thing,* is startling and stirring and in itself moves comic books into new territory.

The same is true of comic artwork. Having reached a peak of illusion-ism with Neal Adams and John Buscema some fifteen years ago, comic book artists have flattened the page again with particular emphasis on surface design. Yet this is a very knowing two-dimensionality, totally dif-ferent from the flatness of the forties. This flatness is a choice, informed by the ability to turn a figure in space. Perspective was long ago mastered and the illusion of depth is part of even the most stylized, innovative artwork, as in *American Flagg*.

Q: Have the social climate and historic events of the past twenty-five years had any direct influence on developments in the comic book? Do comics merely reflect social trends or do they have the power to create and influence them?

Lee: The social climate and the world we live in always affects things that are written and drawn at that period. No artist or writer works in a vacuum, and whatever he does is affected by the times. Comic books are no different in that sense than movies, television, novels, music, or newspapers. But though we are affected by our own world, in writing about things that are happening and in making them dramatic and bigger than life, we probably cause the very things we're writing about to attain greater importance than they would have if they hadn't been mentioned at all. We're not sociologists. Our entire function is to entertain. All we try to do is tell stories that people will enjoy.

Kahn: Ever since their inception, comic books have been visionary, prophets of a sometimes terrifying, often titillating future. Because their province is the realm of the fantastic, comics have predicted everything from space travel to psychic phenomena.

Yet there is no denying that artists and writers—no matter how far ranging their imaginations—create out of their own time period and the culture in which they participate. Every comic book artist and every comic book writer describes the hero or anti-hero he (more than 95 percent of writers and artists are male) wants to be, the woman he wants to be with, and the issues that concern him. The societal undertone of each era means that these perceptions change as times change and we do, too. Men were macho in comics' Golden Age and women were no more than pneumatic window dressing.

Today, our writers allow their heroes to be vulnerable because they wish to be, too. Similarly, the women in today's comics are loving but self-sufficient with ideas and lives of their own.

Where the early comics, propelled by World War II, were militaristic and chauvinistic both, today's comics are the antithesis. The devastation of nuclear war and radioactive waste, the frail hope of global unity—all are themes permeating contemporary comic books.

Certainly comics embody the concerns and social trends of their time. But unlike other media, they don't report them, they dramatize them. The impact of an involving, compelling story can take a theme and drive home its significance with emotional urgency. In this way, comics are instruments of social change.

Q: Have we realized the full potential of the comic book as an educational tool? Do comic books have a place in the four-year college or university?

Lee: Comic books could be one of the most potent educational tools of all time. We haven't even scratched the surface. I used comics when I was in the army and I saw evidence of how they could be used to teach virtually any subject in the world.

If people are going to study movies, TV, opera, ballet, concerts, sculpture, painting, and other media, they might as well study comic books because comic books are just as profound and as strong a factor in shaping, and moving, and molding people's thoughts. They can be used primarily in pop culture courses and contemporary American literature courses. Many filmmaking courses use comics because a comic book is essentially a motion picture story between two covers.

Kahn: Kids learn so much from comics. There's reading. There's the whole realm of imagination. Comics have been a harbinger of the wonders of the universe, of space travel. When something is that good spontaneously, without actually purposely teaching, you hesitate to use it as an educational tool because you're afraid you might take away from people's pure enjoyment. But we've done almost nothing with comics consciously as an educational tool. No one has put his head to getting out very basic kinds of information. I believe a teacher could evolve programs around existing comics but it would have to be done with true gentleness, not to taint the comics, which are kid's own special item, with the stamp of formal education.

You can't get the kind of dense material in a comic book that you should be reading at a college. I would shy away from courses on comic books—the overly scholarly approach—because foremost comics are entertainment and were created for that. On the other hand, comic book characters, the superheroes, are truly mythological figures for our age. Everyone knows about Clark Kent and Lois. How they came to be that and why they had values that people could identify with is an interesting question.

Q: Does the comic book have the same potential as an art form as film, drama, or fiction? If so, has it lived up to its potential?
Lee: If Shakespeare and Michelangelo were alive today, and if they decided to collaborate on a comic, Shakespeare would write the script and Michelangelo would draw it. How could anybody say that this wouldn't be as worthwhile an art form as anything on earth? Comics are merely a method of telling a story through words and art. If the art is magnificent, the words are well-written, of course comics can be as good as any movie or novel. I don't think the present writers have knocked themselves out enough. But I think that we're on the way. I wouldn't be surprised if comics are reviewed by critics and have their Oscars and their Emmies.
Kahn: I think it does, insofar as an art form is limited only by the imagination of its creators and the tools available to it. In each era comics have lived up to their potential. After this past ten-year period it must be about time for another breakthrough.

Q: What is the most significant event in comic book publishing since 1950?
Lee: Probably the creation of Marvel Comics. It sounds selfserving, but I think Marvel really turned the whole field around. We proved that comics could be produced that weren't just kidstuff. We were the first company to use an adult vocabulary, to try characters who were realistic and reacted to situations the way real people would, even if they had super power. We had subplots within our main plots. We had continued stories. We tried to make comics into a more sophisticated method of storytelling than the "Take that, you rat," which had been the level of most dialogues in comics.
Kahn: Comic book characters pick up the unconscious trends of the time and become the spokesmen for those trends. That's why people can identify so fully that the characters can become part of the mythology. Stan Lee's characters did that in the sixties. He picked up on anti-Establishment feelings, on alienation and self-deprecation. Our characters were still carrying the hero mode of World War II and Stan came in with characters with bad breath and acne, punkier, younger, when young people needed symbols to replace many of the things they were rejecting.

Q: What part do you believe the comic book will play in the future of American culture?

Lee: If the people producing comic books are sincere and desirous of improving the art form, comics will play a very important part in American culture. Nothing has more impact than the movie screen. The second strongest impact is obtained through a comic book. In a movie you have words, visual images, and sound. Nothing can beat that. In a comic book, you have words and visual images that don't move, but they can be even more imaginative. You can draw things that nobody can photograph. Unfortunately, you don't get sound. But comics have an advantage in that a comic book can be read at the reader's own speed. A comic can be carried around, it can be read and reread, it can be shared with a friend. Anything that is important to a large segment of the population should be studied and should be taken seriously, whether it's silly putty, the hoola hoop, or comic books.

Kahn: Comics have spewed out characters that speak for society, and I assume the same thing will happen again. New characters will capture our imagination in a new way and become part of our symbols.

The Marvel Age of Comics: An Interview with Stan Lee

PAT JANKIEWICZ / 1987

From *Chaffey College Mountain Breeze*, October 10, 1987. Reprinted by permission of Pat Jankiewicz.

Pat Jankiewicz: Okay, before we begin, I'd like to open on a corny note and say that I've admired you and your work for a long time.

Stan Lee: Well, that's the way it should be! (Laughter)

PJ: Having grown up with Marvel Comics, and the ideas and stories you've created, we were kind of stricken to see today's films, the especially popular ones, lift a lot of the style, pacing, character, and feeling of your old comics. I thought I'd talk to you about that, basically, as a starting point.

SL: Fine. It's actually very frustrating to me, because a lot of the movies and TV shows that we're working on don't have enough of the Marvel style that a lot of people have that aren't connected!

The best example, I think, is the *Superman* movie. The first *Superman* movie had a lot of the Marvel pacing, and yet they never had that kind of stuff in the *Superman* books . . . I used to figure if we ever did *Spider-Man* the right way, the way the books have done him, people would think we were imitating *Superman*! You can imagine the way that makes me feel.

We've had *Spider-Man* on television, live-action, years ago, and it was terrible! It had no similarity whatsoever. And they did *Captain America*, and it was an abomination! It's very frustrating . . .

PJ: It's funny, because we were speculating that a lot of writers may have been influenced by the material you did, and now, as adults, people like George Lucas and Stephen J. Cannell think "That was great," and appropriate it. Does this make you apprehensive?

Tom Jankiewicz: Cannell's really taken a ride, hasn't he?

SL: Cannell has, yeah. But no, it doesn't make me apprehensive. I think the only thing I feel is disappointment in myself. Because "Why did I let all these guys . . ." But we weren't in the movie and TV business, you know. I'm a "Johnny-Come-Lately," having come out here five years ago, and it's taken me two to three years to learn how things work out here—it takes very little time to learn this business. Now I think we're starting to take some strides, but you're right. Guys like Cannell, Lucas, and Spielberg, whether it's because they read Marvel, or we just think alike, I don't know, but their products certainly have a lot in common with our old comic books, yeah.

PJ: Are you worried they might strip-mine the subject, and possibly wear down the audience?

SL: No, no. I feel there's always, always room for a good story. You can see 800 million movies, and you'll still want that 800 million and one. It's like books, you never say to yourself "That's it! I've read all the books I'm ever gonna read in my life. I'm never gonna read another book!" You're always looking for that other book, like a surfer who's always looking for that better wave. You always look for a book or movie that's better than the last.

The only time people worry, I guess, and the only time I would worry is, if I were to run out of ideas. That's it. I would hate to try to live on what I did yesterday; I'm more interested in what I'm gonna come up with tomorrow.

PJ: You're still going strong.

SL: Well, I'm trying!

PJ: Did you ever feel this way in the sixties . . . You know, "I created the Fantastic Four and the Hulk, now I'm washed out!"?

SL: You always hope you'll be able to come up with something else. I think I've sort of convinced myself that ideas are really the easiest things—I could walk down the street and think up ten new movies, or ten new comics. Getting them done is difficult (Laughs), but thinking of them?! So I never worry "Will I run out of ideas?"

The funny thing is, the more you do, the more it seems you're able to do. I remember, a million years ago, I was writing a comic book called *Millie the Model* (Laughter) for about fifteen years, and it was very successful for the company—sort of a female *Archie*. Anyway, after I had been doing it for ten years, my publisher said to me: "Gee, Stan, don't you think you ought to stop doing these? You've been doing it for ten years now, it must be tough for you, you're probably running out of ideas, and I don't want you to get stale."

The strange thing is, I wasn't running out of ideas. I found it easier than when I started because I knew the characters, their motivations, and the type of situations they would get into. The stories came naturally. I've used the same method on the *Spider-Man* strip.

PJ: Yes, you can feel the momentum pick up on the strip. You've dealt with issues like child abuse and computer theft, yet the further it goes, the stronger it gets. Do you ever have trouble coming up with new concepts for it?

SL: No, the more you do something, the easier it is to do it. When I need a new plot for the *Spider-Man* newspaper strip, I sit down and think for five minutes and come up with a hundred of them! The more you do it, the better you know the character, the better you know the character's friends, family, enemies, and the situations that follow. It was much tougher when I started the strip.

What I've been doing with the *Spider-Man* strip lately is try to write it like a soap opera—it just happens that the hero has a super-power.

PJ: Have you ever thought of writing a year's worth of strips, while you're "in the mood"?

SL: Wish I could, but I only have one day a week to do my writing on the strip, because I'm busy with other things the rest of the week.

In that one day, I've got to write a week's worth of story. What I was doing in New York was writing two weeks' worth of strips each day, putting in a very long day, but I got myself a few months ahead.

I haven't written anything in the past two or three months, so I'm getting very worried! I've got to start writing again, or I'm gonna be in big trouble! In case you're interested, they've just released *The Best of Spider-Man*—

PJ: Hey! I've already bought it!
SL: Oh, so you're the one! (Laughs)

PJ: Have you ever received any acknowledgement from admiring film-makers like Spielberg and Lucas?
SL: Lucas and Spielberg have exercised a lot of willpower and restraint in not ever contacting me! (Laughs) Years ago, however, Federico Fellini came to see me in New York! I couldn't believe it! The secretary said, "There's a 'Mr. Felony' or something, here to see you . . ." I said "Okay, show him in," and sure enough, Federico!

I wanted to talk to him about his movies, and all he wanted to talk about was our comics! I was so flattered! We became a little bit friendly for a few years, writing letters to each other . . .

PJ: Did he have any favorites?
SL: No, he liked all my stories and said he was a big fan. Another filmmaker-director you might not have heard of, Alain Resnais—

PJ: Right here! The very next question!
SL: Aw, bless your heart! (Laughs) He came a year after Fellini, and by now I was used to it—"Come right in, what took you so long?" (Laughter) He was very nice, and flattering too. He told me he learned to read English from reading my comic books!"

PJ: A lot of people say that! A Vietnamese friend of mine recalls reading *Spider-Man* as a kid before the North Vietnamese took over.
TJ: Some, of course, got them from GIs, that's how that started.

PJ: I talked to a couple of Viet Nam vets on campus, and when I told them I was doing a piece on you, they said they used to love you and hate you. They'd pass time in 'Nam on a field or ditch reading Marvel, when the hero's life would be hanging in the whole balance, till next month's conclusion, which they would never get!

SL: Aw, gee . . . (Laughs) We used to send them to a lot of servicemen, because every so often I'd get a letter from some guy saying that, so I'd send them a whole pack of books, but they were always continued stories! You couldn't send them everything!

PJ: Did you ever consider sending them the endings?
SL: I never knew what the endings would be, until hours before I wrote them!
TJ: I guess that would explain some of the endings! (Laughter)

PJ: To get to my next question, have you written any scripts for films? I know Alain Resnais approached you . . . What became of that? Have you ever considered writing any scripts of your characters, in an attempt to "do them right"?
SL: It's a funny thing, but I just don't have the time! There's a guy who does a full-page mail order ad—he's run it on and off for years, that tells you how to get rich quick. The headline is "Most People Spend Too Much Time Working to Ever Make Money." That's really been my case—I've kept so busy doing my day-to-day things!

People have asked me to write screenplays, and a lot of publishers have asked me to write novels, but I would have to take a few months off that I can't spare.

PJ: There's a misconception that you penned a certain spy novel—how do you feel about that?
SL: I'm not very happy about it. I don't know if I should sue or what. The guy's name is something like "Stanley R. Lee," but he just ran it as "Stan Lee" . . .

PJ: The book doesn't run a picture of the writer, and it says something brief like "Stan Lee lives in New York." An Upland bookstore was selling it alongside *The Best of Spider-Man*, implying that it was from the same writer.
SL: What I've suspected, and what you've said seems to confirm it, is that he knew and deliberately traded in on my name. He'll probably become the biggest writer in America, and suddenly, I'll be "The Other Stan Lee"! I wouldn't mind having written it, though. It sold well, and I heard they're going to make it into a film.

PJ: It also shows the credibility people give you—that you would write a bestseller. You did write *The Best of the Worst* a while back . . . (Holds out Xeroxed copy)

SL: Jesus! Where do you guys get this stuff? You must be the world's greatest researchers! (Laughter)

My wife just sold a novel, and I would also love to write a novel or screenplay! Now that I've been here, and seen how screenplays are written, I know I could! What I did do is write a treatment for a TV series—the first treatment I ever wrote, and they love it at one of the networks, so we'll see if they buy that. I've been working with writers who are doing screenplays, and I've written outlines for them, but I sold a screenplay with Resnais, geez, twenty years ago! It was the funniest thing in the world, I had never written one, and Alain taught me how.

PJ: You did teach him how to read!
SL: (Laughs) In France, they do screenplays differently. In those days it didn't cost much to make a movie there, and he had me put in everything but the kitchen sink! He wanted a lot of "big scenes," so I put them in. We gave it to a producer who, liked it, and bought it for $25,000. It's pretty petty now, but it was a lot of money then, which I split with Alain! (Laughter)

The producer said, "The only thing is, you're gonna have to cut a lot of this stuff out, or I can't afford to make it," and my nutty friend Alain said (adapting thick French accent) "Shhtan will not change a word!"—one of these moralistic ideas. It's like that joke—"Pay him the two bucks!" (Laughs) I said "Alain, I'll change it, I'll change it!" "No, you wheel not change a word!" Well, the goddam script is still sitting there, on a shelf somewhere.

PJ: What genre is it?
SL: It was called *The Monster Maker*, and it had to do with a guy like Roger Corman, who makes monster movies.

PJ: Corman had the rights to *Spider-Man*.
SL: Geez, he knows everything.
TJ: I'm afraid so!
SL: Anyway, he makes monster movies, and tries to get out of the mold and make a grade A movie, a high-budget, impressive movie. Without giving away the story, not that it matters, it ends up that the only way he can do his good thing is to take all his skills as a monster maker and translate them.

It had to do with pollution and stuff—a crazy movie, but it would have worked if Alain had let me rewrite it. It's still lying around somewhere. I also wrote a lot of army-training films.

PJ: You did those?! "Don't Leave Korea with Gohnorrea"–type stuff?
(Mild laughter)
PJ: How has Marvel Productions been running since the fire?
SL: Pretty good! The fire was terrible . . . I lost a lot of personal things.
I had cartoon books from cartoonists all over the world autographed to
me, and I kept them all in the office, so they were all burned up.

PJ: Was it this place?
SL: No, we had the fire in Van Nuys, a few miles from here. I had video-
tapes of all the lectures I'd done on college campuses, so I lost those,
also. It had no monetary value, but it was a terrible thing.

PJ: I found it a Marvel-styled irony that the fire broke out during
"Spider-Man week" on channel five. (Reruns of the old TV program)
The newscaster came on at the commercial break, and announced that
"Spider-Man loses home, News at ten."
SL: It did?!
TJ: Yeah. I got this vision of a splash page showing Spider-Man standing
in front of a burning building, shouting "Everything I touch is
destroyed!" (Laughs)

PJ: What exactly does Marvel Productions do? Will it eventually break
into live-action movies and TV?
SL: At the moment, we're a cartoon and animation studio, and the feature films we're working on are done outside the studio; other producers
do them and we work in a partnership with them. What I, and the president of our studio, Margeret Loesch, hope is that one day we will be
doing live-action. That would be great, but it's a big investment and
undertaking, so we'll see how we go.

PJ: Maybe if the Cannon Productions go well . . . Speaking of which,
how much input have you had on Cannon's *Spider-Man*?
SL: A little bit—I think they're using a screenplay that's based on
an outline I wrote. So at least the story will be similar to Marvel. But I
haven't had a tremendous amount of input because most movie
companies say, "We want to take your property, thanks a lot, now
don't bother us."

PJ: Why do it if they won't be true to it?
SL: They feel they know better . . . There's a million articles on best-
selling authors whose books are bought by Hollywood and ruined.

PJ: Stephen King was quoted as saying, "When dealing with the American cinema you feel like you won if you just broke even."
SL: And now he wants to direct his own.

PJ: I think he's finished it. There's an article on it in the new *American Film*.
SL: I wish I knew how to direct. I'd like to direct one of mine.

PJ: Well, drop around and look, I guess. Speaking of directing, I spoke with Joe Zito's secretary . . . Zito directed the Chuck Norris film *Missing in Action*, another Marvelesque film that even featured *Spider-Man* in a cameo . . .
SL: He's doing the *Spider-Man* movie, Zito is.

PJ: As a matter of fact, that's what I was leading into.
SL: Church Norris is kind of a friend of mine, although I didn't know it. I had met him some years ago, and just for a few minutes we talked. He also came up to the office once. I figured he'd have forgotten all about me, when later, I was at a party Cannon Films was throwing a few months ago when they opened the new building. Chuck Norris saw me and came running over, and left everyone else in his wake, and said, "Stan, how are you?!" Put his arms around me and broke all my ribs! (Laughter) All of a sudden, everyone in the place is wondering, "Who's that guy with the mustache over by Norris?" Nice guy.

PJ: That's wild! That would explain the film's references, and, like we said, people who admired your work.
Anyway, Zito's secretary said, "Of course there's closeness with Lee on the film," and some of the early *Spider-Man* PR stuff features your name prominently.
SL: I've met Zito, we've gotten kind of friendly, and he's a helluva nice guy. We've talked about the script, had dinner and lunch together, and gone over everything, but at the moment I don't know what condition the script is in. Menahem Golan has gotten involved with it, too, so I don't know where it is.

PJ: The secretary told me that "No screenwriting credit has been determined at this time, of course there is a closeness with Lee on he film, Joe Zito is definitely directing at this moment, as definite as that can be, and there is no cast as of yet." So it sounds like they're at least trying to be close to your name.

SL: Yeah, (Laughs) they're cashing in on me! I can't get over the research you guys have done . . . Now what college is this for?

PJ: "Mighty" Chaffey College!
SL: Where is that?

PJ: It's in scenic Alta Loma.
SL: And where is that?

PJ: I hate do say it, but it's on the rim of the Pomona Valley. It sounds terrible, but—
SL: I hate to say it, but I don't know where the Pomona Valley is!

PJ: That's good! It's right outside the San Bernadino mountains. Joseph Wambaugh and Frank Zappa both went there.
SL: Hey, I know Frank Zappa! Is it north of here?

PJ: Hmmm . . . We came south, so it must be north!
SL: I've heard of all these places, but I still don't know where everything is out here.

PJ: We've only been out here four years ourselves . . .
SL: Where'd you guys come from?
TJ: Sterling Heights, originally . . . a suburb near Detroit.

PJ: A friend of mine from high school used to live in Harlem. He said you were popular with the guys at his high school when you lectured there, while the girls weren't too interested—
SL: The story of my life!

PJ: And gave the guys their complimentary comics . . . He felt your appeal was that you never made the audience feel it was being wrotten down to.
SL: GASP! *WRITTEN* down to!
TJ: "Wrotten down to"? Where'd you get that?

PJ: Uh, sorry!
SL: What's the name of this college again? (Laughs) You're allowed one error—don't exceed your quota! But that's very nice . . . He never felt he was being written down to. I tried not to.

PJ: It was refreshing compared to the DC Comics "Let's explain everything to the audience, because they aren't very bright" approach.

SL: The only reason I didn't, not because I thought the audience was bright, but I never understood it myself so I couldn't explain it!

PJ: Were you ever at the typewriter at three in the morning thinking, "My God—No one will know what I'm talking about!"?
SL: No, I was at the typewriter at three in the morning thinking, "I don't know what I'm talking about!"
TJ: I can imagine somebody lettering it all!

PJ: In the early sixties, your books seemed to focus on American heroes battling evil Russians in Cold War combat. Around the middle sixties, you introduced pacifist characters like "The Watcher" and "The Silver Surfer," while some of your characters went to an unglamorous Viet Nam. Was this a conscious change on your part, and, if so, do you feel Marvel-styled action movies are taking your ideas, but not your themes?
SL: Wow, that's a ten-point question! Yeah, I changed in the early days. I began to think, "What the hell am I writing war stories for? I hate war!" In fact, when I did *Sgt. Fury and His Howling Commandos*, I think I advertised it as "the war magazine for people who hate war magazines"!

I'm not vain enough to think I'm being "robbed" by Norris, Rambo, and all those guys. What people forget is that it's all a business. You come out with a formula like *Rocky*, and say, "Hey, I discovered something people want to see. I've been a struggling actor all my life, and nobody paid any attention to me, and suddenly I figured out the formula to bring people into theaters. I'll be rich and be-come a big star!" It doesn't necessarily mean that Stallone likes to fight and kill people, it's just that's what people want to see.

I remember as a kid, I used to go see all the Errol Flynn movies—*Captain Blood*, *Robin Hood*, etc. In those movies, he didn't kill as many guys as Chuck Norris, because he didn't have a machine gun! But as many guys you could stab with a sword, or shoot with arrows? There they go!

Even little kids, when they play "Cops & Robbers"—"Bang-Bang, you're dead!—or Cowboys & Indians, with the same theme—"I just shot you, you're dead!" It's almost meaningless. I played them as a kid and never found it disturbing.

But I'm sure whatever stories I write are influenced by all the books I read as a kid: H. G. Wells, Edgar Rice Burroughs, Hardy Boys, Sherlock Holmes, Tarzan, King Arthur and the Knights of the Round Table . . .

Cover of *Amazing Fantasy* #15 (August 1962). This comic book features the first appearance of the Amazing Spider-Man. © Marvel Entertainment, Inc.

Cover of *Amazing Spider-Man* #50. Peter Parker rejects (for a time) his superhero persona. © Marvel Entertainment, Inc.

Despite the number, *Captain America* #100 is the first issue of the comic devoted solely to the exploits of this superhero. © Marvel Entertainment, Inc.

Cover of *Daredevil* #7, the first to feature the superhero in his characteristic red costume. © Marvel Entertainment, Inc.

Cover of the *Fantastic Four* #50, which features the first appearance of the Silver Surfer on the cover of a Marvel comic book. © Marvel Entertainment, Inc.

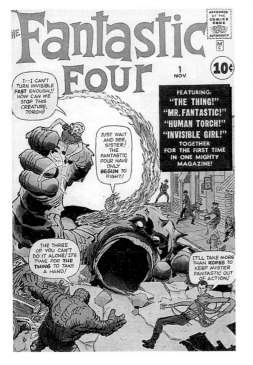

Cover of the *Fantastic Four* #1 (November 1961). Created by Stan Lee and Jack Kirby, this team would become the flagship superhero team of Marvel Comics. © Marvel Entertainment, Inc.

Cover of the *Fantastic Four* #51. © Marvel Entertainment, Inc.

Cover of the *Incredible Hulk* #1 (May 1962). This Lee-Kirby creation has inspired a hit television show and a feature film. © Marvel Entertainment, Inc.

Cover of the *X-Men* #1 (September 1963). This title became one of the first comic books to address social issues such as racial and ethnic prejudice, assimilation, communism, and homosexuality. © Marvel Entertainment, Inc.

Cover of the *Invincible Iron Man* #1 (May 1968). © Marvel Entertainment, Inc.

Cover of *Tales of Suspense* #58, with Captain America and Iron Man—two heroes—fighting each other on the cover. © Marvel Entertainment, Inc.

Cover of *Journey into Mystery* #83, which features the first appearance of the Mighty Thor on a Marvel Comics cover. © Marvel Entertainment, Inc.

Cover of the *Silver Surfer* #1 (August 1968). Lee often cites the Silver Surfer as one of his favorite Marvel characters. © Marvel Enterprises, Inc.

Cover of the *Mighty Thor* #129 (June 1966), featuring Thor, Hercules, and Zeus. © Marvel Enterprises, Inc.

Cover of *Marvel Treasury Edition #6: Doctor Strange*.
© Marvel Entertainment, Inc.

Cover of *Sgt. Fury and His Howling Commandos* #1
(May 1963). © Marvel Entertainment, Inc.

PJ: *King Arthur and the Avengers?*

SL: That's funny! When I write something I'm not trying to steal from something I read, or was influenced by. Even when I wrote Thor's dialogue, I'd get influenced by some biblical or Shakespearean phrases I read, but not conscious copying. I used to love the movie made out of *Omar Khayam*, and the wording there. You realize the dialogue has the same rhythm and quatrain from *Omar Khayyam*, or something from *Hamlet* or Poe. So, I'm sure anyone that's read my comics, and I'm very flattered if that's the case, may have been influenced at some time, and used it for something else.

PJ: That's what I was thinking . . . Not a "rip-off," but a conscious or unconscious homage.

SL: I'm delighted if that's the case. It happens with everyone and everything we see, hear, and read. Some of it sticks. That's one of the things in being a human being. Dogs are no further along than they were a thousand years ago. They don't have the ability to pass on information. No animal does, but human beings write down our knowledge and build on what the previous generation has done, like art and writing.

PJ: Marvels usually ended on truly depressing notes—your characters continually snatched defeat from the jaws of victory . . . Were you having a bad time then?

SL: No, I was doing it to be realistic. In real life everything doesn't turn out great. Say, are you taping this?

PJ: Yeah . . . Would you rather I didn't?

SL: No, I'm just gonna ask you a favor: When you're all finished, could I have a transcription of this? You guys have said such nice things, and so many flattering things, I'd like to have it written down. I don't want to give you a homework assignment or anything. And when the piece is done, could you shoot me a copy?

TJ: Sure, we'll take out all the dumb remarks!

SL: Don't edit anything out—not even him, with his malapropism.

PJ: Are your wife and daughter "Spider-Manned" out, having been around it for so long?

SL: No, they really weren't comic book readers. They love the idea of Spider-Man because they realize there's a little glamour attached to him!

PJ: Do they groan every time you come home with a new idea?
SL: She used to like it when she was younger. Her boyfriends were impressed when they found out who her dad was. It's like those kids you mentioned at the Harlem high school; girls aren't into superhero comics. If I'd written romance stories, my life might have been different! (Laughs)

PJ: That was a wild idea . . . (Looks at Captain America poster) Bringing back a character from the 1940s. Was it a conscious attempt on your part?
SL: (Laughs) Sure . . . Everything I do is a conscious attempt, even when I do them unconsciously! Yeah, I wanted to bring him back, along with the Torch and the Sub-Mariner.
TJ: Is this picture supposed to be an in-joke? They (Capt. America, Torch, Toro, and Sub-Mariner) are blowing up a tanker like the one right outside the window . . .
SL: I never looked at it that closely . . .

PJ: Was it because of the sixties heating up that you thought the time was right to bring them back?
SL: No, it wasn't the sixties. I brought back the Torch when I was doing the Fantastic Four, and I wanted four characters because it was the FF. I had come up with the Thing, Mr. Fantastic, and Sue, so I wanted something totally different for the fourth guy, and I wanted a kid-brother for Sue, when I remembered the Torch. I didn't want the typical teenager, so when Reed and Sue married, he'd be the brother-in-law.

PJ: They get along so well! (Laughs)
SL: Well, I never knew a comic that had a brother-in-law. I figured the Torch had been an adult, so I'm not really copying it totally, because he's no longer an android.

With Sub-Mariner, I was looking for something that would be fun for the FF, and thought, "What if I brought him back, also?" He could be the enemy of the FF.

PJ: The politics of that is extremely funny—he's very arrogant and vengeful, almost like a Black Muslim, or Middle Eastern power in the sixties.
SL: I also planned to have him fall in love with Sue, and have some interesting complications, but I married her off to Reed too soon. With

Capt. America, I needed somebody to fill the Avengers, and I thought he'd be good.

PJ: How do you feel about the *Howard the Duck* project?
SL: Oh, I can't wait for it to come out! It's gonna be a big movie!

PJ: On Your twenty-fifth anniversary, it seems your company is finally being recognized.
SL: I have no complaints; we're being recognized. They're doing *Howard the Duck*, *Captain America*, *Spider-Man*, and they're getting ready to do *The Fantastic Four*, *The X-Men*, *Dr. Strange*, and *Daredevil*.

PJ: Who's handling the FF?
SL: A guy named Byrned Ikeinger . . . He did *The Never-Ending Story*, and also produced *Das Boot*. He's in his mid-thirties, and he's loved the FF for all his life!

PJ: That's great! Do you still narrate the cartoons here?
SL: We haven't done any new ones, so I don't know. They're still on the air with my voice.

PJ: It works well . . . With the inflections in your voice, it sounded like you're writing the story aloud. I pictured that narrative in your style of writing.
SL: You know, the funny thing is when I'd go to do the voice-overs, the directors would say, "More Energy! More Energy!" I don't normally talk that way, and they had me practically shouting!

PJ: Speaking of that, have you had any more offers to do commercials? I remember you doing a shaving spot a while back . . .
SL: Geez, you're wonderful! Like *Spider-Man*, that story had a tragic, unhappy ending! I did the commercial for Persona Blades, and I ad-libbed the last line that they loved, and kept in. I said, "I like this blade so much I may create a whole new character—Persona-Man!"

They said it was terrific. Then I got a call from the advertising agency about two weeks later, and they said, "We've decided we want to start a whole new campaign—you create a character called "Persona-Man," and we'll do ads for it in the newspapers that publish your strip, and you can announce the TV ads like you did!" I figured I had a whole new show business career, and would you believe that one month later the company went out of business?!?

PJ: Wow, that stinks! Now, my final question: Your comic book characters have gone through many changes since you left. Do you ever feel the urge to delegate your ideas to the current writers, when they make radical changes, like Spider-Man's black costume?

SL: Yeah, they do it all the time. My name's still on them, but I don't do the comics anymore, and they're quite a bit different. I never feel it's right to boss people around if you won't take the responsibility. I don't, so I let (Marvel Comics Pres. Jim) Shooter do what he wants. It may be a good idea, having a black costume—they may decide to keep it permanently, whatever they do is fine as long as they keep the sales up. If the sales get terrible, and they start losing their readers, they better think up a way out, and get the book doing well again.

I think DC, sooner or later, may start competing with us. Their "new Batman" and "new Superman" could create some interest. I know this *Batman* graphic novel is selling out, so we'll see.

Graphic Mogul: Stan Lee

ALASTAIR MABBOTT / 1991

From *The List*, December 1991.
Reprinted by permission of *The List*
and Alastair Mabbott.

For anyone who began devouring Marvel comics as soon as they could read—who preferred them, for goodness' sake, to *television*—he belongs as much to the world of myth as the superheroes who made him his fortune. But here he is, spreading ketchup evenly and meticulously over an omelette with the flat of his knife: Smilin' Stan. Stan the Man.

To understand Stan Lee's place in American popular culture, you'd have to think in similar terms to Walt Disney, and when he opens his mouth to gush about how exciting it is to live in LA and do lunch with Coppola and De Vito, you're likely to be reminded of Andy Warhol's boyish "golly-gee" ingenuousness too.

Now in his mid-sixties, grey and balding, he looks less like a publishing giant than a retired small businessman who's glad to have the pressure off his back. Bloomsbury's *Cultural Icons* has Lee pegged as "super-rich," but his slightly stooped frame is clothed today in an unassuming black V-neck and jeans. Perhaps he just liked dressing down for signing sessions. Despite his relocation to California, he speaks with a perfect New York twang and seems slightly self-conscious about it, putting down the lack of flavor in the American accent while praising the Scottish and Irish lilt. "It's like music. It really is, listen sometimes," he urges, between bites.

The day-to-day comic book work in the New York offices far behind him, the Chairman of Marvel Entertainment Group now supervises movie adaptations of the company's characters. After a series of embarrassing disasters (like *Howard the Duck*), Marvel looks set at long last for a block-buster that will even the score with DC (their "Distinguished Competition"), who have the *Superman* and *Batman* movies to their credit. *Terminator* and *Aliens* director James Cameron is turning his considerable talents to a Spider-Man movie, and several other Marvel projects are under way. Even the Black Panther, hardly one of their biggest smashes, is being nurtured by Columbia in the hope of cashing in on recent Afro-American box-office successes.

The glittering lights of Hollywood—the dream of every boy who grew up in the Depression. If there had been any money in it, Stanley Martin Lieber (he later legally adopted his pen-name) would have tried to become an actor—he belonged, he says, to the WPA Federal Theater, as did the young Orson Welles—but his father was unemployed, his mother needed money, and Lee discovered it was easier to make ends meet by working on comic books.

In 1940, when he was seventeen, he was taken on by publisher Martin Goodman's Marvel forerunner Timely Comics to help with the increasing workload brought on by the success of the superhero title *Captain America*.

"I answered an ad in the paper. It said an assistant was wanted in a pub-lishing company. I didn't even know it was a comic book company," says Lee, perhaps momentarily forgetting that Goodman was his cousin-in-law and had already recruited several members of his family into the business. Also working at Timely then was aspiring novelist Mickey Spillane, and Lee himself had plans to move into "proper" writing. (Lee scripted training films during the Second World War, and was one of only nine men in the U.S. Army to hold the military classification "playwright.")

For the next twenty years, however, he busied himself with whatever material Timely thought would sell—Westerns, war, romance, funny ani-mals, monsters—then, in quick succession, he and veteran Golden Age artist Jack Kirby came up with the Fantastic Four, the Hulk, Spider-Man, Thor, Iron Man, the Avengers and the X-Men. All were heroes who had flaws to their make-up which made them that bit more interesting than the competition. Sales snowballed and, with unprecedented reader response, the company started producing more and more books per month. So many were on the go that Lee could not script them all and would only give a brief summary to the artist, who would draw the story however he (invariably he, rather than she) saw fit. Lee would get the pages back and add dialogue to suit the pencilled pages. So the disputed legend goes, anyway. Thus was born "The Marvel Method."

"It was totally born out of necessity," says Lee, "but then we found out it's a great system, because the artists could use their imaginations to the fullest."

"Method" turned out to be a fitting name for the process considering that long-term Marvel artist John Romita has dramatically described it as "digging into my insides and pulling it out." If you can capture that solipsistic movie-brat effort in print, it's no wonder that the books started to pick up sales among legions of alienated, sensitive Baby Boomers.

The original Marvel creators were a generation too old to write convincingly for them, but Spider-Man could nonetheless be found rubbing shoulders with student dissenters while Doctor Strange devoted himself to Eastern lore in Greenwich Village and the Silver Surfer pondered the meaning of life as he drifted through the heavens on a flying surfboard. Lee admits to being "a little worried about these so-called hippies" and had Thor tell a bunch of them that they should get more active in society rather than drop out of it.

Marvel stories were usually told with a humanitarian, liberal slant. "Knowing that so many children were reading these stories," he says, "I tried to give them a decent moral tone. I tried to preach against things like hate and bigotry. Today, when I go to conventions, or I do a lecture, or I come to a store to do a book signing, people say to me, Stan, I wanted to meet you because you had such an effect on me when I was young. But at the time I had no idea at all. I was just writing them and publishing them and I hoped that someone would read 'em."

His special talent though, was and is in being a figurehead—developing a strong image for the company and promoting brand loyalty by making Marvel seem like a club for its readers—a club that, even today, is built around the personality of Smilin' Stan Lee with his mysterious motto "Excelsior!"

The whopping tome he is over to promote, *Marvel* by Les Daniels, is a good gloss of "Five Fabulous Decades of the World's Greatest Comics," but by printing only four complete stories it doesn't do its subject full justice. Lee, who hasn't actually read the book in detail, praises Daniels for his objectivity, but there are some who will take it as just another example of Stan Lee rewriting history.

In the 1980s, Marvel's reputation was dragged through the mud somewhat by dispute about his old partner Jack Kirby's copyrights and original artwork. Lee, of course, denies that it harmed them at all. Perhaps if I'd asked about his personal credibility the answer might have been a little different.

"I think Jack was wrong." The affable Lee suddenly turns very abrupt. "He felt we didn't want to give him back his pages. We were very happy to give him back his pages. Most of the pages had been lost. It all got stolen or we threw 'em away. We never saved that stuff in the beginning. Then we did have some pages, but Jack was making weird claims, like he created Spider-Man and that he created this and he created that. So our lawyer said, "We're not gonna give you back your artwork unless you admit that you didn't create those things, because you didn't." Finally, he signed some sort of a statement saying he wouldn't make claims on things he didn't create and we gave him back his artwork. That was the end of it."

Not quite. So "very happy" was Marvel to return Kirby's artwork that it had taken them five years' legal pressure, a publicity campaign, and a petition signed by 150 comics professionals to do it. Eventually, Marvel backed down and gave Kirby 2,100 pages out of an estimated 13,000 that he had drawn for them over the years (refusing to pay the $800 insurance freight). Marvel retained the lucrative copyrights. Kirby felt he had a right to be bitter and gave a lengthy interview to *The Comics Journal* in 1990, disputing Lee's claim that he, Smilin' Stan, had created all of Marvel's greatest characters. "I created the Fantastic Four," raged Kirby. "I created Thor." Worse was to come: "I've never seen Stan Lee write anything," Kirby maintained. "If Stan Lee ever got a thing dialogued, he would get it from somebody working in the office."

"That was when I called the lawyer," Lee recalls, "and I said, 'Should we sue him?' He said we could, said it'd cost a lot of money, but Marvel could afford it, and it'd cost Jack a lot of money to defend it. I said, 'Well, forget it. I don't want Jack to go broke.' Because most of the people who read it have written to me and they said, 'Look, we know it isn't true, we've worked with you, we know what stories you wrote.'

"He had a lawyer call me months after that, saying, 'You know, Jack would really like to make up, what do you say?' I said, 'It's fine with me. All Jack has to do is write a letter to *The Comics Journal* which says that the things he said weren't true, and I'll be happy to make up.' But how can I make up with him now? If I'm friendly with Jack, it'll sound like he was telling the truth. Like I'm not angry about it. So I never heard from the guy again."

He's glad to move along to other topics, and practically shakes with excitement to find out that one of his former British editors, Neil Tennant, reinvented himself as a Pet Shop Boy and became one of the country's biggest pop stars.

"My God, really?" he exclaims. "Is that the same Neil Tennant? Wait a minute, I've got to write that down, I didn't know he was the same one!"

As he speaks, he reaches beneath his pullover, slips out a tiny notebook from his shirt pocket and takes down what he's just learned in one of the margins. It's so incongruous, this "super-rich" big shot with all his Hollywood contacts relying on a tiny notebook. Not a Filofax man, then, Stan?

"Too big," he grins. "I like this because I don't have to carry anything. I just keep it in my shirt pocket—and my hands are free to fight the bad guys."

Stan Lee

JUD HURD / 1997

From *Cartoonist Profiles*, no. 113
(March 1997), pp. 12–20. Reprinted by
permission of Claudia Hurd.

Recently we talked with our longtime friend, Stan Lee, whose newspaper comic strip, Spider-Man, is celebrating its 20th Anniversary.

Hurd: Stan, your approach to writing *comic book* stories was quite different from the technique you used in preparing the newspaper Spider-Man strip wasn't it?

Lee: Yes. For the comic book, I would first discuss the story with the artist. I would tell the artist what story I wanted and then he would draw it in his own way. When he later sent me the artwork I would then put in all of the copy. I enjoyed working that way because I never had a chance to be bored, since I was never quite sure what I would be getting from the artist. Sometimes I wouldn't like what the artist did, and I figured that he should have done it differently. However, I never asked him to change his work, but would just figure out how to write the copy so it would look as if that was the best way it could be done. More often I would love what the artist did and that made it fun.

However, on the newspaper strip I work differently, because we're talking about only two or three panels a day. In this case, I have to make sure that the panels are *precisely* what I have in mind from the point of view of the story flowing the right way from day to day. So I write a *complete script* and tell the artist *exactly* what to draw. At the present time, my brother, Larry Lieber, pencils the daily strips, and then they are inked by Fred Kida. Fred is also penciling the Sunday pages which are inked by Joe Sinnott. Fred used to work for Marvel many years ago and was one of our very best artists in the fifties and may be even in the forties. And Joe Sinnott was one of our best inkers all during Marvel's *glory days*, during the sixties.

Hurd: Can you say something that would particularly help a young person who is ambitious to write for newspaper comics? (How to keep the brain wheels going, etc.)

Lee: I can tell you this: For many, many years, before I started the strip, and I started it I guess in 1977, newspaper syndicate editors were asking me to do a Spider-Man newspaper strip. I always refused because I couldn't figure out how to do it so that it would be successful. As you may know, Jud, many other superheroes have starred in newspaper strips, and none of them are there any longer.

So, at the present time, there are no superheroes from the comic books in papers today other than Spider-Man. That's because transferring from comic book to newspaper has been a very difficult thing to do. It wasn't until 1977 that I thought, finally, that I had figured out the way to do it. Most of the superhero stories depend on elaborate fight scenes which are carefully choreographed by the artist, and they go on for page after page. Now, as you can imagine, in a daily strip which has two or three panels, it is almost impossible to figure out how to do an interesting fight scene. By the way, this limitation isn't the same with the Sunday page—you can solve the problem a little better there. As for the daily strip, if in panel 2 or 3, somebody punches somebody, the reader would have to wait till panel one the next day to see the victim fall down! And if a character is about to get punched at the end of a day's strip, by the time you read the next day's strip, the matter doesn't seem as urgent. You need a time continuity to be constant. But, as I said, I finally thought I'd found a way to lick this problem. Apparently I must have been right because the strip has been in the newspapers all these years. And we've pretty well maintained our base readership of about five hundred newspapers—daily and Sunday.

Hurd: And specifically how *did* you solve this problem?
Lee: I had an idea that you would ask. I decided to treat the superhero adventure strip as though it's a *soap opera* story that just happens to be about a superhero who has to defeat villains. But rather than predicating it on great action scenes, I determined to predicate it on characterization, and on whatever personal problems a superhero might encounter living in a realistic world—in today's world. So I play up Peter Parker's personal problems every bit as much as the problems of having him fighting a villain. Even when he is Spider-Man, rather than resorting to one fight scene after another, I try to put him in unusual situations, and I try to have him come up against villains who are unusual. And I try to make the themes as contemporary, and as relevant, as possible. As an example, some years ago I did a story about a woman who realized that Spider-Man is a very popular superhero and then decided to do something about it. This was a woman who was a manufacturer who wanted to make Spider-Man bluejeans. She thought of some such slogan as, "they fit as tight as Spider-Man's webbing," or something like that. Now in this story, Spider-Man got very annoyed because he felt that nobody had the right to do that, i.e., the manufacturer wasn't paying him royalties. This was the continuing thread of the story. For the adventure part, we had a villain who tried to hijack a truck carrying the jeans and, of course, Spider-Man had to catch the hijacker. But to me, the interesting and the important part of the story dealt with a superhero who was upset about somebody using his name and licensing a product without him being compensated. I thought it was a nice relevant and satirical story.

Incidentally, I find the Sunday pages are the most difficult, although the most gratifying, to write. Here's the reason for the difficult part. There are a few newspapers which don't carry the Sunday page—they just carry the dailies. So when I write the strip, I can't put anything in the Sunday page that advances the story, because then when somebody picks it up Monday (and his paper doesn't carry the Sunday page), that reader will be a bit confused. As a result, on Sundays, I have to find a way to write something that is interesting, and seemingly new for the reader, but which still doesn't move the story forward to any degree.

The reason that I say I enjoy doing it is that the Sunday page for the most part gives me the chance to inject a little bit more humor. This is because I can use those six or seven panels to probe more deeply into Peter Parker's personal life, or even write panels that show Spider-Man's reactions to something with thought balloons. On Sunday, the strip can flow in a more leisurely fashion, and I can put in more dialogue. As you know, the more dialogue you have, the more you can display the person's character and personality. So, I enjoy the Sunday pages, but they're diffi-cult to do because you don't want the reader to think, "Hey—I just read this Saturday, it's the same thing!" Nor do you want your reader on Monday not to understand what's going on because Sunday's page moved the story ahead.

Hurd: I think you wanted to mention another type of story you some-times do.
Lee: Yes, I try to do these as much as possible, but I can't do too many because I don't want to lose the readers who enjoy the super villains. One of this kind of story I enjoyed had to do with somebody who wanted to produce a television series called *Spider-Man*. Peter Parker thought that this would be his way to make some money, so he decided that he himself would apply for the job. Of course, he would get it because who else would they hire but the real Spider-Man! So, he put on his costume and applied, but it happened that the TV network had a teenage boy who, they felt, represented the average viewer. So they based all of the shows on what this teenager felt . . . how he reacted to things. But actually he didn't care for the real Spider-Man. He thought he was too corny, etc. I thought it was a deliciously humorous little story. I won't tell you how it ends . . . not that I'm trying to keep it a secret, but I don't remember.

Here's something that's changed recently: I used to keep the stories going for four months, five months, six months—sometimes seven months, if I really enjoyed a plot. That's because it gave me a chance to show every angle that I could and to bring in all the little gimmicks that I wanted to. But I began to think, "Maybe in a way, the readers lose inter-est when a continuity goes on that long." So for the past year, I've adopted a policy of limiting every story to just thirteen weeks, which I think is the general average of these strips. I've enjoyed doing this because it's a whole new regimen for me, trying to condense everything. I hop back and forth between using super villains and trying to get the more "every day" type of plots with a little bit of humor, satire, parody or whatever you want to call it. In the plot that's running right how, Spider-Man meets one of our other superheroes, the Sub-Mariner. The story is structured so that the Sub-Mariner thinks Spider-Man is doing something evil, and Sub-Mariner is battling Spider-Man who in turn is trying to convince him he's fighting the wrong guy. This is the typical superhero adventure story. Now the next one I do will probably be a little more "off-the-track."

Hurd: How do you divide your time these days, Stan? Do you presently do any writing for comic books?

Lee: Actually, my main job involves serving as chairman of Marvel Films and of Marvel Comics. Marvel Comics, however, is located in New York, and my title, I think, is more of an honorary one. I stay in touch with the comics that Marvel produces and I give suggestions that aren't really involved in the day-to-day operations since I moved out to Los Angeles fifteen or sixteen years ago. However, I do spend most of my time working on the various motion picture, television, and animation projects which involve Marvel characters. We have about a dozen of our major characters now in development as live-action, big-budget features at the various studios around town. For example *The Fantastic Four* is going to be directed by Chris Columbus at Twentieth Century–Fox. We have *The Hulk* in development at Universal, *The X-Men* at Fox, and on and on.

As far as the newspaper strip is concerned, I take one day a week on that. It might be a Saturday or a Sunday, or I might stay home from the office on a Tuesday or a Wednesday. I then spend that day writing a week's installments. If I'm really going strong, I might write two weeks during that day. And there have been days when I've written three weeks! Using this system, I can never fall behind. I think the latest thing I wrote was for May 1997.

Hurd: I'm sure you remember the first conversation we had many years ago which resulted in an interview with you in our Issue #4 in 1969. And you've been a good friend of *Cartoonist Profiles* ever since!

Spider-Man in the Marketplace

JULES FEIFFER / 1998

From *Civilization*, June/July 1998, p. 57.
Reprinted by permission of Jules Feiffer.

Writer and editor Stan Lee created *Spider-Man* and the *Fantastic Four* for Marvel Comics in the 1960s, thereby triggering a dramatic reversal of fortune for the sagging comic book industry. This spring the two of us sat down in Los Angeles to discuss the current state of his art.

Stan Lee: Marvel didn't start until 1961, when we had the *Fantastic Four*, the *Incredible Hulk*, and *Spider-Man*. Until that point we were just doing ordinary comics, and they were the same as the competition, nothing special. The good guys were all noble. With the *Fantastic Four*, I decided to change all that by making the characters more three-dimensional. It was probably the first time that we tried to do a comic book the way a movie would be done—with real characters.

Next we did the *Hulk*, in which I made a hero out of the monster. Then came *Spider-Man*; I wanted him to be a teenager. My publisher said, "You can't have a teenager as a hero. A teenager can only be a sidekick." We made him a teenager.

Then I told my publisher I wanted Spider-Man to have problems. I wanted him to worry about making a living, and girls wouldn't be so crazy about him. He'd have trouble getting dates. And he'd get ingrown toenails or an allergy attack while he was fighting. "You're crazy, Stan. That's not a hero, that's supporting character. That's a comedy character." But I didn't listen. I did it. And Spider-Man turned out to be our most popular character. Since then everything we did I tried to do offbeat.

Jules Feiffer: I look at all the superheroes, and it's clear that most of them, before Jack Kirby, were influenced by Alex Raymond's *Flash Gordon*.
SL: Nobody drew like Jack Kirby. He was not only a great artist, he was also a great visual storyteller. I would say, "Look, Jack, here's the story I want you to tell." And Jack would bring back the story that I had given him, but he would also add a lot of imaginative things of his own. He should have been a movie director. He knew when to make a long shot, a close-up. He never drew a character who didn't look interesting or excited. In every panel there was something to look at.

JF: Comic books today appear to be radically different from the strips that you and Kirby did.
SL: Unfortunately, there are some artists who concentrate more on drawing impressive illustrations than on telling a story in a clear, compelling way.

JF: So the story goes out the window, and all the heroes look like they're on steroids.
SL: Some companies, I admit, tend to think in clichés. They seem to feel that all heroes must look as if they can bench-press a locomotive with one hand. Another place where things can be overdone is in the coloring. Sometimes they put in too much color, making it difficult to see what's happening in various panels. Even in the lettering, some letterers use so many different fonts in their blurbs and captions, you can hardly read them. It's all done by computer now, and everything has equal value so you don't know what you're looking at. The words might catch the eye more than the picture. I feel today's books lack cohesion. For clarity and drama, it would help if the covers tended more towards poster art, the way they did years ago.

JF: In the last few years, the circulation of comics has suffered, hasn't it?

SL: Kids like comics as much as ever, but a very unusual thing happened. There used to be a very big collectors' market; all of a sudden people were paying high prices for back issues of comics. Houses like Sotheby's would have big auctions, and kids would read that a comic book, which originally cost a dime, was sold for $20,000. There were newspaper articles: "Comic books are a better investment than stocks." So, instead of buying one issue of a magazine, they'd buy twenty. They wouldn't even read them, never took them out of the cellophane. Suddenly a book that sold 200,000 was selling a million or half a million. It was the greatest thing. Then the market crashed.

The kids buying the books found they couldn't get a nickel for them. They didn't realize it's only when a book is in short supply that the market value goes up. If there are 100 million copies around, nobody's going to pay for them. This was maybe five or eight years ago. But another bad thing happened at the same time. Years ago, comic books were sold in neighborhood shops. There are no more mom-and-pop stores like that. The only place where you can count on buying comic books today is in a comic book store. At the height of the market, there were about 6,500 comic book stores around the country. Now, there are only about 3,000 because when sales started plummeting these guys went out of business.

The enthusiasm among readers is still there. Young people love comics. The problem is there aren't enough places to buy them, and even when you can find them the storytelling art in comics has declined. Too many adventure comics, the superhero comics, they don't even think of young kids when they write these things. They're written for the guys who were young kids back in the sixties, the baby boomers. They're written for the artists themselves. We're not attracting enough of the new generations coming along.

Stan the Man and Roy the Boy: A Conversation between Stan Lee and Roy Thomas

Roy Thomas / 1998

From *Comic Book Artist*, no. 2 (Summer 1998), pp. 6–19. Reprinted by permission of *Comic Book Artist*.

What follows is less an interview and more a conversation between the two most prominent creative forces working at Marvel Comics in the early 1970s: the legendary "Smilin'" Stan Lee and "Rascally" Roy Thomas. The discussion was conducted via telephone in two sessions during May 1998.

Stan Lee: What on earth could you possibly ask me that hasn't been asked before?

Roy Thomas: The magazine's theme for its second issue is Marvel from 1970–77, but still we'll need a little background from the forties through the sixties.

Stan: You just ask and I will answer.

Roy: You started working at Timely as a teenager under Joe Simon and Jack Kirby. Were both of them counted as editors, or was it just Joe?

Stan: My memory is not the best, but I thought that Joe was the editor and sort of Jack's boss. I got that feeling. Generally, Jack would be sitting at the drawing board drawing and chewing his cigar, muttering to himself. Joe would be walking around, chewing his cigar and mumbling, and also handling whatever business there was to handle under Martin Goodman.

Roy: So you didn't see Joe draw a lot?

Stan: No, but I know that he did draw. I didn't see him draw a lot at all.

Roy: When Simon and Kirby left Timely in 1941 to go to work for DC with the deal that had them doing *Boy Commandos, Sandman*, etc., was there some bad blood between them and publisher Martin Goodman? Or did he just accept the fact there was more money to be made over at DC?

Stan: I would imagine there had to have been some bad blood, or why would they have left? I have a feeling that there was some problem. Either Martin found out that they were doing work on the side, or they started to argue about who owned Captain America—both of these things may be wrong. But it was something like that. There was some unpleasantness.

Roy: John Buscema once told the editor of *Comic Book Artist* that, sometime in the late forties, Martin Goodman once opened a closet door and discovered "an enormous pile of discarded (but paid-for) art that was never published." John says that Goodman promptly put all the staff artists on freelance status. Do you recall that?

Stan: It would never have happened just because he opened a closet door. But I think that I may have been in a little trouble when that happened. We had bought a lot of strips that I didn't think were really all that good, but I paid the artists and writers for them anyway, and I kinda hid them in the closet! [*laughter*] And Martin found them and I think he wasn't too happy. If I wasn't satisfied with the work, I wasn't supposed to have paid, but I was never sure it was really the artist's or the writer's fault. But when the job was finished I didn't think that it was anything that I wanted to use. I felt that we could use it in inventory—put it out in other books. Martin, probably rightly so, was a little annoyed because it was his money I was spending.

Roy: The revival of Captain America, the Human Torch, and Sub-Mariner in the fifties was done, everyone assumes, because of the success of the Superman TV show. Bill Everett told me in an interview how some TV producers approached Martin Goodman and Timely in 1954 about a Sub-Mariner TV show to star Richard Egan. Bill said comedian Herb Shriner was part of the deal, and that Arthur Godfrey put up the money. Bill mentioned a producer named Frank Saverstein or Saperstein. Did you know anything about that?

Stan: No. It's a funny thing: Martin never discussed business deals with me, and that would have fallen under the heading of a business deal. This is the first that I've heard about it

Roy: You were just the peon that kept things running? [*laughs*]

Stan: I was just the guy in the other room, trying to do the comics.

Roy: A couple of years after, the American News debacle happened— that's when Timely/Atlas collapsed. Bill told me that someone forewarned him. Did you have any warning that this total collapse was coming?

Stan: Absolutely not. The only thing I did know was that Martin had given up his own distribution company and had gone with the American News Company. I remember saying to him, "Gee, why did you do that? I thought that we had a good distribution company." His answer was like, "Oh, Stan, you wouldn't understand. It has to do with finance." I didn't really give a damn, and I went back to doing the comics.

And then, very shortly thereafter—maybe two weeks later—the American News Company went out of business! We were left without a distributor, and we couldn't go back to distributing our own books because the fact that Martin quit doing it and went with American News had got the wholesalers very angry—I don't know *why* it got them angry, but this is what I heard—and it would have been impossible for Martin to just say, "Okay, we'll go back to where we were and distribute our books."

It ended up where we were turning out forty, fifty, sixty books a month, maybe more, and the only company we could get to distribute our books was our closet rival, National (DC) Comics. Suddenly we went from sixty, seventy, eighty books a month—whatever it was—to either eight or twelve books a month, which was all Independent News Distributors would accept from us. We had to try and build ourselves up from that until we eventually went to Curtis Circulation.

Roy: Didn't Independent have a contract that basically said that in order to start one new title, you had to drop something else?

Stan: I don't remember that for a fact, but that could very well have been the case. I know that it was very tough for us; we were down to almost nothing.

Roy: That's the period when Jack Kirby came back to Marvel. Jack mentioned in an interview [in *The Comics Journal* #136] that he came to work offering his services when people were literally moving out the furniture. Do you recall that?

Stan: I never remember being there when people were moving out the furniture. [*chuckles*] If they ever moved the furniture, they did it during the weekend when everybody was home. Jack tended toward hyperbole, just like the time he was quoted as saying that he came in and I was crying and I said, "Please save the company!" I'm not a crier and I would never have said that. I was very happy that Jack was there and I loved working with him, but I never cried to him. [*laughs*]

Roy: During that period when you put out very few books, did you feel that your days in comics were limited and that maybe the whole thing was going to die?

Stan: Believe it or not, I think I felt that way until we started Marvel Comics. I never though that this would last! [*laughs*] When did I start? '40? I think it was the third issue of *Captain America*.

Roy: That would have been in very late '40 or early '41, in terms of when the issues left the office. Less than a year later you became the temporary editor; that lasted for decades. Now, skipping ahead to 1961: The story has often been told of this infamous, legendary golf game with Martin Goodman and [DC President] Jack Liebowitz in which Liebowitz bragged about the sales of *Justice League of America*, and Goodman came back and told you to start a superhero book. Was that story really true?

Stan: That's absolutely true. He came in to see me one day and said, "I've just been playing golf with Jack Liebowitz"—they were pretty friendly—and he said, "Jack was telling me the *Justice League* is selling very well, and why don't we do a book about a group of superheroes?" That's how we happened to do *Fantastic Four*.

Roy: Was there any thought at that time to just bringing back Cap, Torch, and Sub-Mariner?

Stan: No, I really wanted to do something new. You probably heard this story: I wanted to quit at that time. I was really so bored and really too old to be doing these stupid comic books; I wanted to quit. I was also frustrated because I wanted to do comic books that were—even though this seems like a contradiction in terms—I wanted to do a more realistic fantasy. Martin wouldn't let me and had wanted the stories done the way they had always been done, with very young children in mind. That was it.

My wife Joan said to me, "You know, Stan, if they asked you to do a new book about a new group of superheroes, why don't you do 'em the way that you feel you'd like to do a book? If you want to quit anyway, the worst that could happen is that he'll fire you, and so what? You want to quit." I figured, hey, maybe she's right. That's why I didn't want to do the Torch and the Sub-Mariner; I wanted to create a new group and do them the way I had always wanted to do a comic book. That's what happened.

Roy: I assume that Joan said this *after* you were given the assignment to do the superhero group and not while you were doing the monster books.

Stan: It was after I told her that Martin wanted to do a superhero group but I thought that I would say to him, "Forget it. I want to quit."

Roy: So you were actually thinking of quitting instead of doing the *Fantastic Four*? I hadn't heard that before! *That* would have changed comic book history.

Stan: Maybe. If Martin hadn't come in to me and said, "Liebowitz said the *Justice League* is selling well, so why don't we do a comic book about superheroes?"—if he hadn't said that to me, I might've—in the next day or two, I might've just quit.

Roy: Timing is everything.
Stan: Luck, too

Roy: By *Fantastic Four* #1, you had developed what later came to be called "the Marvel style." But you were doing this all along for some monster stories, some time before this. How far back does that go?
Stan: You mean just doing synopses for the artists? Was I doing them before Marvel?

Roy: I know that you did it for *Fantastic Four*. So I figured with Jack as the artist—and maybe Ditko, too—in these minor stories that you mostly wrote, along with Larry Lieber, you must have been doing it since the monster days.

Stan: You know something, Roy? Now that you say it, that's probably true; but I had never thought of that. I thought that I started in with the *Fantastic Four*, but you're probably right.

Roy: You probably didn't write full scripts for Jack for *Fin Fang Foom*.

Stan: I did full scripts in the beginning, but then I found out how good he was just creating his own little sequence of pictures—and I did it in the beginning with Ditko, too—but when I found out how good they were, I realized that, "Gee, I don't have to do it—I get a better story by just letting them run free."

Roy: The amazing thing is, not only could you get Jack and Steve to do it, but that other artists who had always worked from scripts—Dick Ayers, Don Heck, and others—could also learn to do it and be quite successful with a little training from you.

Stan: I will admit that a lot of them were very nervous about it, and very unhappy about being asked to do it. But then they loved it after a while.

Roy: I think that John Buscema, too, thought it was a little strange at first, but got to really like it. Then, when someone would give him a full script, he didn't like that.

Stan: Absolutely right. John Buscema is amazing. He was never thought of—it's not the popular idea that he was the most *creative* guy, story-wise. And yet, he was as creative as anybody else—probably as creative as Jack. Well, *you* worked with John.

Roy: Sure, quite a bit: *Conan*, *Avengers*.

Stan: He only needed a few words. He didn't even want a big synopsis; he wanted the skimpiest outline, because he wanted to do it his way. And his way was always great!

Roy: I remember plotting the first story of this villain called the Man-Ape in *The Avengers* with him for five or ten minutes over the phone. I wanted to give him more, and he said, "Nah, that's enough." [*laughs*]

Stan: That's exactly what he did with me. And I was never disappointed.

Roy: How did you feel about being distributed by Independent? Especially after Marvel became successful, were you antsy to get out from under?

Stan: It would be like if you were working for Ford, and General Motors was selling your cars! I could never prove it, but we were sure—it's just human nature and psychology—that National Comics wasn't working as hard to sell our books as they were to sell theirs. Even more, it was the fact that we were only able to do so few books in the beginning, which meant we had to let a lot of artists and writers go. That was always the worst thing that could happen.

Roy: I do remember when we began particularly to have suspicions during the *Not Brand Echh* days, when every issue of that book seemed to sell, until the one where we had a takeoff on Superman on the cover. Suddenly the sales went down! [*laughs*] In the early days, it's now well known that Larry Lieber, your brother, wrote the dialogue for a number of stories, after they were plotted by you and drawn by Jack or whoever, on some series like *Thor* and *Iron Man*.
Stan: Well, it's in the credits and I always put his name in. If not, I'd say, "Plot by Stan Lee." Larry definitely did the first *Thor*, and he *may* have written the copy for *Iron Man*. What I did was give him the plot and he wrote it.

Roy: Was it that you were just too busy, or did you just think that it wasn't that important that you do the dialogue?
Stan: Both. And you know that both *Thor* and *Iron Man* were only ten-, eleven-page stories and not a feature book. I was very busy, and I liked the way that Larry wrote, and so I thought I'd give him a shot at it.

Roy: The mere fact that people assumed for years afterward that you did the dialogue shows that he imitated your style pretty well. The thing with Larry is that he was just a little slow.
Stan: He was like Romita; he was never that fastest one.

Roy: We used to say that if we'd change *Rawhide Kid* from monthly to bimonthly, Larry would just take twice as long to draw it. [*laughter*] I'll never forget the day I walked into one Marvel office not long after Ditko quit, and here's John Romita drawing *Amazing Spider-Man* and Larry drawing the *Spider-Man Annual* and Marie Severin drawing *Dr. Strange*, and I joked, "This is the Steve Ditko Room; it takes three of you to do what Steve Ditko used to do."
     [Production Manager] Sol Brodsky told me that, right from the start, you thought Spider-Man was an important character, even if he was just

in the last issue of *Amazing Fantasy*. But Larry Ivie, someone else who worked there at the time, feels that you considered him a throwaway character. Did you feel that Spider-Man was big from the start?

Stan: I'm trying to remember, but I think I must have felt that he was a good character or I wouldn't have fought so much to do him. I wanted to do Spider-Man as a book, But Martin wouldn't let me. Therefore I sneaked him into the last issue of *Amazing Fantasy*.

Roy: Because Goodman said that spiders wouldn't sell?

Stan: He said three things that I will never forget: He said people hate spiders, so you can't call a hero "Spider-Man"; then when I told him I wanted the hero to be a teenager, as he was in the beginning, Martin said that a teenager can't be a hero, but only be a sidekick; and then when I said I wanted him not to be too popular with girls, and not great-looking or a strong, macho-looking guy, but just a thin, pimply high school student, and Martin said, "Don't you understand what a hero is?" At the same time, I also said that I wanted him to have a lot of problems, like that he doesn't have enough money and he'd get an allergy attack while he was fighting. Martin just wouldn't let me do the book. Normally, I'd have forgotten about it, but when we were doing the last issue of *Amazing Fantasy*, I put it in there. So I must have felt that he was important somehow, or I wouldn't have bothered.

Roy: You started right off joking about superheroes being "long underwear characters," so it had a different tone at the very beginning. It was obvious that there was a lot of thought going into it. I noticed that the day I bought it, in 1962.

Stan: I don't know if there was *that* much thought, or if I was just uninhibited when I wrote it.

Roy: There could be that, too: the opposite!

Stan: There wasn't much thought in anything, because there wasn't *time* to give anything that much thought; we were working too fast!

Roy: Sometime, not too long before that, you had some alien "Spider-men" in a story you did with Jack.

Stan: Maybe. I know Jack once said that he had done a Spider-Man comic years ago and said that I had copied it. I never saw it and, to this day, I don't know what was going on.

Roy: C.C. Beck and Joe Simon worked on the Silver Spider, but there are few similarities, it seems to me, between the two. Besides, there had been *The Spider* before, anyway, in the pulps.

Stan: That's probably what influenced me with the name. I used to read *The Spider* pulp magazine—which of course was nothing like Spider-Man—and I always thought that it was a dramatic name.

Roy: The funny thing is that the pulp Spider was more like The Shadow; he didn't have any kind of web. But when they did the movie serials, he had a costume that had webbing on it.

Stan: I didn't see the serials. When they started to do the *Spider* paperbacks a few years ago, whoever the publisher was sent me a letter asking if I'd give some sort of testimonial for the book. You know I'd always write a few lines for a book, and I wrote that it's great to see *The Spider* back again. I thought it was nice and tried to do what I could to help those books sell. One day not so long ago, I got a letter from Jay Kennedy, the editor-in-chief at King Features, and it said that in the Spider-Man newspaper strip I must not use the term "The Spider" in the title, in one of the coming-next-week blurbs. I wrote something like, "The Spider at Bay." They protested and thought I was trying to pull a fast one. Since then I don't use the term "The Spider" anymore.

Roy: Various people like Gene Colan, Frank Giacoia, and Mike Esposito started wandering over to Marvel in the mid-sixties, and they used pseudonyms. Was this so DC wouldn't know that they were working for Marvel?

Stan: Maybe not in every case, but as far as Gene and Frank, I don't think there was any other reason for them to use different names.

Roy: Everyone's heard tales of you physically playing out stories, jumping on tables, and acting out "Thor" stories.

Stan: I used to enjoy doing that. I always had a lot of energy in those days and it was hard for me to sit still. I think I never really grew up and I loved acting silly. I got a kick out of it. Writing comics—you know how it feels, but maybe you don't feel that way—writing at the typewriter, hour after hour, got kind of boring. I would do whatever I could do to jazz things up. I liked to feel that there was excitement in the air at the office. If I could sing out loud or play my ocarina—I was the worst player in the world, but at least it made a lot of noise.

Roy: Maybe I'm more inhibited because I'm short, and as a high school teacher for several years, I had to get the students, some of whom were taller than I was, to take me seriously.

Stan: [*laughs*] Being a teacher probably toned you down!

Roy: When you started those letter columns with that friendly tone, were you inspired by the EC letters pages?

Stan: No. You know what inspired me? When I was a kid, there used to be these hardcover book series like *The Hardy Boys, Tom Swift, Tom Sturdy*, but nobody ever heard of the one I read: *Jerry Todd and Poppy Ott*. I think Poppy was a friend of Jerry Todd's who was spun off into his own series. They were not periodicals or magazine but real books.

At the end of each book, there were letters pages where the writer, Leo Edwards, would write a little message to the readers and print some of their letters with answers. He had a very informal style, and the books themselves were wonderful because they were adventure stories. But unlike *The Hardy Boys* and the others, there was a tremendous amount of humor—the way I tried to do with *Spider-Man* and some others. I was a big fan of these books, and I loved the fact that they had letter and commentary by the author. Leo Edwards was the only guy that did that. Maybe I remembered the warm, friendly feeling of those letters.

Roy: When I came aboard in mid-'65, you were coming into the office only two or three days a week. Was it because it was getting too busy?

Stan: That's a little bit of a story: A few years before that, I was doing so much writing and I couldn't finish it in the office, so I said to Martin, "I have to have one day a week off to get my writing done." So he said okay, and I took Wednesday off because it was right in the middle of the week and it broke it off into two two-day weeks.

Then, as I got more and more into writing, I said to Joan, "I'm gonna ask him for another day off." She said, "You can't do that! How can you have the nerve to ask for two days a week off and he's paying you a weekly salary?" Hey, the only thing he can do is say no. So I asked him, and he must have had a good golf game that day, and he said okay. I took off Tuesdays and Thursdays.

Then I still seemed to feel that I had too much writing to do, so I said to Joan, "I'm going to ask him if I can take Monday, Wednesday, and Friday off!" She said, "Stan, I'm going to head for the hills! *Nobody* can ask for something like that!" I said, "Hey, what can I lose?" And he actually said okay! So there was a time when I came in Tuesdays and Thursdays.

The funny thing is that people still say to me, "Boy, you're lucky to stay home those days," and there's no way to explain that I'd rather be in the office! When I'm home, I'm working all the time; when I'm in the office, I'm talking to people, making phone calls, acting like a boss—being in the office is fun! Being at home, I'm sitting at the goddamned typewriter or, now, the computer and I'm working. But it still sounds to people like such a cushy deal.

Roy: There were a couple of people who worked in the office in a vague editorial capacity in '65 before I came along. One of them was Larry Ivie. Was he working there as an assistant editor at the time?
Stan: I remember his name—he wrote books, didn't he? But I really don't remember. I just recall the name.

Roy: Now—about the famous "Marvel Writer's Test": Sol Brodksy and Flo Steinberg told me that you put an ad for writers in the *New York Times*, and had hundreds of people applying.
Stan: It's news to me, but it sounds like something we might have done.

Roy: Did you have to read a lot of the tests?
Stan: I probably gave them to somebody else to read. I really don't remember.

Roy: The reason I'm curious is that supposedly I was hired on the basis of taking this writer's test while I was working at DC.
Stan: Then I must have been reading them.

Roy: We met the next day after I turned it in. You offered me a job a few minutes later, but you never referred to the test then or at any other time, so I never knew if you actually read it or if I was hired because I was already working for Mort Weisinger over at DC. [*laughs*]
Stan: I think I liked your personality.

Roy: It was always strange to me: I went in there expecting to discuss this writing test and figured that I must have passed—but you never mentioned it! And I'm still waiting!
Stan: [*laughs*] Maybe that's the case, Roy. I just don't remember.

Roy: We're actually going to print one page of that test in *Comic Book Artist*. The test was four Jack Kirby pages from *Fantastic Four Annual # 2*. . . .

Stan: Oh! When I wanted people to put dialogue over the pictures? That was a good idea!

Roy: You had Sol or someone take out the dialogue. It was just black-and-white. Other people like Denny O'Neil and Gary Friedrich took it. But soon afterwards we stopped using it.

Stan: That was a clever idea! I'm proud of me! [*laughs*] You know, I probably did read yours and most of the others, because I know I hate to read scripts, but if it was just pictures with dialogue balloons, I could have read that very quickly, and chances are that I did read them all. And chances are that I'm a lousy judge, so I probably liked yours! [*laughs*]

Roy: I was startled to learn in '65 that Marvel was just part of a parent company called Magazine Management. A lot of people from other departments went on to fame and fortune during Marvel's early days: [humorist/playwright] Bruce Jay Friedman, Mario Puzo, Ernest Tidyman (who created Shaft), and [gossip columnist] Rona Barrett. Do you remember when Puzo—before he came out with *The Godfather*—wanted to write for Marvel?

Stan: Yeah. Either he came to me or I heard that he was kind of strapped for money and he would like to see if he could write a comic book. At any rate, I spoke to him and I gave him an assignment because I knew he was a good writer. He came back to me a few weeks later and he hadn't done the assignment. He said, "Stan, I didn't realize that writing comics was so hard! I could write a goddamned novel with all the work that it would take me to do this!" The next thing I knew, there was *The Godfather*!

Roy: That was his third novel, but I imagine he could have been working on it at the time, so he eventually would have left us anyway. [*laughs*] I remember that when we started the Academy of Comic Book Arts in 1970–71, he sent a message to the first public meeting thanking Marvel Comics "for teaching my children to read when the public schools failed."

Stan: Aw, gee, I wish I had a copy of that.

Roy: I was sitting in the audience with Tom Wolfe at the time. I'd invited Wolfe because he was an idol of mine. So we had some nice heavy names for that first big public ACBA meeting.

Stan: I would love the chance to start ACBA again. The industry could certainly use that. With all the contacts I now have in TV, if there were an ACBA, I'll bet I could get the awards ceremony to be televised once a year.

Roy: Now that we wouldn't win anymore! [*laughs*] In the two weeks I worked for DC in '65, I learned they had an editorial meeting in which they were discussing the Marvel competition, because Marvel had begun to outsell DC in percentages. This was the second time—since EC had done it in the fifties—that Independent was distributing a comics company that was out-selling DC, percentage-wise. When did you begin to realize that Marvel was becoming a sensation?
Stan: I would guess that (A) when I read the fan mail—would you believe that I read every damn letter! (Which is why I wear glasses now!)—and (B) Martin probably told me. I could tell how well we were doing by the letters where the kids would write, "You're our favorite magazines and we love these characters." Martin was very happy and proud about it and would tell me.

Roy: In 1968 Marvel expanded. Every superhero had his own title—*Iron Man*, *Sub-Mariner*, *Captain America*.
Stan: I was drunk with power.

Roy: And soon after that, there was a downturn in sales in general. Do you think there was an over-expansion?
Stan: I don't even remember. Well, you were there long enough to know that sales have their ups and downs. Even the best books—*Fantastic Four*, *Spider-Man*, *Hulk*, *Thor*—some months they didn't sell as well as other months. The same went for *Superman*, *Batman*. Today the same goes for *Spawn*, which isn't selling now what it sold a year ago. They go up, they go down. It's hard for me to remember specifically any particular event or why it happened.

Roy: You may recall that in 1971 Martin Goodman suddenly made the decision to jump the page count to 48 pages for 25¢. Then, after one glorious month of these big books, they were suddenly dropped back down to 32 pages for 20¢. I understand the motivation to give 50 percent off the cover price to the wholesalers, but I was wondering how you felt about this jumping around of page size.
Stan: I had so little to do with that. The orders would just come from Martin's office. This month the price would be this, or this month this is how many pages we had. My only job was to make sure somebody got good stories to fill those pages. I was never really consulted when they

would raise the price. The only time I was consulted was when he wanted to put out the "Treasury Editions"—that may have been my idea. I think that I went to him once and said, "Why don't we put out a big book that people would notice?" But when he made these decisions, he made them all himself.

Roy: I remember that one of the few times I met with Martin Goodman was when I was there with John Verpoorten [Marvel's production manager] and Goodman was talking about how suddenly we were going to cut all the books down in size and that DC was going to take a bath if they didn't follow suit right away—and they *did* take a bath, because they kept the giant-size books for a year and Marvel just murdered them. So it was a very smart move, but I remember him then saying, "Well, I'm sure that the artists and writers will like it better with the smaller books." And—this was the only time that I talked up to Mr. Goodman—I said, "Actually, we prefer the bigger books." And he just sort stared at me blankly. That was the end of our conversation. [*laughs*]
Stan: And almost the end of your job!

Roy: [*laughs*] It probably was! I was polite, but once in a while you have to speak your mind. . . . You were writing less in the seventies, and that's the time you began working with [French New Wave film director] Alain Resnais on the film *The Monster Maker*.
Stan: That never was made. Y'know, we sold that screenplay, but it was never produced.

Roy: You had another movie you worked on in the late seventies called *The Inmates*. Have you ever thought about taking one or both of those properties and turning them into graphic novels?
Stan: No, but I'm working on selling *The Inmates* as a movie now. It needs some revision, but I'm going to start showing it around. *The Monster Maker* would require so many changes that I just don't have the time. Maybe someday when I retire, which will probably be never.

Roy: As we entered the seventies, the fans were writing in for us to do *Tarzan* and *John Carter of Mars*, Tolkien, *Conan*, and *Doc Savage*. All those properties were starting to be big in paperbacks in the late sixties. I remember us talking about *Conan*, and you had me write what turned out to be a two- or three-page memo to Martin Goodman to persuade him as to why we should seek the rights to a sword-and-sorcery hero. I've never been able to figure out why we didn't just make up a character!

Stan: It was because of *you*. You were too persuasive and you wanted to do *Conan*! I was not a big *Conan* fan. I had heard of it, but I don't think that I ever read it. To show how little I know, I had that much confidence in you, and I figured that if Roy wants to do it that badly, well, let's try and do it!

Roy: We originally tried to get the rights to *Thongor* by Lin Carter, because we didn't think we could afford *Conan*, but it worked out all right—certainly for me. [*laughs*]

Stan: You were the guy who was totally responsible for doing *Conan* and for its success. That was one book that I had *nothing* to do with!

Roy: I remember that you said that when I completed an issue that I thought was good, I should show it to you. So I gave you the make-ready of the fourth issue, which was *The Tower of the Elephant*—based on one of Howard's best stories—and you took it inside your office for a few minutes, brought it back, tossed it limply on my desk, and said, "Well, okay, that's it—not my kind of thing." I felt bad because that was a particular story in which Conan didn't do any rescuing or fighting at the end of the story.

Stan: Maybe that's what I missed.

Roy: If I had been making up the story, I wouldn't have done it that way, I'll admit. I was a little worried about that myself, but it turned out to be quite popular. About 1970, ACBA was formed, and [DC publisher] Carmine Infantino and you were the official starters.

Stan: It was all my idea, but I knew that I needed some support. I wanted it to be like the Motion Picture Academy of Arts and Sciences, and I felt (and I feel this way to this day) that comic books are a great literary and art form that isn't appreciated enough in this country. I felt that why the hell shouldn't we have an *Academy of Comic Book Arts*? Even back then I felt that if we had an awards ceremony every year, we could probably get it on the radio and eventually, after we got a little more prestige even have it televised. I knew there were a lot of celebrities who were into comics, and that's all you need to get something on television—to get this actor or actress to serve as master of ceremonies. So I formed it and we were successful beyond my wildest dreams in the beginning, because every company joined and virtually every writer and artist joined.

Unfortunately, Neal Adams, whose work I respect greatly—he's one of the geniuses of the business—wanted to turn the damn thing into a union. At these meetings, Neal would get up and start talking about pay raises, benefits, and ownership for the artists. I remember saying to him and to the gathering in general, that he might well be right in everything he said, but this was the wrong forum for that sort of discussion. They don't discuss those matters in the Television Academy; that's the kind of stuff you discuss in a union meeting.

If Neal wanted to form a union, he should go ahead and do it, but the purpose of ACBA was to give our industry prestige, not to discuss the fact that artists don't have ownership or things like that. I was never able to convince him, and ACBA became divided into two camps, it seemed. I wasn't interested in starting a union, so I walked away from it. Neal was elected president, but it didn't last. The whole thing collapsed. I'm not saying this to put down Neal Adams, for most of the things that he was pitching were very worthwhile things, but, as I said, I just felt that he had picked the wrong forum. I think now it could be much more successful than ever before, because it's a bigger field and there are more celebrities involved.

I had done my best to build up Marvel, and as much as I may have contributed to Marvel's success with any stories, editing, or creating characters, I think equally as valuable was the advertising, promotion, publicity, and huckstering that I did, traveling around the country and talking about Marvel, trying to give it the right image. The reason I mention that is, *that* is what I wanted to do with ACBA; but I wanted to do it for the whole industry, not just for Marvel. That was the purpose. I wanted to make people feel that comic books are really great. I was very frustrated and disappointed that in some way I couldn't get everybody to have the same vision that I had for ACBA.

Roy: The early seventies were a time when you started to move away from actively being a writer because of other things you had to do.
Stan: Yeah, guys like Roy Thomas edged me out!

Roy: [*laughs*] Right! I was so eager to do *Spider-Man* in those days! Much as I loved the character Spider-Man, what I wanted to do was *Fantastic Four*—though nowadays it would be great to write *Spidey* and get those royalties! The main reason I wrote *Spider-Man* #101–104 and Archie Goodwin wrote *Fantastic Four* was because you were working with Alain Resnais on *The Monster Maker* for about four months' worth of books. Did it feel odd to return to *Spidey*, *F.F.*, and

Thor after leaving them for four months and for the first time not writing any comics for a period of time?

Stan: No. I think you can compare it to riding a bicycle; no matter how long you stay away, you get on the bike and it's just like you never left it. For example, if I were to go back to writing a book now, I don't think that it would feel odd at all; my problem would be that I haven't carefully read the preceding issues, so I wouldn't know where the hell I was in the storyline. Or I might write a character in such a way that I think is the way to write him, but I wouldn't be aware that three other writers before me had changed the character totally, so I'm now writing it in the wrong way.

Roy: So when you write the *Spider-Man* newspaper strip, you ignore what goes on in the comic books?

Stan: Of course. I couldn't cope with that, because we do the newspaper strip so far in advance, and there's no way that I could make it compatible with the books—impossible.

Roy: Another event in 1970 that had considerable impact at Marvel was Jack Kirby suddenly leaving. Do you remember his phone call?

Stan: No. I know it must have happened, but I don't specifically recall it. I don't know who he called; it may not have been me. Maybe he didn't even call, but I just remember that at one point he just stopped working for me.

Roy: I remember that he called, because you called us in and told us. In light of all that has happened since, do you think that the relationship could have been salvaged at some point?

Stan: I think it certainly could have been salvaged if I knew what was bothering him. He never really told me, nor did Steve Ditko when *he* left. You can't salvage something if you don't know the cause.

Roy: I remember the day that Steve quit, a few months after I began to work at Marvel. He just came in, dropped off some pages, and left. Sol Brodsky then told me he had suddenly quit. Sol had a memo on his desk to add $5.00 to Steve's page rate, a considerable raise at that time, so it certainly wasn't over money. He wandered off to do work for Charlton, which paid half of what Marvel was offering.

Stan: As you know, I have the worst memory in the world, but maybe I knew why he left at the time. But right now, I absolutely cannot remember. The one thing I remember and felt bad about when Jack left, was that I had been thinking about—and maybe I even talked to him about it—that I wanted to make Jack my partner in a sense; I wanted him to be the art director and I though that he could serve in that function and I would serve as the editor. Maybe this was way earlier, but I was disappointed when he left because I always felt that Jack and I would be working there forever and doing everything.

Roy: For some months when you became publisher, you needed someone to be art director, so Frank Giacoia came in [as "assistant art director"], and, very soon, John Romita succeeded him, becoming art director.

Stan: But I wasn't thinking of Jack being art director because I would be leaving; I just thought that it would be great working with him in that capacity. I was serving as art director and thought that he could take it off my shoulders, so I could just worry about the stories. It probably wouldn't have worked out anyway, because I might have disagreed with him about things—not about his own work, but if we started critiquing other artists' work, Jack and I might have looked at it differently. So it might just be that I never could have worked with any art director who would function the way I did, because I guess no two people see anything the same.

Roy: Also, with Jack being in California, there would have been a geographical problem. I have a memory that, sometime before Jack left, Jack called you up about some new ideas he had for characters. I don't think it went any further than that. Do you recall that at all? I was always curious if those were the same ideas that appeared a year or so later as *The New Gods*, and wondered if they could easily have ended up as Marvel characters.

Stan: I don't know if he told me the ideas and I had said that I didn't like 'em! [*laughs*] I just can't remember.

Roy: The last few months Jack was working for Marvel, he ended up doing the writing on a couple of series—*Ka-Zar* and *The Inhumans*. Did you invite him to write at that time?

Stan: I am probably the worst guy in the world for you to interview! (A) I didn't realize he *had* written them; and (B) I can't remember if I invited him to or not. I don't think that I ever would have specifically said, "Jack, I would like you to write," because I never thought of Jack as a writer (but he was certainly a great plotter). Certainly 90 percent of the

"Tales of Asgard" stories were Jack's plots, and they were great! He knew more about Norse mythology that I ever did (or at least he enjoyed making it up!). I was busy enough just putting in the copy after he drew it.

Roy: I was always curious about those three buddies, Hogun, Fandral, and of course enormous Volstagg. Were those characters your idea or Jack's? That's one of those ideas that I could see either you or Jack making up.

Stan: I made those up. I specifically remember that I did them because I wanted a Falstaff-type guy, a guy like Errol Flynn, and then I wanted a guy like Charles Bronson who was dire and gloomy, riddled with angst. Those three were mine.

Roy: When Marvel was acquired by Perfect Film, run by Martin Ackerman—because of the *Saturday Evening Post* debacle, where they dismantled the magazine, were you apprehensive about that, or were you thinking mostly about the fact that now you'd be free to put out more books?

Stan: I was just curious to see what was going to happen next. I didn't know what was going to happen. It was the first time that we were owned by a conglomerate and not by Martin Goodman, so it was a whole new experience for me. I was just hoping that I could keep my job, probably—that was the thing I always worried about! Then, of course, Ackerman left after a while and Sheldon Feinberg came in. There was something wrong with Perfect Film—I don't know what it was—but the stockholders or the bank or the board of directors got Martin Ackerman to resign and they put Sheldon Feinberg in his place. Feinberg changed the name of the company from Perfect Film to Cadence Industries, and then he was in charge for quite a while.

Roy: Was it Feinberg's decision to make you president and publisher?

Stan: Yes. But I didn't stay *president* very long.

Roy: Do you remember when we had problems during the Wage and Price Freeze during the Nixon administration, over the fact that we dropped down in size after one month of those giant-size 25¢ comic books? We had to put a slick, color, four-page insert in one issue of *Fantastic Four*; supposedly this was to make up for the fact that the Wage and Price Control Board had decided it was right on the cusp of whether we had, in a certain way, actually *raised* prices by charging 20¢ for 32 pages.

Stan: How the hell do you remember that?

Roy: Because I was the guy who had to write that insert! [*laughs*]

Stan: That was what was so great about having you there; I let you worry about it. I don't even remember it.

Roy: Do you still have the letter from the Department of Health, Education, and Welfare which prompted you to write the narcotics issues of *Spider-Man?*

Stan: There used to be a scrapbook in the office, and if it's still around, the letter would be in there. I haven't seen it in a million years. I got this letter—I don't remember the exact wording—and they were concerned about drug use among kids. Since Marvel had such a great influence with young people, they thought it would be very commendable if we were to put out some sort of anti-drug message in our books.

I felt that the only way to do it was to make it a part of the story, and we made that three-parter of *Spider-Man.* I remember it contained one scene where a kid was going to jump off a roof and thought he could fly. My problem is that I know less about drugs than any living human being! I didn't know what kind of drug it was that would make you think you could fly! I don't think I named anything; I just said that he had "done" something.

Roy: It was just a generic kind of drug. Just the same way we used to make up the names of countries. You made up Latveria.

Stan: You're right! [*laughs*] Doesn't Latveria sound authentic?

Roy: I take it that you didn't do a lot of research on drugs, then?

Stan: I have never done research on anything in my life. Out here in Los Angeles, I work with and know so many screenwriters, and it amazes me the amount of research these guys do. I was going to do something about a prison, and I gave up the project because I realized I don't have any idea what the rituals are inside a prison and I just couldn't be bothered to look it up. But these guys would go and spend a week visiting a prison—even talking to the warden! I'm just no good at that.

Roy: Back in 1965 I took a phone call at the office sometime after 5:00 P.M. from somebody who asked me what you and Steve Ditko were on—because you *had* to be taking something in order to do those

Dr. Strange stories with the fights. I said, "I don't think Stan or Steve do anything like that." (I wouldn't have admitted it if it had been true, of course.) Then he says, "It has to be, because I had a fight like that when I was high on mushrooms in Mexico City a couple of years ago! It was just like the one Dr. Strange had with Dormammu!"

Stan: It's just a testimony to Steve's ability to make things look real. I can't speak for Steve (who probably also was not on anything), but I never even smoked a marijuana cigarette. I never took anything.

Roy: After John Romita became too busy to draw or even lay out *Spidey* on a regular basis, you worked with Gil Kane and even Ross Andru. Do you have any thoughts about those artists?

Stan: They were great! Gil came first, and he was just terrific! And he was *so fast*! It was such a pleasure working with him, because he was fast. I missed John because I had such a great relationship with him—everything that John did I thought was perfect—but it really was a pleasure working with guys who were fast. I always loved Gil's stuff—very stylized, but very good.

Roy: My four issues of *Amazing Spider-Man* were with Gil. He and I had been friends ever since we had worked on *Captain Marvel*. We had a lot of fun together, too. You'll be glad to know I'm not going to ask you about who killed off Gwen Stacy. We'll skip that entirely, as we've had enough of that.

Stan: [*laughs*] It's funny, because obviously my memory is wrong. I think Gerry Conway has said that I told him to kill her off, but I don't remember saying that.

Roy: Actually, what he said was that evidently it was John Romita's idea. All Gerry said is that we okayed it with you, but he never claimed that it was your idea. I don't think you would ever have come up with that idea.

Stan: The memory I have is him asking me how to write the thing, and I said, "Hey, it's your book, just keep it in character and write it." I took off, came back, and she was dead! I think he was quoted somewhere as asking me whether he could kill her off and I said yes. I don't remember that and can't believe I would have. The reason is not that I have an aversion to a character dying in a series, but that I always wanted her to marry Peter Parker. But even more than that, only a short time earlier we had killed off her father and I didn't want it to look like I had something against the Stacy family!

Roy: I do remember you agreeing to it. You probably felt that it was our ball—me as editor, and Gerry and John—and it was our job. I don't think you wanted to stand in the way, but you were never enthusiastic about the idea.

Stan: If I agreed to it, it was probably because I had my mind on something else. I was careless, because if I had really considered it, I would have said, "Roy, let's talk this over."

Roy: The final time you came back as a regular writer in the comics, after you spent those four months working with Alain Resnais.

Stan: Did I really take four months off?

Roy: Yeah. You wrote up to *Spider-Man* #100, which you ended by giving him four extra arms and tossed it to me, saying, "Take it, Roy." I was stuck with a six-armed Spider-Man for a couple of months! [*laughs*]

Stan: I thought *you* gave him the extra arms!

Roy: No, that was at the end of *your* story, so I can get out of that one! You were still involved editorially though, because this was right after the Code was liberalized, and you told us you wanted Spidey to fight a vampire. Gil and I were going to bring in Dracula, who was not yet a Marvel character, and you said, "No, I want a super-villain vampire." So we made up Morbius, the Living Vampire.

Stan: It worked out great.

Roy: Did you feel strongly at that time that the Code needed to be changed?

Stan: As far as I can remember—and I've told this to so many people, it might even be true—I never thought that the Code was much of a problem. The only problem we ever had with the Code was over foolish things, like the time in a western when we had a puff of smoke coming out of a gun and they said it was too violent. So we had to make the puff of smoke smaller. Silly things. But as far as ideas for stories or characters that we came up with. I almost never had a problem, so they didn't bother me. I think the biggest nuisance was that sometimes I had to go down and attend a meeting of the [CMAA] Board of Directors. I felt that I was killing an entire afternoon.

Roy: Do you think that there were any bad feelings on the part of the Code over the *Spider-Man* drug issues?

Stan: That was the only big issue that we had. I could understand them; they were like lawyers, people who take things literally and technically.

The Code mentioned that you mustn't mention drugs and, according to their rules, they were right. So I didn't even get mad at them then. I said, "Screw it" and just took the Code seal off for those three issues. Then we went back to the Code again. I never thought about the Code when I was writing a story, because basically I never wanted to do anything that was to my mind too violent or too sexy. I was aware that young people were reading these books, and had there *not* been a Code, I don't think that I would have done the stories any differently.

Roy: The only difference was that, technically, you could not do a vampire or werewolf story.
Stan: We couldn't do vampire stories?

Roy: No, they had been forbidden since the mid-fifties when the Code arrived. The Morbius story was done in the vein of just like any other super-villain—we even gave him primary costume colors of red and blue, just like Spider-Man. Very soon after that, we began the whole gamut of those creatures. *Werewolf by Night, Man-Thing, Frankenstein.* Many of these concepts flowed from you. Man-Thing was a sentence or two concept that you gave me for the first issue of *Savage Tales.*
Stan: That came after *Swamp Thing*, didn't it?

Roy: No, it came at the same time as the first one-shot "Swamp Thing" story, but before the regular series.
Stan: So we didn't copy it from *Swamp Thing*?

Roy: No, or vice versa. In fact, I had done a character a little earlier in *The Hulk* that was also a takeoff on the Heap character from the forties comics. I had called it "The Shape," but you insisted that name sounded feminine, so you changed it to "The Glob."
Stan: It's funny that you mentioned the Heap, because when I did the *Hulk*, I had the Heap in mind when I made up the name. I thought "The Hulk" sounded like "The Heap" and I liked it.

Roy: The Heap was one of the great old characters; he's been copied more than most characters. Man-Thing ended up looking a lot like him. Do you remember how *Savage Tales* came about? I always got the impression that Goodman wasn't wild about doing black-and-white books. Were these something you pushed?
Stan: I wonder why I wanted to do black-and-white books. I *did* push them, but I can't remember why.

Roy: Well, there were the Warren books getting a share of the market that we weren't getting into, perhaps?
Stan: Were they cheaper to do?

Roy: Well, no color, so they were cheaper per page, certainly. They were also more expensive and we could, without the Code, go a little further. The first issue of *Savage Tales* had a little nudity in the Conan story and in your Ka-Zar story.
Stan: I was looking to grab older readers.

Roy: There was a little more violence, but nothing really salacious. I remember a story by Denny O'Neil and Gene Colan where, by the time the book came out, all the nudity had been covered up. We were feeling our way back and forth, because we didn't know exactly what we were doing. There were all sorts of distribution problems. There was a year between *Savage Tales* #1 and #2. Do you remember why that was?
Stan: No, but that seems to indicate a distribution problem.

Roy: I heard that we didn't get into Canada at all because somebody complained that it was salacious material, but I've never seen anything in writing about that. But I did get the impression that Martin Goodman was very happy to see *Savage Tales* die the first time.
Stan: Martin never had any interest in those books.

Roy: When *Savage Tales* came back, it quickly spun off *The Savage Sword of Conan*, and there were all those black-and-white books starting with *Dracula Lives!* that you heaped on my shoulders over a two-day period.
Stan: Well, you were good at it.

Roy: I was good at it because I got Marv Wolfman and other people to help a lot. This happened after you had become publisher, and you used to always tell me that we needed to do these extra books to pay my salary. Except that I never noticed getting a big raise! [*laughs*]

One day you came in and said we were going to do a new book called *Dracula Lives!* which was about sixty pages of black-and-white material to fill. The next day you came in and said we're going to do a second black-and-white, too, because we can't fit non-vampire material in *Dracula Lives!* so we'll do *Monsters Unleashed*. I said that made sense, so I called in Marv, Gerry Conway, Len Wein, and we all got started on this. Then I came in the next day and you said, "Guess

what?" I said, "Don't tell me, you have a third book to add." You said, "No, *two* more!" You wanted to do *Vampire Tales*—vampires that weren't Dracula—and *Tales of the Zombie*.
Stan: Didn't Bill Everett do that cover?

Roy: No, what happened was that, not too long before that, in the warehouse when we were doing one of our searches, I found this story from *Menace* that you and Bill had both signed—a five-or six-page wonderful zombie story from the 1950s.
Stan: *That's* the one that I remember.

Roy: The image on the splash page was one of the all-time great drawings of a zombie. I decided to make that the template of the title character, but you may have been thinking of that story, too, and just never mentioned it. I made up the name Simon Garth and turned it over to Steve Gerber, and it sort of went from there. So, in less than forty-eight hours, we suddenly had four gigantic books coming out and that didn't even count the *Conan* black-and-white!
Stan: I just wanted to make sure that we needed you.

Roy: It was a challenge. Some of the stories were good and some not so good, but all the mags lasted for a while—*Savage Sword of Conan* lasted for over two hundred issues. . . . Next I wanted to ask you about a few people from that period. What's your main impression of Jim Steranko?
Stan: I loved him and was incredibly impressed by him. He was such a multi-talented guy. One of the most important things is to have a certain style, not only to be able to write or draw well but to do it with style and distinction. His style was so distinctive that he just seemed more hip, cooler, and more cutting-edge than any other artist at that time.

Roy: This is the guy who walked in one day and told me that he had just come in from his fencing lesson. I don't know if that was hip or not, but it was cool.
Stan: That happened probably after his magic show. He was a great guy who knew what he wanted and was very definite. He was the kind of guy who, after you got to know him, you were willing to give him a project and let him do it his way. I had a lot of confidence in him.

Roy: After writing the first few *SHIELD* stories that he drew, I was happy to let him write them, as well, because he had his own ideas and I had other things to do. *SHIELD* was never a big seller, but it was one of the influential books. Steranko and Neal Adams were influential beyond of their selling power.

Stan: It was a big loss to us, and the whole business, when Jim decided to quit and do his magazine.

Roy: Do you remember how Barry Smith got his job?

Stan: No, but he had a very distinctive style and, at first, it took a little getting used to on my part when he developed into being so different from some of the other artists. He was more quietly illustrative. One thing I remember about Barry was a Dr. Strange story that he did with me. I was so pleasantly surprised at how well it tuned out; when I had to sit and write the copy, it was so easy to write and it worked so well. I was very impressed and I think Barry is another guy who is very, very talented.

Roy: The nice thing about people like Barry and Steranko is that they're not just artists, but real storytellers. They don't just draw a lot of pretty pictures. I've never had much patience for artists who just draw very pretty because it's often either totally dull, like still photos, or else it's so illustrative that you practically have to connect the dots to tell a story.

Stan: That's one of the problems with some of the artists in the business today—they do nice, impressive individual pictures, but they don't have enough feeling for continuity—letting one picture run into another so that it tells a story.

Roy: Another artist, whom I don't think you worked with, was Jim Starlin.

Stan: There you go! There's another creative, stylized, very, very talented guy. I was so impressed with that strip in *Epic* magazine, featuring that character with the long nose.

Roy: How do you remember Herb Trimpe, with whom you worked for a long time on *the Incredible Hulk*?

Stan: I liked Herb. He was a nice guy, dependable, with a style that was nice, simple, and clear. He told a story well. Herb was a pleasure. He was good.

Roy: I had a very good time working with him on *the Hulk* after you. He's teaching now.

Stan: If you speak with him, give him my best.

Roy: Coming up from coloring, there was Marie Severin, with whom you worked on *Dr. Strange.*

Stan: Marie is worth an entire interview just to talk about her. You talked about being multi-talented. She was great at humorous cartoons; she did *the Hulk* and all these serious strips; one of the best colorists in the business; she's a wonderful person with a great sense of humor; always cheerful and great to work with. She was also stylized; you could always recognize her work with that slight touch of cartooniness in the serious artwork that gave it a certain charm, I'm crazy about Marie.

Roy: She and her brother John combined her style and his realism in *Kull* that are considered classics of the early seventies.

Stan: Of course, you could do a whole interview about John, too; he is one of the real greats in the business.

Roy: It must have been the money. [*laughs*] You also worked with Bill Everett over the years.

Stan: Bill was great, and he was also very, very stylized. You could spot an Everett drawing, and he had his own way of telling stories. He was imaginative and talented, but the amazing thing was that he was very easy to work with. When I worked with him, there was no show of temperament at all. For a guy that talented, you would think he would have argued constantly—"No, Stan, I don't like that! Let's do it this way!"— but no, he was a joy to work with.

Roy: Do you remember waking up one morning and realizing that Marvel had finally surpassed DC in total sales?

Stan: I can't remember the exact moment I realized that, but I know it was very pleasant to hear it. I must admit that I expected it, Roy, so it didn't come as a surprise. I could tell by the fan mail we were getting, the write-ups we received in various newspapers and magazines—everything was Marvel and nobody was talking about DC. Just by talking to people myself when I went to conventions or lectures, I thought that we were outselling them before that became officially the case.

Roy: I've heard that there was a great dropoff in female readers in the early seventies. We came up with three strips for which you made up the names and concepts: *Shanna the She-Devil*, *Night Nurse*, and *The Claws of the Cat.* Were we trying to woo the female readers back?

Stan: Yes, and also to appeal to the male readers who liked looking at pretty girls. Unfortunately, we weren't able to draw the girls the way they're drawn now, because I think if we had been, our sales would have soared much more than they did!

Roy: People know that I'm the one who assigned three women to write those books—Linda Fite (now Herb Trimpe's wife); my first wife Jeanie; and Phil Seuling's wife Carol—but I can't remember if that's something you suggested.

Stan: You're so strong-willed, you wouldn't have taken my suggestion. I don't know [*laughs*] if I had to guess, I'd say that it was your idea, because I don't think I was telling you who to use.

Roy: Probably not. Of course, in some ways, I could have gotten more experienced writers, but I don't know if that would have helped the books, because the market didn't seem to be there at that time. We did everything we could. We got Marie Severin to draw *The Cat* and Wally Wood to ink; we got Steranko to do the covers to *Shanna*.

Stan: The failure of *The Cat* was my biggest disappointment I really thought that that would have worked.

Roy: Strangely enough, the one that is collected now, for a reason I cannot figure out, is *Night Nurse*, by my ex-wife Jeanie and Winslow Mortimer.

Stan: Martin Goodman always thought there was something inherently sexy about nurses. I could never get inside his thinking there.

Roy: Considering the "men's-sweat" magazines he published with those ill-clad nurses, that's where it probably came from. Hadn't Timely done *Linda Carter, Student Nurse*?

Stan: We even had *Nellie the Nurse*, a humor book.

Roy: And *Tessie the Typist* and *Millie the Model*, my first assignment at Marvel.

Stan: Not to mention *Hedy of Hollywood*.

Roy: And probably your peak moment in comics, *Ziggy the Pig and Silly Seal*.

Stan: Oh, that was our high point, [laughs] We peaked! That was with Al Jaffee.

Roy: In the early sixties you had done that *Willie Lumpkin* newspaper strip. You used that name again for the mailman in *Fantastic Four*.

Stan: That was just for fun. Mel Lazarus had done a strip called *Miss Peach*, which used not panels but one long panel instead. I liked that idea very much, so when Harold Anderson, the head of Publishers Syndicate, asked me to do a strip, I came up with *Barney's Beat* which was about a New York City cop and all the characters on his patrol who he'd meet every day and there would be a gag. I did some samples with Dan DeCarlo, and I thought was wonderful.

Harold said it was too "big city-ish" and they're not going to care for it in the small towns because they don't have cops on a beat out there. He wanted something that would appeal to the hinterland, something bucolic. He said, "You know what I want, Stan? I want a mailman! A friendly little mailman in a small town." I don't remember if I came up with the name Lumpkin or he did, but I hated it. I think I came up with the name as a joke and he said, "Yeah, that's it! Good idea!"

It was the one strip in the world I didn't think I was qualified to write, because I liked things that were hip and cutting-edge, cool and big city. I always wrote *Seinfeld* and that kind of thing. Here I'm writing about a mailman in a small town! Even though it was not my type of thing, it lasted for a couple of years. Unlike today, when I do the *Spider-Man* daily strip and never heard from the syndicate (I gotta call them a few times a year and say, "Are you guys aware that we're still doing this?"), in those days Harold Anderson passed on every gag, looked at every panel, and I worked with him. He was a lovely man, but as an editor, he was a nightmare! [*laughs*]

Roy: You said that you didn't stay president very long . . . just a few months, maybe a year.

Stan: I found that I was expected to—and did—go to a lot of financial meetings where they would discuss costs and financial reports. We would have to come up with a five-year financial plan—things like that. I only stayed as president for a year—maybe less—because I would say to myself at those meetings, "What am I doing here? There must be a million people who could do this as well as or better than I." The thing that I enjoy the most and do the best is working on the stories, and I wasn't doing that! At some point I walked in to Feinberg and said, "I don't want to be president any more." I think I'm one of the few people who resigned the post of president. But I kept the title of publisher, though I'm still not sure what a publisher's duties are!

Roy: That's when Al Landau, not one of my favorite people, succeeded you as president of Marvel. His company. Trans World, had been selling Marvel's work in other countries.

Stan: He came in because Martin knew him and dealt with him for years; they had been friendly. But then Martin and he had a falling out—I don't know. I always got along fine with Al. He leaned on me a lot, so I helped him when he was president—he came to me for everything. I know that he wasn't all that popular. He died a few years ago.

Roy: Al Landau was president a couple of years; then Jim Galton took over. The only time Al and I were on the same side (and it took me a minute to realize why) was when both of us wanted to get back one of the pages of story we had lost in our books. I wanted the page back just because I wanted it back, for better stories—and he wanted it because then his company Trans World could sell another page abroad. We had a community of interest only that once during the year or so he was there and I was editor-in-chief.

I also remember when I was supposed to fly over to the Philippines and talk to the artists there. I would have had to spend twenty-four hours in the air, a day or so there when this revolution was going on, and then another twenty-four coming home. I remember you telling me that Al Landau didn't want me to go because it would have been too much like a vacation! [*laughs*] Some vacation! I was happy not to have to go!

Stan: Al was a very strange guy.

Roy: Between my leaving in '74 and Jim Shooter's ascension in '77, a period of three years, there were four editors-in-chief, counting the three weeks of Gerry Conway. Len Wein, Marv Wolfman, Gerry, almost me again, and then Archie.

Did that musical chairs of editors bother you?

Stan: Yeah, I wish that any one of those guys would have stayed for a while. But it didn't affect me that much; I just thought it didn't look good for the company—that we didn't know what we were doing. But they were all good. I was disappointed that Gerry didn't stay, because I always liked him and thought that he would do a good job.

Roy: That's the only time the job didn't automatically go to the next person in line. I suggested bringing Gerry back from DC and thought that it would work out, but after three weeks he just couldn't handle it.

Here's a question phrased by the *CBA* editor: "Arguably, the DC Comics under Carmine Infantino were art-driven—beautiful to look at, but maybe the art overwhelmed the storytelling. But Marvel seemed influenced by your legacy that, no matter how great the artwork, the story was paramount. Sales seemed to prove that out. What, is it, do you think, that made Marvel the industry leader for the last quarter century?"

Stan: I would like to think that we had a good marriage of art and script. I think that the art has always been at least as important as the story. Because you can tell the best story in the world, but if the artwork is dull—it's like a movie: If then photography, acting, or directing is bad, you can have a great story but it's still not going to be a great movie. By the same token, you can have the best artwork and if the story isn't there, you're only going to appeal to people who like to look at nice drawings. To me, a comic strip should be a beautifully illustrated story, not just beautiful illustrations.

I would never say that the story itself is paramount; and as far as a style, I would think that one thing that made our work a little different from anyone else's is the fact that we tried to make our characters as real and believable as possible. Even though they were in fantasy stories, our formula always was, "What if somebody like this existed in the real world, and what would his or her life be like?"

We always tried to have dialogue that sounded as if real people might say it, and we always tried to give our characters different personalities so they weren't cut from the same mold. We tried to have each one talking differently from the others. But, getting back to the original statement, we never concentrated more on script than art, nor did we concentrate more on art than script. The two are indivisible: they had to work perfectly together.

Roy: And now I have what Evans and Novak would call on their show, "The Big Question," which the editor requested me to ask you: Which is stronger, Thor or the Hulk?

Stan: I would have to guess that Thor is stronger, only because he *is* a god and probably can't be killed. Again, I don't know how the guys have been writing him lately, but I thought of him as invulnerable. I would think that with his hammer and everything, he'd probably beat the Hulk. But what's interesting with the Hulk is, the more he fights and the more he's beaten, the stronger he gets, so maybe it would be a draw.

Roy: It was really a facetious question—but, on the other hand, it's one of those things you could argue about forever. It's amazing that, after twenty-five, thirty years, people still think of that as the archetypal Marvel question.

Stan: The thing I loved writing was having our heroes fight, and for me to figure a way to end the story without denigrating either one or making one seem stronger than the other. The best example of this was in one issue of *Daredevil*, where DD was fighting Sub-Mariner. Oh, I loved the way that story turned out! That was just so perfectly done. Daredevil was beaten, but he was just as heroic as Sub-Mariner.

Roy: Thanks, Stan.
Stan: Anytime, Roy.

Writing for Himself: Stan Lee Speaks

JAMES CANGIALOSI / 1999

From *Comics Buyer's Guide*, no. 1324
(April 2, 1999). Reprinted by permission
of James Cangialosi.

Where do you begin to describe how much Stan Lee has given to the comics industry? You could read any one of the countless stories he has written and find yourself taking a trip to another universe that is populated by an abundance of characters including a hulking green monster and a young man who swings on a web. You could marvel at the wondrous characters he and Jack Kirby gave life to and be astounded by the imagination and intelligence that brought each and every one into existence. The adventures of Spider-Man, the Fantastic Four, Iron Man, Thor, and so many others were the nourishment sought by countless "Marvel Zombies" over the years.

In each super-character Lee helped to create, readers find a complex individual who must deal with the trials and tribulations of everyday life as well as cope with unusual powers and responsibilities. The terms "hero" and "villain" took on new definitions with Lee's reign during the Silver Age. They became synonymous with fun and adventure.

CBG: What made you decide to bring superheroes back in the 1960s?
Stan Lee: Actually, my publisher came in to see me one day and said, "*The Justice League of America* seems to be selling well. Why don't we try putting out a superhero comic book? Why don't we do a team of superheroes?" I didn't want to just copy DC's Justice League. I wanted to created a different type of team that went beyond what was being produced at the time, and that led to the creation of the Fantastic Four.

CBG: Where did the idea for the Fantastic Four come from?
Lee: People always ask me that, and it would be great to have a stock answer, but who really knows where ideas come from? I was sitting and I thought, "What powers would be interesting for these characters to have?"

One thing I remembered was that when I was younger I loved the original Human Torch and I thought I would like to bring him back. I also liked the idea—and I don't know how I particularly thought of the idea—of a scientist who was a little bit stuffy. This character became Mr. Fantastic.

Then I wanted to have another guy on the team who was always bored when the scientist was trying to explain things, and this character became the Thing. Then you had to have a girl, but I figured instead of having just the usual type of female character who doesn't know that the hero is the super-character she admires, I figured I'd let her know who the hero was. And I'd let them be engaged. In fact I'd let her be a part of the team.

And I wouldn't give anyone on the team any secret identities; I'd let everybody know who they were. I figured that would be fun, because I know, if *I* had a super power, *I* sure wouldn't keep it a secret.

CBG: With the publication of *Fantastic Four* #4, you re-introduced the Sub-Mariner. Do you think that the mix of old and new characters was more appealing during the 1960s than during the 1950s, when some of Timely's Golden Age heroes were reintroduced for a short time?
Lee: I never thought about that. I was only thinking about what would *I* like, and I knew I would enjoy seeing the Sub-Mariner back.

In fact, that has always been the way I operated all my life: People have always said to me, "What group do you write for? Do you write for young kids or older people or men or women, etc.?" I don't write for anybody except for myself. I ask myself what type of story would I like to read, and what type of character would I like to read about. That's what I write, and then I hope that there are a lot of people with the same tastes as mine.

CBG: During the Silver Age you worked a great deal with Jack Kirby. How much of a collaboration actually existed between the two of you?
Lee: A tremendous amount.

In the beginning, I would give Jack the idea for the character. I would describe the characters and give him an idea on how I wanted them to be. Jack would then draw the story and give me the exact rendition that I was looking for in the character.

After a while he was so good at it that I only had to tell him a few words. I mean I would say something like, "In the next story let's have Dr. Doom capture Sue and have the other three come and get her." I would tell him a couple more things, and that was about it. He would then draw the whole story and add a million things that I hadn't even told him. I would get the story back, and some of the things in it I would have liked, and some other things I would have felt he shouldn't have done. It didn't matter though, because it was fun—even the parts that he drew which I felt weren't quite right for the story.

I would try and figure out a way when I was writing the story to make it seem as if I wanted those parts included from the start. I made them seem as if they fit in perfectly. I think we had a great collaboration. Whatever he drew, I was able to write and I was able to enjoy writing it.

CBG: With Spider-Man, it took the death of his uncle to really motivate him toward the heroic life. Why did you add this tragic element to the hero's origin?
Lee: I didn't add it. That was there all the time. That was the first thing I thought of when I was sitting down to write the story—because, again, in trying to be realistic about the superheroes, my feeling was that the character needed to be driven into the role of a hero. Why would a guy with super-powers spend all his time risking his life trying to fight bad guys? Why wouldn't he just go on the stage and make a fortune, be an entertainer, or go into sports?

In order to be realistic, here's a teen-age guy, I think he was seventeen at the time, who was suddenly just about the strongest guy around. He could climb on walls and shoot webs and do just about anything he wanted. Why would he want to risk his life all the time fighting super-villains? I had to give him a motive. I had to give him a reason why he's going to be a hero.

I figured if somebody close to him died, and he felt responsible for that death, then he would perhaps want to spend the rest of his life atoning for that. I say that the death of Uncle Ben was an integral part to Spider-Man's origin, not an add-on.

CBG: How important to the flow of the story is it to have a truly dangerous villain?
Lee: Very important. The villain is really the most important one, as the series moves along. There are very few surprises that are left for the hero, because, after a few issues have gone by, the reader knows pretty much all there is to know about the hero.

The villain, on the other hand, is, it's to be hoped, interesting and exciting in every issue. It's how the hero will beat the villain that will keep the readers coming back, so the villain has to be somebody who is very interesting and very appealing.

CBG: Did you ever think that the Silver Surfer and Galactus would become so important to Marvel history?
Lee: I never thought that *any* of this stuff would become as big as it has.

When you write something—or, at least, when *I* write something—I've never said to myself, "Wow! This is going to be big! This is going to live for years!" You just write it and hope people will like it.

CBG: Did you think that having advanced social concepts in comics aimed at children were beyond the understanding of some children?
Lee: No, because I feel children are mostly smarter than many adults. They get concepts that many of us don't.

One of the biggest problems in the world is that people always downplay a child's intelligence. Children are very sensitive and they're very perceptive. And not just children, but young people, as well. Their minds are very sharp.

I was never worried about that. In fact, I had an argument with my publisher at the time, because I wanted to call the series the Mutants, and he said that no one would know what the word "mutants" meant. I said, "Then they can look it up. It's a great title." Unfortunately, he didn't want to do it.

Then I figured out I'd call the team the X-Men, because they have eXtra power. I went to my publisher and said, "How about the X-Men?" He said, "Well, OK. That's better." I thought to myself, "If nobody knows what a mutant is, then how are they going to know what an X-Man is?" I didn't argue, though, so that became the name of the series.

CBG: How did you come with those characters, especially their unusual qualities?

Lee: Well, again, I don't know how to explain it.

When you write, you want variety, so I wanted about five or six characters and I wanted them all to be different. I wanted one guy who flew, and that became the Angel. As I said, I always liked the Human Torch, but I didn't want to do another hot guy, so I figured; Why not a cold guy? And we came up with Iceman.

Then a girl with mental powers, who became Marvel Girl. Professor X, of course, was another character. I always liked Yul Brynner, so I pictured Professor X looking like him. Again, he would be the leader, and—just to make him interesting—I thought he should be in a wheel-chair so physically he was pretty helpless but mentally he was one of the strongest men on Earth.

Then I wanted someone else who was strong, so I came up with the Beast. I wanted to go against type with the Beast, so I thought that he would not only be strong, but he would also be the most agile and most articulate of the group. I also thought it would be interesting having a character like Cyclops, who could shoot power bolts from his eyes. Then I would have him have a crush on the girl and vice versa, and I'd let the Angel be the third member of the triumvirate, and maybe they would both be jealous, and this and that.

You just work out all the details and concepts in your mind. It's hard to explain where ideas come from. You just sit and think about it.

CBG: The Marvel bullpen is legendary for having the greatest assortment of artists in the industry. Jack Kirby, Ditko, Dick Ayers, and John Romita all worked for Marvel at some point. What were your hiring criteria?

Lee: An artist who could draw well and tell a story. An artist who could make the characters interesting to look at. The way Marvel works, the artist has to be a storyteller, too. There are a lot of artists who can draw beautiful pictures, but they don't know how to put them together so that they get an interesting story.

If you look at the old Marvel comics, as well most of the present-day Marvels, you'll see that they resemble a movie. The pictures come together beautifully and cinematically. In fact, years ago at New York University they were teaching a course in filmmaking, and I was very happy to see that they used a Spider-Man story in one of the text books, drawn, I think by Steve Ditko, with all the panels. They were explaining how the comics panels were laid out the way a motion picture would be photographed.

CBG: You frequently had one comics story lead into another in a different title—for instance, the way Loki helped to create the Avengers and the way Marvel's characters would constantly meet one another. Was it important for the success of Marvel to show readers that these characters existed in one universe?

Lee: I think so. Remember, I was writing virtually all those comics myself, and, by writing them all myself, it was easier to hold them all together. It made the characters more real to me by having them meet each other. I used to imagine that the characters lived in their own world. They lived in the Marvel universe!

I remember I wrote a particular story once which had nothing to do with Spider-Man, but in a scene I told the artist to put Peter Parker in there as a photographer who was covering the event that was going on for *The Daily Bugle*. So Peter Parker was placed in a scene that wasn't part of a Spider-Man story, and a lot of people didn't notice him—but those who read the story carefully noticed him and got a big kick out of it. They felt it was very realistic.

We've also had stories where characters like the Fantastic Four or Spider-Man needed a lawyer, and they would go to Matt Murdock, who was also Daredevil. Those instances where they would go to Murdock were not taking place in a Daredevil story; it might have been a little scene in another story in another title. The character would be seen in this story talking to Matt Murdock, who was acting as their lawyer. I think these types of meetings made the reader feel that these were real characters that you might bump into in the streets, and it made me feel that way, too.

CBG: As an editor were there any decisions that you really had difficulty making in connection with a story?

Lee: No. Stories were always easy. There were personal decisions that were tough, such as what artist was right for a particular series. There were two times in my life when business got bad when Marvel had to let a lot of people go. Those were two of the worst times for me in the business. Fortunately, stories were never a real problem.

CBG: Which is more important, art or writing?
Lee: The art is every bit as important as the writing—if not more important—because the artwork is the first thing you see.

The art could also ruin a story. I mean, you could write the greatest story in the world, but, if it isn't drawn well, it's not going to come across well.

It works in the opposite way, also. You could have the greatest art and, if the story is no good, unless you're either an art connoisseur or an art critic who just loves art, you'll be bored with the story. You won't want to read it. So both aspects are equally important.

I would say if either of the two, story or art, had to be rated to evaluate which was the most important, I would be inclined to say the art. It is what you see first and, in most cases, it is what makes you pick up the comic book. There has to be a drawing that interests you. You could also say it was the writer who told the artist what to draw and, had he not given the artist the direction to take, then he might not have drawn an interesting picture. But I'm inclined to think that the art has the edge over the writing.

CBG: Would you say that your stories from yesteryear are still relevant today?
Lee: I would hope so, but I think that is for the public to say more than me. I think anything is relevant, if it is well written and if the characterization is good.

Sherlock Holmes was written many years ago, and it is still relevant to me. Books like that are relevant because they're about "real" people, and they showed how life was during different periods.

My ultimate goal was to write stories that people would enjoy. That is all any writer ever tries to do. You try to write something, and you hope the public will like it. I've written everything. I've written Westerns, romance, war, horror, humor, animation, love stories, and on and on.

At the time I was specializing in superhero comics and what I was basically trying to do was make them somewhat believable. The thing to figure out was here were characters with fantastic powers, and, if we could accept the fact that they have those powers, then we could try to make everything else as realistic as possible. In other words: If there was really a guy with green skin and super-strength living in my neighborhood, what would his life be like? How would people treat him? What would he do? What would he do in his spare time? I wanted to make the characters believable.

CBG: What do you see in the future of the comics industry?
Lee: I don't know. I'm no great prophet. I just think there are so many talented people in the business now. Sometimes I read some stories, and I say, "Wow! These guys can really write."

I look at some artwork, and it really knocks me out at how beautifully it is done. You wonder how some of the artists do this many pages in a month and make every panel so beautiful.

It just seems to me that any business that has so many talented people as practitioners today can't have too much to worry about. There is always going to be good stuff. People are always going to enjoy reading comics. There will be good ones, and there will be bad ones, as there are with movies and television shows.

As long as there is a lot of talent in the business, I don't think there are too many problems to worry about. Whatever problems there are business-wise or distribution-wise or whatever will be ironed out sooner or later.

CBG: Who's your favorite character?
Lee: I can't say. Usually, it is whatever character I am reading at the time. I like so many of them. I have absolutely no idea who my favorite actor is, my favorite singer, or my favorite band. I'm not good with favorites. There are so many people and so many things that I like.

People are always saying to me, "Who is your favorite artist?" I might want to say John Buscema and then I think of John Romita and then I think of Gene Colan. You can't pick a favorite, because they're all good.

Stan Lee Looks Back: The Comics Legend Recalls Life with Jack Kirby, Steve Ditko, and Heroes

WILL MURRAY / 2000

When Stan Lee scaled down his involvement with Marvel Comics in summer 1998 to pursue his own Internet-based company, Stan Lee Media, he altered a relationship that spanned nearly sixty years. From the time he was hired as an office boy for Martin Goodman's Timely Comics in 1941 to his replacement of Timely's first editor, Joe Simon, in that same year to his ascendancy as publisher of the Marvel Entertainment Group, Stan Lee has been everything from editor to chief spokesperson of the company he ultimately remade to his own creative vision.

Lee has given many interviews over the years. *Comics Scene*, in fact, published one in each of the first issues (1981, 1987) of this magazine's previous versions. Back during the last *CS* incarnation, we sat down for another lengthy chat. Some quotes were culled for other articles, but the bulk of it, an exploration of Lee's roots and feelings about his career, has never seen print. For this first issue of the revived *Comics Scene 2000*, we thought this lost look at the one-time Master of Marvel Comics more topical now than it was when first done.

Comics Scene: You were the editor of Marvel Comics for twenty years before you stepped out of the relative anonymity of your given name to make a lasting impact on the field with *Fantastic Four*. Why is that?
Stan Lee: I never took comics seriously. It was just a way to make a living. I was always waiting for my chance to get out of comics, and do *real* writing. Then for whatever reason in the 1960s, I really was getting ready to quit and my wife said to me, "Before you quit, why don't you once do a book the way you would *like* to do it? Get it out of your system. You're going to leave anyway. What can they do to you?" So I tried to write *Fantastic Four* differently, just to get it out of my system. This is the way I liked to treat characters. It worked! And it got so popular that Martin asked for another hero. I think the next one was the Hulk, and I tried to do that a little differently. Then Spider-Man. By now we had started getting fan mail and it got interesting. I had never gotten feedback from readers before. I figured I would stay a little longer and see where it led. Then it was like a whole new resurgence.

CS: You almost didn't get your chance. Comics were in tough shape in 1961. And only a few years before, in '58, Marvel almost went under.
Lee: What happened was: Martin Goodman made one of the biggest publishing decision mistakes that was ever made. He had his own distribution company, Atlas. The books were doing fantastically. His business manager talked him into giving up Atlas and letting the American News Company distribute him. Very shortly after he did that, American went out of business. We had *no* distribution. Martin could not go back to his own company because the wholesalers, whom the distributors sent the books to, got very angry at Martin because he had left them and gone to American. He couldn't form his own company any more. So he had to go to DC and say, "Will you guys distribute me?" They said, "Yeah, but only eight books!"

CS: Was that why you switched from Atlas to Marvel Comics?
Lee: When we saw how well the books were starting to sell, I figured we ought to change our name and give ourselves a whole new image. So we thought a while and came up with the name Marvel, because that

was the name of the first book that we ever published, *Marvel Mystery Comics*. Also, I thought Marvel was a great word. You could make up slogans with it, like "Make Mine Marvel" and "The Marvel Age of Comics." All that kind of corny stuff, which I'm famous for—or *infamous*.

CS: Eventually, DC followed Marvel's lead.
Lee: DC decided to change the name of their company. They were called National Comics. Now we came up with Marvel Comics, which kind of says something. What did they come up with? And they spent thousands on experts to research this. They came up with the great name— DC. DC has about as much sex appeal as a rusty doorknob. "I'm with DC." Big deal.

CS: Once you rivaled them in sales, was it a problem staying ahead of DC?
Lee: No I don't know why, but they never realized what we were doing in our stories that was grabbing the reader. I had a lot of friends there and they used to tell me they would have an editorial meeting once a month and put our books down on the table and say, "Let's see if we can figure out why the Marvel books are outselling ours." They would look at the covers and one genius would say, "I know why! It's because there's more dialogue balloons on the covers." So the next month they would put a lot of dialogue balloons on their covers. The minute I found out about it, I took off all the dialogue balloons. It didn't make *any* difference in the sales. That wasn't what did it. But it must have driven them crazy! Then they would say, "It's because they use a lot of red on their covers." So that next month we would stop using red! We played this little game for months. They never caught on.

CS: Old-time DC editors have said that they would look at Jack Kirby or Steve Ditko's unrestrained art, and think fans were suddenly going for what the editors perceived as "bad" art. So they tried to copy that.
Lee: One of the toughest things in the world is really to know what bad art is, and what good art is. If you look at *Dick Tracy*, you would say this [Chester Gould] is not one of the world's greatest artists. It's kinda cartoony and awkward. But it's wonderful art because it's perfect for that kind of strip. There used to be an artist named Alex Raymond, who did *Flash Gordon*. *Flash Gordon* was colorful and exciting. But Raymond also did *Rip Kirby*. It was one of the best-drawn strips you'll ever see. Other artists used to use it for reference. But *Rip Kirby* was never successful because even though it was beautifully drawn, it was dull as

dishwater. It was just nice drawings. So when you talk about good or bad art, every strip requires a certain *style* of art. Sometimes something that is good for one strip won't be good for another.

I'll give you one difference in artwork it took them years to catch on to at DC. I tried to get our artists to exaggerate everything. For example, if a monster was approaching a hero or heroine, and our character is supposed to look scared like this [*reacts*] and our artist would draw it that way. I would say, "That's no good. When our character is scared. I want him to look like this!" [*bigger reaction*] "AUGHHH! Exaggerate it! And if somebody is punching somebody, you don't want this," [*throws a weak punch*] "because this is what you got in the DC books. You want this!" [*throws Kirby-style punch*] "I want that arm coming out of the socket." It's like in animation. There are directors, animators, and in-betweeners. The director does the key action drawings. The animator does middle poses. And the in-betweener does all the little poses in between. At DC, they would do it like the in-betweener. It's a simple thing, but even today I don't think they fully understand it.

CS: It's interesting how Kirby flowered as an artist once he left the restrictive atmosphere at DC for Marvel.

Lee: At DC they also had a lot of rules. They told the artist everything to do. The only thing I used to say was, "Be exciting. Do it your own way. You want six panels, do six. You want to make a full-page spread, do that." Ditko, on some of the Spider-Man stories, he would have nine panels, twelve panels, tiny little figures—a lot going on. I feel the best rule was no rules at all. Just let an artist do it the way he wants.

CS: Wasn't there more to Marvel's resurgence than art style?

Lee: Philosophically, there was another thing, and I had a big argument with Kirby about this once. We were being interviewed by Barry Gray in New York. He had a talk show. Jack and I went up there. He wanted to talk to us about Marvel and how it was selling. This was in the middle 1960s. Barry said, "I understand you people are starting to pass DC." And I said, "Well, we're doing the best we can, but they're such a big company and so rich, and we're just this little company." And Jack said, "That isn't true, Stan! Why don't you tell him we're better than them? And bigger than them." And I'm trying to shut him up. I said, "Jack, nobody likes anybody who's bigger and better. Let them think we're Avis. We're just trying harder." And Jack never understood that. You've got to use a little psychology.

CS: Why did it take you so long to come into your own as a writer?
Lee: Well, the reason I think is because I was doing everything the way my publisher wanted me to. I was very much a company man. I wasn't a rebel. "Hey, that's the way you want 'em. You're paying my salary. Fine." The industry never thought much of comics. It was a business, a way to make a buck. I'm afraid I felt the same way. Once or twice I wanted to try new things, and the people I worked for didn't want me to. They used to tell me I had to not use words of more than two syllables, and if I tried anything that was a little sophisticated: "Stan, don't do that. This is a children's medium. Don't write over the kids' heads. We won't make money. We won't sell the books." And I went along with it.

CS: Considering that you're known for your emotional writing, that's amazing.
Lee: Well, you can't be emotional when you think you're writing for young kids, or for idiots who are old but haven't got the capacity to understand. That was the mood of the industry in those days, really.

CS: Looking back, do you feel those twenty years of toiling in relative obscurity as a comics writer-editor were wasted?
Lee: No. I learned a lot, a hell of a lot! I learned a lot about artwork. Strangely enough, I've always been more interested in the art than the writing. In fact, even later on I always served as art director even when I became editor of publisher. The artwork was the thing. It was hard for me to tell writers how to write. It's hard to tell *any* writer how to write. But it's easier to say to an artist, "Your work is getting too convoluted. Simplify it." Or: "Use masses in your inking more than all that line work." Or: "Tone down your layouts," "Give me more long shots" or whatever. Somehow it's easier to work with artwork and it's more fun. I am very interested in the art. My big regret is that I have never drawn the strips. I wish I had studied art a bit more.

CS: You were an artist in your early days.
Lee: A cartoonist. In the Army, I illustrated training manuals and I did posters. But I never really worked at it after I got out of the Army.

CS: Tell me about the creation of the Fantastic Four. In hindsight, it looked as if you were reviving and reinventing old Golden Age Timely superheroes like the Human Torch, Flexo the Human Rubber Band, and the Blonde Phantom, giving them new twists.

Lee: Flexo? I don't remember him. There was Plastic Man. But I don't know any Flexo.

CS: He was a minor forties Timely character. You didn't ransack old Timely comics to create your Fantastic Four?

Lee: It's a strange thing. I've never done reference. I hate research. I never keep old books. If I wanted to go back, I wouldn't know where to look. Even today, if I'm doing a story and I have to find something out, I will call the office and ask one of the guys at Marvel. But I'm the first guy to admit it.

I liked Plastic Man. That's a great power, and nobody was using it. So I gave Reed Richards Plastic Man's power. The Human Torch I always felt had been a great character. We weren't using him. So I brought him back. As for the Invisible Girl, she's a girl so I don't want her to be strong. I don't want her to be Wonder Woman and punch people. So what power should she have? I figured, "Gee, what if she's invisible?" I knew there had been invisible people. There was *The Invisible Man*, the movie with Claude Rains. All I was trying to do was think of four powers that were totally different. The Thing was my favorite. I wanted to really work on him. I told Jack, "I want somebody who turns into a monster. The other three are able to change back so it does not affect them, but I want the Thing to be *bitter* because he's a monster and can't change back."

CS: I'm surprised you made one of the FF a monster. You had been scripting monster titles for years at that point. Weren't you sick of monsters?

Lee: No. But I didn't want to treat the Thing the same way. Actually, the Thing really did not come into his own until issue #3 or #4, when I started to get into his personality. In the first issue, I didn't write him the way I was going to write him later. It took me a while to get the feeling of it. But I knew what I wanted to do with him.

CS: Speaking of the monster titles like *Tales to Astonish* and *Amazing Adult Fantasy*, you seemed to write only those little five-pagers you did with Ditko. Why is that?

Lee: I was prouder of the ones I did with Ditko. I tried to make those the more O. Henry ones. I liked them the best. I liked working with Ditko on that stuff. He was wonderful! It's funny. When the *Twilight Zone* TV show came out—and there were two others like it, *One Step Beyond* or something [perhaps *Thriller* or *Alfred Hitchcock Presents*]—I used to get letters from readers "Hey, I just saw *Twilight Zone*, and they used one of your stories from issue so-and-so."

CS: What about the big monster stories Kirby drew? You never signed them. Who did those?
Lee: Oh, a lot of guys did 'em. I only did the ones I signed my name to. But there were some that I did that I didn't sign because I wasn't thinking of it. But there were other writers like Ernie Hart, Robert Bernstein, and Larry Lieber. I don't remember if they were writing the big ones or the little ones, but it might have been a combination. In those days, we weren't always signing them.

CS: Most people think you wrote the lead fantasy stories, like "Fin Fang Foom," even though you didn't sign them.
Lee: I did that one. If my name was on them, I did them. I *never* put my name on anything that I didn't write.

CS: "Stan Lee" started off as a pen name for Stanley Martin Lieber, then you changed it legally. Would it be fair to say Stan Lee is a creation of Stanley Martin Lieber?
Lee: Well, no. Stan Lee is the *same*. I didn't want to use my real name because I thought comics were just little kids' stuff and I figured some day I was going to write the Great American Novel. So I was saving my name.

CS: But the true Stan Lee writing style didn't seem to emerge until you starting doing letters columns and the Bullpen Bulletins. I'm inclined to think Stanley Martin Lieber wrote all your pre-Marvel comics and Stan Lee came to the fore in the 1960s.
Lee: Even though I was signing it "Stan Lee," you could probably say it was Stanley Lieber who was writing all the early stuff, and then I really decided to play up the "Stan Lee" for what it was worth. I didn't think of it that way consciously, but you do have a point.

CS: You grew up during the Great Depression. You've said in interviews that *The Spider* pulp magazine inspired your Spider-Man. You must have read other pulps like *Doc Savage*.
Lee: *Doc Savage* I loved!

CS: Did Doc influence the Fantastic Four? I'm thinking in particular of the idea of a skyscraper headquarters, which they both had in common.

Lee: I read *Doc Savage*. I liked it. I remember characters named Monk and Renny. I don't remember it that well. The only reason why I put the FF in a skyscraper headquarters was that I wanted to definitely base them in *New York*. So I figured there were three things: they could be in a brownstone, in a subterranean subway or in a skyscraper. I picked the skyscraper. It had nothing to do with *Doc Savage*.

CS: What other pulps did you read?
Lee: *G-8 and His Battle Aces*. I liked it. There was one you probably never heard of called *Captain Fury*.

CS: Cap Fury starred in a book called *The Skipper*.
Lee: What I remember of it was he had a boat, and it looked like a seedy, sleazy little wreck of a ship. But when he pushed a button, it turned into this high-speed, diesel-powered, fastest boat in America.

CS: It sounds like Cap Fury's name inspired Nick Fury.
Lee: I know what influenced me in some areas with Sergeant Fury. It didn't have a whole squad, but it was a movie called *What Price Glory?* [1926]. Edmund Lowe and Victor McLaglen played Sergeant Quirt and Captain Flagg. They were always fighting. They loved each other, but they were always fighting. I tried to get that feeling into *Sgt. Fury's* squad.

CS: If you loved *The Spider*, surely you read *The Shadow*.
Lee: It's a strange thing. I don't ever really remember reading *The Shadow*. I knew there was a Shadow. Either I did not like it or I just never got around to buying it. *The Spider* I read when I was eight years old. He punched people in the nose and left a spider mark. It was so dramatic.

CS: What else did you read?
Lee: I was a big science fiction fan. I read almost every SF pulp for a while—*Amazing Stories*, *Astounding* which later became *Analog*. *Astounding* was wonderful. [Editor] John W. Campbell was great. Strangely enough, I was never really into sword and sorcery. It was Roy Thomas who gave me the idea to do Conan. I had heard of Conan [whose adventures appeared in the pulp *Weird Tales*], but I didn't know anything about it. Roy said, "We ought to do Conan. We ought to do Conan." Just to shut him up, I said, "Do Conan." It turned out great. I loved horror stuff. *Dracula*. *Frankenstein*. I know I was influenced by *Jekyll and Hyde* and *Frankenstein* when I did the *Hulk*. I loved H.P. Lovecraft.

CS: Obviously, Lovecraft influenced Dr. Strange.

Lee: Not the way you've implied. I mean, if I were coming up with a name, I wouldn't go back and look at Lovecraft, and find a name. I loved the words! Like Liggoth and Ugulug.

CS: Who are your favorite writers?

Lee: Oh, I had so many. Believe it or not, William Shakespeare. When I was a kid, I didn't understand a lot of what he was writing, but I loved the language. I used to read it out loud. I love the Bible, and I'm not a very religious guy. But I loved the way it was written, just the phraseology. I used to think, "Who was this writer? I wish I could get him." When I did Thor, I remembered you would put a certain verb before the noun in the Bible. I loved Mark Twain, Edgar Allan Poe, Alexandre Dumas, Edmond Rostand. I loved *Cyrano de Bergerac*, *The Rubaiyat of Omar Khayyam*. I loved whatever all kids loved. I wasn't that different.

In terms of popular writers, Edgar Rice Burroughs, Sir Arthur Conan Doyle, and H.G. Wells. Burroughs was much better than he was given credit for. I read the Mars books as well as Tarzan. The way he would do a chapter and then leave off and go to something else and then leave that off—there were *always* cliffhangers—he had four or five cliffhangers going at the same time. He would keep coming back to them and I would think, "How can he keep it all in mind?"

Of course, one of my all-time favorites was Conan Doyle. Sherlock Holmes to me is a great a thing as you can get. He's the *ne plus ultra* superhero because a superhero should be believable. There was never a more believable character than Sherlock. There are still people today who go to look at 221 Baker Street in London. Sherlock Holmes was "alive." Doyle's writing was so great. Not only were his plots wonderful, but his characterization. If he was just telling you Sherlock Holmes went to the store, and he entertained someone at home, the dialogue! This guy drew characters with words that were fantastic. To me, Conan Doyle was a real master.

CS: Anyone else?

Lee: There was a guy named Leo Edwards. He wrote Poppy Ott and Jerry Todd. They were wonderful! You know what was great about them? They were humorous. They were like the Hardy Boys but funny. Edwards did something that probably gave me the idea for the Bullpen Bulletins. You never saw this in a book—these were hard-covers—at the end of each book, there were letters pages and they were fascinating!

CS: What entertains Stan Lee these days?

Lee: Oh, I like adventure. I like things with a *touch* of fantasy. I don't like them when they are too crazy or too far out. I like good drama. I hate depressing movies, though. On television, I will not watch the illness of the week or the tragedy of the week, these mini-series things. I've been too busy and it's to my everlasting regret, but I only read newspapers and trade magazines now, and I only watch movies on TV. I don't have time to watch the other shows.

CS: They say your favorite artist in the days before Kirby was Joe Maneely, who died tragically a few years before you started *Fantastic Four*. If Maneely had lived, where would he have fit into the Marvel Age of Comics?

Lee: If Joe Maneely had not died, he would have been the stellar artist in the business today. He was one of the fastest artists I ever knew, and among the most versatile. He did war stuff. He did weird historical stuff. Westerns. Probably the one thing he didn't excel at was romance, although he could do it. He also did comedy. In fact, he did a newspaper strip with me called *Mrs. Lyons' Cubs*. When he died, Al Hartley took it over. Joe could do *anything*. He was so fast, he could do a strip almost without penciling it. He would draw the borders, put a little stick figure here and there, and then he would take his pen or his brush and start inking. He was incredible. He was also the nicest guy you could ever find.

CS: It boggles the mind to think but for that fluke, Joe Maneely might have been the originating artist on *FF* or even *Spider-Man*.

Lee: If Joe had lived, we would have been doing many different magazines because I would probably have come up with other types of books for Joe to do. Very often I would come up with books for a certain artist. I would have an artist in mind for a book. I don't know if I would have done *Sgt. Fury* if Jack hadn't been available. Jack was the one guy I thought of for *Sgt. Fury*.

CS: I've always wondered about your choices on who inked Kirby. For example, Joe Sinnott, a very moody inker, inked the first Dr. Doom story in *FF* #5. did you choose him because his style fit that story, or was that coincidental?

Lee: It was probably a coincidence. The strange thing about it, I cared much more about who inked Kirby than Jack did. We used to discuss in the office the fact that Kirby never seemed to care who inked him. This is a guess on my part because I never asked him, but I think Kirby felt his style was so strong that it just didn't matter who inked him, that his own style would come through the way he wanted.

CS: Did you have a preferred Kirby inker?

Lee: I liked all of our inkers. Dick Ayers was very good on Kirby's stuff. Sinnott I felt was wonderful. I liked Sinnott, Ayers. Paul Reinman, and Sol Brodsky even, because all four of them could also pencil. Reinman was good because he was also a painter and he inked in masses like a painter.

CS: Tell me about working with Ditko on *Spider-Man*.

Lee: Steve Ditko was the best. He and Kirby both were so much alike. They were like Maneely, two of the greatest guys to work with your could ever want. If there was ever anything that Steve did that I felt ought to be done differently, or that didn't work out right, I would pick up the phone: "Steve, could we just do this over or change it?" He would do it in one minute. Quick. Uncomplainingly. It was done. He wasn't temperamental. He's the guy who designed the trademark we had in the upper left of our covers. I thought it was brilliant the way he came up with that. I can only say good things about him.

CS: So what brought about your parting at the peak of *Spider-Man's* popularity?

Lee: I don't know. But after a few years, something happened between Steve and me—and it was all on Steve's part. I mean, I felt the same, but he got angry. He was angry about something and I never knew what it was, really. Specifically. He never told me. He came in one day and he did say, "Stan, I don't like the way you're putting in the sound effects." I put in all the sound effects. "You're ruining my artwork with those sound effects." "Fine, I'll leave them out." I never wanted to get Steve angry. I left them out. A little later, he would come in and say, "Stan, I don't like the plots you're doing." "Plot them yourself, Steve." Whatever he didn't like, I said, "Fine. I'll change it." But it didn't help. I could sense he was unhappy about something. Then, one day—I don't ever think he told me himself—I heard from somebody that he had said he wasn't going to do any more *Spider-Man*. And that was it!

CS: Unlike Kirby, Ditko didn't like others inking his pencils.

Lee: He preferred inking his own. No one could ink Ditko as well as he could ink himself. Nobody. He was wonderful! And he was an absolute joy and delight to work with. And a nice guy. I didn't know him that well because he didn't come to the office that much. He worked at home and he was a very private person. I think he still is.

CS: Of all the comics you've scripted, does any stand out as your favorite?

Lee: I really don't know. I don't remember *everything* I've written. There might be one that I would love that I would answer if I remembered what it was. But there are so many stories. I liked the Galactus trilogy [*FF* #48–50]. I loved the *Silver Surfer* that I did with John Buscema. I loved that *Spider-Man* story [issue #33] where he is lifting up the things in the sewer, whatever the hell that was. There was a Thor story that nobody remembers where he's lecturing a bunch of hippies on why they shouldn't be hippies. There was a *Daredevil* story about a blind guy that I loved [issue #47]. There are so many . . .

CS: It sounds like you don't look back much.

Lee: You know the only time I look at my old stories? When I'm signing autographs and a kid will put a book up. I'll say, "Did I write that? It looks good." I have a few books at home, but I couldn't even find them. They're buried in closets.

CS: Which of your characters stand out as the most innovative?

Lee: It's tough to say. I would like to think they're *all* innovative. Spider-Man is probably the most successful, so I've got to be proud of him. I have a very warm spot in my heart for the Silver Surfer, because I have a chance to give vent to a lot of my corny philosophy in that strip. I like Thor, Dr. Strange. Whichever one I think of, I suddenly decide, "Gee, I like that one." I never think much of the Fantastic Four, but the other day I was reading some of *FF*s as though I had nothing to do with them. I thought, "Gee, these are great!" So I suddenly think those are good.

CS: Did you ever create a character you didn't like?

Lee: One. I needed a villain very quickly for a *Fantastic Four*, and I came up with the name Diablo, which I thought sounded great, like the Devil. I said, "Gee, Jack, you can draw this guy all black and scary and mysterious-looking." And then I realized I didn't know what to do with him. Jack drew the guy. I couldn't think what power he had or how to use him. But the book had to be drawn quickly because it was due to go to the engravers in a few days. I don't even remember what the story is now, but I know I wasn't too proud of it when I wrote it. And I wish I hadn't come up with that, because that was dumb.

CS: Ant-Man certainly wasn't among your most successful creations.
Lee: I'm going to tell you what I think is the reason Ant-Man never
became one of our top sellers or had his own book. We had him in *Tales
to Astonish*. I loved Ant-man, but the stories were never really successful. In order for Ant-Man to be interesting, he had to be drawn this small
next to big things and you would be getting pictures that were visually
interesting. The artists who drew him, no matter how much I kept
reminding them, they kept forgetting that fact. They would draw him
standing on a tabletop and they would draw a heroic-looking guy. I
would say, "Draw a matchbook cover next to him, so we see the difference in size." But they kept forgetting. So when you would look at the
panels, you thought you were looking at a normal guy wearing an
underwear costume like all of them. It didn't have the interest.

CS: The role of comics creator has changed radically from when you first
entered the field.
Lee: We people in comics are very lucky because we have fans. In the
early days, there were no such things. I used to do a little radio work in
the early days, and I would talk into that empty microphone and wonder, "Is anybody listening?" When I wrote comics years ago, I would
wonder, "Is anybody reading them?" You never got a fan letter. And
today to be in a field where there are conventions where you can go and
talk to the people you are writing for, and you get mail. I mean, this is
better than the novelists, newspaper writers, screenwriters. We're very
lucky to be in this field. I hope all the people appreciate it. I sure do!

CS: At your peak, you were one of the most prolific scripters in comics.
Do you miss that?
Lee: No, because I was working so damn hard. I made up so many,
many plots in my life—probably as much as anybody who has ever
lived—and I got tired of doing it. By the time I became publisher I said,
"Thank God I don't have to dream up any more stories!" You know
what I *do* miss now? What I love to do because it comes easy to me is
get somebody to draw a strip and give it to me to put the dialogue in. I
could do twenty pages in a day. That's fun. It's like doing a cross-word
puzzle. There are the panels in front of you. Very often you don't like
what the story is and you say, "I'm going to find a way to make it
good." In the later days, I did that with Kirby a lot. Most of the plots, he
had much more to do with them than I did. When he did give me the
artwork, a lot of times the plots were not the way I would have wanted

to do it. So I would change them in the copy and the story ended up *not* being what I'm sure Kirby expected. It was fun doing them. But I don't miss the sitting and dreaming up the plots.

CS: And you work differently with your brother Larry Lieber on the syndicated *Spider-Man* strip.
Lee: It's a funny thing. I do it now the old-fashioned way. I write a complete script and I give it to Larry or to whoever does the Sunday pages. They draw it and they send it back to me to proofread before it goes to the syndicate. I *always* find things to change. My own story! I'll read a balloon and think, "I should have said it this way." Cross it out and have it relettered. Every story at Marvel I wrote I edited myself, and I was probably tougher on them than another editor would have been. I always rewrote them. If there had been time to read it again, I probably would have found more things to change, but there was never time.

CS: What motivates Stan Lee?
Lee: Greed.

CS: Can't be just that.
Lee: I don't know. I like to work and I like people. One reason I *don't* like to write is that it's such a lonely thing. You are by yourself. I love what I'm doing now. We're talking. I'm a very gregarious person.

CS: When you look back at your long career, what gives you the most satisfaction?
Lee: You know, it's a funny thing. And this sounds like a self-serving remark, but it not only goes for me but for everybody in comics. So many people come up to me and say, "Stan, I want to thank you for your stories. Your books changed my life." Or: "They've made me decide to do this or that." Or: "They've made me interested in this." I have a feeling you can be a novelist who has written a bestseller and as many people won't come over to you and say. "I want to thank you for being such an influence on my life." It's something we in the comic book business should appreciate and feel good about, because in our own crazy way, we seem to affect a lot of people and their lives. We're important to many people.

An Afternoon with Stan Lee

JEFF MCLAUGHLIN / 2005

January 21, 2005, Beverly Hills,
California. Previously unpublished.
Printed with permission of Jeff
McLaughlin.

We headed out for lunch on Beverly Drive before Stan had to meet the folks at ABC Television for discussions of a possible upcoming project.

JM: I hope we can find a quiet place.
SL: Lunch hour around here? I hope we can find a table.

We proceed into one restaurant and there's a tiny bit of a wait, but we're quickly seated after I request a booth at the back. I spread out my papers and get the tape recorders set up while the waiter comes by to take our order.

Even though it's almost 1 p.m., Stan orders an omelette (but later regrets ordering it with cheese since it seems to stick to everything). He glances at his watch.

We have one hour and four minutes before we need to get going. We can continue the conversation in the car there and back. I'll try to talk fast.

JM: I brought two tape recorders just in case . . .
SL: Good idea.

JM: . . . because this one doesn't work well. I brought this long, long list of questions, and one reason I sent the list to you [earlier via email] is that this is a rare opportunity to meet with you so I have a lot of questions.
SL: It terrified me. But go ahead. Ask the important ones.

JM: Last night I pared the list down.
SL: Oh, that will be great.

JM: And simplified the questions. I tried to provide you with a lot of background . . .
SL: And another thing if we don't have time to cover everything . . . You use email . . . email me some questions that I can send answers back, or you can phone me, but email is better so I can answer them when I have the time.

JM: Exactly.
SL: Okay

JM: First question. Are academics justified in looking at comic books as an art form?
SL: I think that anyone is justified in looking at anything which is written or drawn or sculpted as a true art form. It merely depends on how well a thing is done. For example, it's conceivable there could be a comic book that is worthwhile as a Shakespearean play. As a matter of fact if Shakespeare and Michelangelo were to get together years ago and say, "lets do a comic book," and Shakespeare wrote it and Michelangelo illustrated it, who would say that this isn't a valid art form. So it really depends on who does it and how it is done. There can be bad novels, good novels, bad ballets, bad operas, and good ones. Everything depends on the quality, not on the manner in which it is presented. That was profound. (*He smirks.*)

JM: You've used that analogy before.
SL: I always do.

JM: But people can say, "I know Shakespeare was a writer *before*, and I know Michelangelo was an artist *before*," so how do we promote that the actual writers and the artists NOW that you've worked with . . .
SL: But the analogy holds because if you take a really good artist today and a really good writer and if they do a comic book, I would think it would be a very worthwhile, valid art form.

JM: Can you think of any examples?
SL: No, I don't. You know why? I don't like to. Because if I give an example, half of my friends will say, "Why didn't you mention me?" but I think what I'm saying is clear.

JM: Given that, what sorts of things do you think comic books add to our experiences?
SL: The same as any form of literature. You read a story, you either like it or don't. It either stays in your memory or it doesn't. Everything you hear and read and experience adds to your own body of experience whether it be a comic book or a bubble gum wrapper or Dostoyevsky. My conversing with you now is adding to my experience. The sums of my experience.

JM: Do you think there are any unwritten truths or universal truths that come out in comic books?
SL: Conceivably they could come out in anything. And it depends on whether the writer is skillful enough to put them in. Again, a lot of people get things out of a story whether it's a comic book, or a novel or a play or whatever, that the writer didn't even know was in there. I can't tell you how many people have read stories of mine and said, "Gee, Stan, I didn't know you were influenced by the writings of Nietzsche or someone." I certainly am not aware that I was influenced.

JM: For example, the Silver Surfer is often seen as being a "Christ-like figure."
SL: Oh, so often. I didn't think of that originally.

JM: In terms of [people reading in things that the writer didn't intend], when the Comics Code came out, and was put in place after the fifties' situation, you said once that it really didn't matter to you because you wouldn't do the kinds of things that they didn't want you to do anyway. How do you feel about that whole issue of a ratings system or going even further to the issue of censorship?

SL: I'm not as opposed to ratings systems as most people are. I think there are things that children shouldn't have to be exposed to—very young children. But that's the only caveat. I mean if someone is old enough, then I don't believe in ratings systems. It didn't affect me because mainly the comic book code was against sex and violence, and I tried not to have any undue sex in our stories, and I never believed in violence. To me our stories had action, and there's a difference between action and violence.

JM: What is that difference?
SL: Well, to me violence is something unpleasant, it's torture or people getting injured in ways that makes you grimace when you look at it. With the stuff I wrote, it was just usually super-powered people fighting super-powered people. Very rarely did someone get hurt. If someone got hurt, it was in a very normal way; it was usually a villain and he deserved it. I mean he'd get shot or something, but we didn't have torture, we didn't have anything that would make you turn away and say, "Oh, that's revolting."

JM: What do you think of comic books now?
SL: I can't answer that because I don't read them. I don't read them at all because I don't have time.

JM: You mentioned the villains deserving punishment. But they always come back, it seems, three issues down the road.
SL: It's very difficult to create new villains, just as it is difficult to create new heroes, so if you come up with a villain that the readers enjoy, you'd be crazy to kill them off forever. Just like Professor Moriarty in *Sherlock Holmes*. I'm a big fan of Sherlock Holmes. I wish he had written many more Sherlock Holmes stories in which he was opposed to Moriarty with the two of them battling. I love that.

JM: After the Reichenbach falls?
SL: Yup.

JM: I found letters in your archives that were very touching, moving letters from people, from children or parents commenting, "My son wonders why there are no (quote) 'negroes' in comic books," and so on. How have things changed since the sixties on that particular issue?
SL: Oh, they've changed tremendously since then. I like to think I was one of those who started the change. I introduced a black character a million years ago called the Black Panther. And a few others who I don't

even remember who they are now. Today you have people of all colors and nationalities, and that's how it should be.

JM: Women are well-represented in comic books, but their outfits tend to be a little more revealing than the male suits. It's hard to image them fighting without popping out, so to speak.
SL: That's something I always thought was very amusing. If I was a superheroine and I was going to go into battle, I would want to wear the most protective clothing I could. I wouldn't go semi-nude. However, that's sort of a convention of comic books. It's just a case that the publishers always felt that predominately comics are read by boys; boys like to look at drawings of voluptuous girls, so they took that liberty.

JM: Do you think that's a good message to be sending to boys?
SL: Nah, I don't think it's any message at all. I don't think kids think that people fight in bikinis.

JM: Here's a question that's a bit more philosophical . . .
SL: Excuse me, but I do think it's very stupid [to have women shown this way].

JM: I noticed when I came back to comic books after many years—because they got so expensive—it's only after I got a real job that I could start buying them. And reading back issues I thought, "My, how comics have changed over the years!"
SL: You mean with the semi-nude women?

JM: Yeah. Wearing the thong . . .
SL: I think it's stupid.

JM: My favorite is *X-Men*. I had a colleague over on the weekend and was showing him my copy of No. 1.
SL: You'll notice I didn't have Marvel Girl semi-nude. (*We both chuckle.*)

JM: One of the letters in your archive that I laughed at was from a professor who wrote you about *Fantastic Four*; he said, "Stan, did you know it cost me $12.50 to buy FF #1!"
SL: I do now!

JM: Wouldn't it be nice to purchase it for that price? Does that shock you, the price?
SL: No, no, I'm used to it. I've lived through it for years.

JM: Did you ever conceive that what you were doing would become so valuable?

SL: Of course not, of course not. I had no idea. I only hoped that the books would sell and I would keep my job. Nobody dreamed that comics would come what they are today. No, never.

JM: It was just a job to put food on the table.

SL: Exactly.

JM: A bit more philosophical. What role do you think religion plays in comic books? For example, given you have aliens, superheroes, different worlds, it doesn't seem to capture any specific . . .

SL: I can't speak for comic books in general. I can only speak of mine. As far as mine, I never thought of religion. There was only one moral concept or precept that I tried to follow, I tried to portray and to proselytize. That was, "Do unto others as you would have them do unto you." I never tried to make it look like the characters were Catholic or Jewish or Muslim. I wanted every reader to relate and enjoy the story.

JM: You didn't want to isolate people.

SL: Right. Not at all. Unless there was a story point. I can't remember all the stories I wrote, but maybe there was one where somebody had to be Catholic. I think in *Sgt. Fury* I made one of the members of the platoon Jewish, I called him Izzy Cohen, but only because I wanted the platoon to be multi-racial. In fact I had a black man, a Jewish man, an Italian, a Norwegian, an Englishman . . . I forget, but that was the only reason. But I never played it out. I never thought it was my place as a comic book writer to emphasize religion.

JM: In your writing, and this relates to others' writings too, the superhero tries to save the day, but they don't really try to change the day, they don't try to improve the world.

SL: But I would think that by saving the day, you are improving the world. It's just like the policemen whose job is to just catch the criminals. I don't know how you can improve the whole world. If there is a way to do that, I wish someone would show me. You can be a Mahatma Gandhi, you can be a Jesus Christ, you can come along with philosophy that would make people think differently and behave differently, but our heroes were not philosophers particularly. They were action heroes because that's what sold, so it was just our stories were all, at least my stories were just a good guy versus a bad guy. Now I tried to put in, whenever I could, beneficial themes. I remember when we had a lot of hippies in this country, I guess it was the sixties . . . I didn't care for them. And I had this story dealing with them starring Thor, god of thunder, and there was this one scene, and he was in this ice cream parlor, I think, talking to a bunch of kids, hippies, and he's saying, "If you're dissatisfied with this world, you're not helping by dropping, why don't you plunge in and make it better?" I said it better when I wrote it. And every so often, I put in what was my philosophy, but again I tried not to make it religious or parochial. I did that a lot with the Silver Surfer mostly—I tried to let him say things like, "What is wrong with the human race? Don't they realize they are living in a veritable paradise? Why don't they appreciate it?" And so forth. Again, I worded it better than that, but that kind of thing.

JM: Was the Silver Surfer your mouthpiece?

SL: In a way, in a way. It gave me the chance to write a lot of things I thought and felt. Because he was from another world coming here, and I was able by his reaction to things to show how I felt we would seem to somebody who wasn't used to us, because I always think that somebody from another world coming here would probably think we were all insane.

JM: Well, I don't know if you want to deal with this question right now, but you might want to think about it. Obviously, you're famous for one line that everyone knows that you wrote that has significance that is very philosophical. I want to know if you want to expand upon that particular issue.

SL: I don't know what more I can say about it. I mean it really speaks for itself. I feel that if you do have great power, you have great responsibility not to misuse it. And to use it the best that you can to do good. I mean it's so obvious that I'd be gilding the lily if I tried to add anymore. I wrote another line that I had forgotten about, and I had read it and somebody showed me the other day. "Stan, this is as good or better than 'With great power comes great responsibility.' " "What? What?" and he showed me. And it was a line, I think it was in the *Fantastic Four*, when somebody is talking about power, and I have one of the characters saying something like "the one with the greatest . . . there's one man, who nobody . . . nobody is all powerful except one and he . . . he only used his power for peace." Oh shoot, now I don't remember the exact line. It was a good line, I have to admit. "Oh, and his greatest power is . . . peace" . . . not peace, but something like that. [The line is: "All-powerful? There is only one who deserves that name! And His only weapon—is love!" spoken by the Watcher in *Fantastic Four* #72.]

JM: You mentioned the Silver Surfer a moment ago. This is out of your screenplay on the Silver Surfer, the last paragraph . . . (*I hand him a copy.*)
SL: You know something? I was good. I was really good.

JM: What was interesting about this script that you wrote is that the script reads very much like poetry.
SL: Well, I used to talk about that. I don't know if a lot of readers are aware of it but I tried to write some stuff like prose poetry. I'm very conscious of the rhythm of words. I always knew what I wanted to write. I'm a fast writer. I don't have to spend a long time thinking of what to say, but sometimes I would spend a lot of time thinking of, "Should I put this word first or that . . . would the rhyme be better . . . wait a minute, I think it needs a word of two syllables rather than one to give it the right flow." I'm always thinking that way, half the time subconsciously. That's the reason I loved Shakespeare when I was young. I didn't understand most of it but the words were like music. I mean they had a rhythm to them that was magnificent.

JM: Another thing I came across in the archives is a poem that you wrote, "SUPERHERO." (*I pass it on to him.*) Remember that?
SL: (*reads it and starts to laugh*) I was really good! (*says this as if he was genuinely surprised by this new awareness*) How did these things get to the archives? Who puts them in there? (*laughs*) Do you have a copy of my poem "God Woke"? It's like the most important thing.

JM: It's not in the archive.
SL: Oh, it's not? You got to ask me to send you a copy. It's a long poem, and I think it's my all-time classic.

JM: It was fun digging through all your papers. I was like a child in a candy store. And it was funny because once and a while the archivist would come over and be excited to see what I was looking at.
SL: I'm very impressed.

JM: I came across your original outline of the *Fantastic Four*.
SL: I even wrote a treatment for a *Spider-Man* movie.

JM: Yes.
SL: Do you have that?

JM: Yup.
SL: Good. With Doctor Octopus?

JM: Uh huh. One thing I did notice in the archives was that there were no scripts . . .
SL: What scripts?

JM: For your comics. You never saved them?
SL: Why would I save them? Who knew? And now it doesn't mean anything to save what I write because it's on a computer.

JM: It's almost like that story that I heard from my parents, "Oh I remember my mom threw out all my comics; oh, if I only had them."
SL: My mother never threw them out. She was very happy that I had them. I threw them out, like a moron.

JM: I know children's literacy is very important to you.
SL: Do you have the information about when I tried to start the Entertainers for Education?

JM: I have to check on that one.
SL: I was going to start, what to call it, a charity or an organization, the point being so many kids today are bored in school. They feel the curriculum is irrelevant, and even if it wasn't, it's boring. And here in Los Angeles: the center of the entertainment world. If we could make teaching entertaining, just think what a good thing that would be. So I wanted to start an organization that would have entertainers, and we would do two things. We would teach teachers how to be entertaining. So many teachers simply get in front of a class and say what they have to say, not like an entertainer, but just drone on. Like how often have we gone to hear a speech? Some speakers are wonderful, and some speakers put you to sleep. They just read the pages. And there so many things that teachers can do. If you are teaching about Christopher Columbus, instead of saying, "I want you to remember that he discovered America in 1492 and Queen Isabella gave him the money and blah blah blah"—if a teacher would say, "Alright class, we're going to do a little play. Johnny you'll be Christopher Columbus. Mary you be Queen Isabella. You are the admirals; you are members of the court. The rest of the class, you are members of the court. Christopher, or rather Johnny, I want you to convince Queen

Isabella to let you sail around the world—that the world is round—even though everyone knows that the world is flat. How would you convince her? And Isabella, you decide whether he convinces you or not. And the rest of the class, you judge." And make it exciting; make it a contest like the kids feel they are participating.

There's nothing you can't make interesting if you create it as entertainment. And when I was in the Army, I wrote training films and training manuals, and I wrote them in humorous ways. When I had to do . . . you have the information? When I had to do a book about finance, and I created a character named Fiscal Freddy? So that's what I mean. Unfortunately things happen, and I never got around to finishing Entertainers, to doing that. I got too busy. But in the beginning I thought it would be great. We had a lot of big movie stars who wanted to be part of it. If I were retired now, that is probably what I would work on now. I mean what could be more interesting than history and geography and science? If it isn't taught in a dull way. Every inner city kid would want to be a scientist if people would teach it the right way. Sorry, I didn't mean to take so long.

JM: That's one reason why I think philosophy and comic books can work together . . .
SL: Philosophy goes together with everything when you think about it.

JM: Here's a note you wrote. (*I pass him a note that reads, "Write an adult philosophical novel as a child's story."*)
SL: Wow. Yeah, I was always making notes for things that I wanted to do but never got around to doing them.

JM: But it struck me, that "write an adult philosophical novel in the form of a children's story," and that captures some of the work you do with comic books.
SL: In a way.

JM: Jack Kirby said that he doesn't have any messages in there [comic books], but "I just do it as entertainment." But if you look back at *Captain America* during the Second World War, if there isn't a message in there . . .
SL: The point is that Jack and all of us, we were mainly writers writing interesting stories, exciting stories. We based them on something going on, but the message wasn't the first thing, the exciting story was the first thing.

JM: What sorts of things were you writing on?

SL: Well, if were fighting a world war against Hitler and this is the thing uppermost in everyone's mind, how can you not write stories about it?

JM: Another quote I had from the late great Will Eisner . . . he said that he started writing graphic novels because he couldn't tell children about heartbreak in comic books. He couldn't do this for kids.

SL: Well (*shrugs*) . . . Okay . . .

JM: Are you suggesting that you can do it a different way?

SL: (*Doesn't answer*) How we doin' on time? We have a half hour. Be sure to eat. While I'm talking I want to see you eat. Have we covered all the important stuff?

JM: Oh, no. If we can go back to "with great power comes great responsibility." How do you think that applies to the government, police, people who are wealthy and so on, who have great power in different fields?

SL: I think it applies to everyone. I think a wealthy person who has more money than he needs to live comfortably should think of good things to do with his extra money. I think a person in government who is in a position of power should be trying to do the best he can for his nation. Of course, they all claim they are and they do . . . (*I chuckle.*) You won't find an elected official who says, "I'm not trying to do the best for my fellow man." Some are just more successful than others.

JM: Do you think some go too far though, trying to exercise that power?

SL: How can you go too far to try and do good? Unless you're crazy and your idea of good isn't good. I will add, that obviously you can go too far— it is quite possible, though hard to believe, that Hitler was doing good by everything he did. So the point I said, you got that crazy person . . .

JM: One of the things that comes up in literary criticism and philosophy, and something you mentioned a while ago, that you might write something and not intend a certain message, and rightly or wrongly someone reads into it, sometimes okay, sometimes not. When you are coming up with your characters, your major characters that people know you for, do you ever look back and say, "the Incredible Hulk is a great representation of the beast that's in us all, that you have to control it or let it loose," or that Spider-Man, who is altruistic to a fault . . .

SL: No, never thought of it. I just thought, "Gee, I bet the readers would enjoy stories about this character." It's just again . . . pictures for entertainment.

JM: Do you have anything against people trying to read it that way?
SL: No, it's just that so many people do, and I'm used to it. I guess we all do. You read something, and everyone takes something different away from what they read or what movie they see. We all have our own way of looking at things and interpreting things.

JM: In one of your Soapboxes, where you bring up the notion of "do unto others . . ."
SL: I think that should be the universal religion. If everybody adhered to that, it would be impossible to do wrong.

JM: Actually most religions do have something like that.
SL: Do they?

JM: [We were talking earlier about] messages and relating the comic book to World War II. Some people criticize comic books for being too simplistic a venue for that sort of thing. Do you think that's a just concern?
SL: Well, comic books are simplistic because . . . when you are writing a novel you can take page after page to explain a point. In a comic book, you have to do it in a few words. No doubt about it. You can't put as much in a comic book as in a novel or even in a movie. You do the best you can with what you have to work with.

JM: One of the aims I have is to raise questions that people haven't raised with you.
SL: Great.

JM: I'm sure after almost seventy years in the business, it gets a little tiring answering the same questions.
SL: I don't know how you are going to come up with too many new ones, since I think I've answered everything. (*He draws out the word so that it sounds like "evvvverrrryythiinng."*)

JM: One thing I saw in your archive—and I think I have it with me—is quite humorous . . . it is a list of all the questions that Stan gets asked time and time again.
SL: (*to waiter*) Check please.

JM: But then with the infamous *Spider-Man* drug story—I also found a copy of the letter that they wrote to you to ask you if you would have some kind of impact on . . .

SL: Really? That's wonderful! (*reads it with great interest*) I'm so glad you found that!

By the way, that poem I wrote, "God Woke," I recite that on a DVD that I did with actor-director Kevin Smith. We did a DVD together where he interviews me, it goes on forever. There's a picture of the two of us on the cover. I think it's called "Marvel Monsters" and something else beginning with "M," and one of the added features is me reciting the poem. So if you can get a hold of that . . . if you can't, ask my assistant Mike to get one for you. (*A cell phone rings nearby.*) Is that you or me?

JM: Not me . . . Another thing that I thought you might find enjoyable . . . (*I hold up a picture of a woman on a cover of a book.*)

SL: That's my wife!

JM: I know!

SL: You know, I enjoyed doing those books so much.

JM: Lucky man . . . (*We both laugh.*)

SL: Wow, you got everything. I don't know if you found out about this, but I printed the *Blushing Blurbs* and golf books myself. I printed ten thousand copies and sold out, and it never occurred to me to do more. I was only about twenty years old. I was stupid, but I loved doing that . . .

JM: In the thirties, when you first started out, there were many new immigrant families in the comic business. Was there an attraction . . .?

SL: When you think about it, we got into every business, every business. I don't think there was a disproportionate amount. I got into it accidentally. I heard there was a job opening in the company, and I didn't realize I'd be put in the comic book department, and I walked up and they did comics, and I thought I'd stay a while and get some experience and get out into the real world. I never said to myself that I wanted to be a comic book writer. It was the last thing I wanted to be.

JM: And at that time comics weren't viewed that well.

SL: They were viewed terribly. I was ashamed to admit I did comics. People would thumb their noses at it. Well, not that bad. Almost like a pornographer. Everybody thought they were for very little kids or stupid older people. I think one reason that people got into it, not so much the writers but artists . . . if you were an artist, what could you do to make a living? The most logical thing is to do comics, you know what I mean? That's why in the beginning a lot of artists wrote their own stuff, because there weren't many writers. Here's a bit of information that nobody's been told before.

JM: Looking back, one of your comments you made is that you changed your name because you wanted to save your real name for when you write that great American novel.
SL: Yeah, I thought I would write something great, and I was so embarrassed to be doing comic books.

JM: But the impact you have had is far more than had you written the great American novel.
SL: No, I might have written the next *War and Peace*.

JM: But then no one would have read that either! (*We both laugh.*)
SL: Good. Good.

JM: When I mentioned to people I was coming to meet you, everyone I spoke to had a smile on their face. They always connected your name with something in their past . . .
SL: That's very nice. (*He is visibly moved.*)

JM: Someone asked me why some people still read comic books when they grow up, and others say, "Oh, that's part of my childhood."
SL: Silly question for people to ask you that. Who can account for what people enjoy? Some people enjoyed them, and as they get older they still enjoy them. Some enjoyed them, and then when they get older they lose interest. Some people like to play certain games. When I was a kid I enjoyed playing checkers on a board. I don't now. It depends on everyone's individual taste.

JM: You never really created a strong solo heroine like Wonder Woman. Is that because comics are geared to young boys?
SL: That's the reason. Boys as a rule were the ones who bought comic books. It's that way today, although they are trying to get more girls into it. There are now some books that are more aimed to girls. These new Japanese Manga comics have a much larger girl readership than the average American comic. It's a strange thing. Remember there were those two sets of books, the *Hardy Boys* and *Nancy Drew*? Now, girls could very well enjoy reading the *Hardy Boys*, but no boy is going to

pick up *Nancy Drew*, because that would be considered sissy. For some reason, boys will read what boys read and sometimes girls will, but a boy would hardly ever pick up a girl's title. And that's one of the reasons. And that's one of the best explanations you'll ever hear. (*He laughs.*)

I can see when you write the book, after you write my answer you add "and Stan Lee conceitedly added . . ."

JM: (*I laugh.*) Well, I would hope once I pull this all together, I'd send it back to you . . .
SL: Oh no, no, don't make me. I don't have the time . . . I have confidence in you. Send me the book when you finish. Trust me.

JM: Okay, I just wanted to make sure [that I represent Lee well].
SL: You don't know how little time [I have] to reread the stuff I write to see if I made mistakes. I'm up to here with the stuff I have to do.

JM: Why are you so busy?
SL: I love it. I love doing lots of things. First of all, it may be psychological, but if I'm working on a lot of projects and if one doesn't sell, if two don't sell, it's no big deal because I have a lot of others. But if you concentrate on one thing and it bombs, you're devastated. So I got about forty different projects going on around here and there, and it keeps me busy, and I like being busy, and its fun . . . wondering each time the phone rings or I get a new e-mail, what will it be.

JM: You've branched into so many areas. Many creators, artists, novelists, etc., stick to one thing.
SL: Matter of taste. Do what you like to do. I can't speak for other people . . . Hey, we're making progress here!
(The waiter comes back and takes our plates.)
JM: Looking at the fan mail you got, not only the range, but what impressed me was the seriousness in which you responded to people.
SL: I tried to answer every single fan letter I ever got. I do it today. I answer it immediately so I know it's answered. I'd hate to think that there is someone out there who tried to contact me and never heard from me. I know when I was a kid, I would write letters. There was one guy named Troy Gibbons—he was a columnist and he later died in an airplane crash, but he had a column in the *New York Journal* at that time, and to me he was like a god. He was a man who wrote a column, and his name was in the paper, and his column was on the comics page, and so I always saw it when I was

a kid. And I don't know why, but one day I wrote him a letter: "Dear Mr. Gibbons, I am a fan, I like your column . . ." And I got an answer: "Dear Stanley Lieber, Floyd Gibbons asked me to thank you for your letter. It was nice to hear from you." I know now it was obviously a form letter. But I ran to my mother, "Look! I heard from Floyd Gibbon's secretary! He must have read my letter!" It kept me going for weeks. I don't want any kid or anybody to be disappointed.

JM: Perhaps somewhat related, you started the practice of giving credits to the artists and writers and inkers and so on. Is that to make a connection between the readers and who was doing the book?
SL: Two reasons. One, I thought it should be because they deserved the credit. Two, like the movies, it would help. In the movies there are fans of the directors, actors, screenwriters maybe. Nobody could be a fan of comics because nobody knew who did them. Put the name of the writer, or the artist, then the reader could say, "I like Joe Blow." "Yeah? I think Tom Smith is better." And it gets them involved. I, of course, like to do everything lightly or humorously. So I used to write "written with great aplomb by Stan Lee, drawn with magnificence by Jack Kirby." I tried to always write things that would give them a chuckle and surprise them. We gotta go.

(We dash from the restaurant and proceed to meet up with Stan's business partner, Gill Champion. The two of them are scheduled for what will turn out to be a very short (and successful) meeting at ABC Television. So even though it's a gloriously sunny day, we decide it's best to keep the roof up on Stan's 1995 black Mercedes convertible so we can continue our talk.)

JM: How do comic books differ from movies? What do they do better?
SL: I don't think they do anything better than movies, but there is one thing they do that you can't do well in a movie, and I'm one of the people that really started it, doing the most of it. And that's thought balloons. I think I'm the one who really started using thought balloons in order to show what the characters were thinking, which helps the reader get to know the character, and that's one thing a movie can't do or does with great difficulty.

JM: Sort of like voice-overs. It works for a while and then gets annoying.
SL: You can't do it a lot, right. But other than that, whatever you do in a comic you can probably do better in a movie. Today. It didn't used to be

true, because years ago you could draw things that they could never put on the screen. But today so many directors have told me that there's nothing you can imagine that can't be put on a screen.

JM: That unique combination of images and words—not just a novel with words or a painting, just an image—what do you think the two of them bring together? What kind of synergy do they have?
SL: Obviously you can see what is being described, instead of relying on your imagination. Now, a lot of people have said that they don't like people reading comics because it stifles your imagination—when you read a book you can imagine what everything is, but in a comic you see it. But I don't think that's a valid argument, because nobody criticizes the motion picture, and nobody says you should never go to the theater to see a Shakespearean play, you should only read it as a book.

JM: We were talking earlier about comics being similar to a movie in recognizing the people who are involved, but if I'm watching a movie, I'll say, oh, that's a Spielberg film, that's a Julia Roberts film. How do we separate the creator from everyone else who plays a role in it?
SL: Well, you can't, because the same holds true for a movie. You might say that's a Spielberg film, but somebody else says that's a Harrison Ford film. Somebody might read *Spider-Man* and say that's a Stan Lee script or somebody might say a Steve Ditko script. It depends on what the readers are interested in. Obviously, like a movie, comics are a collaborative venture.

(The COO of POW! Entertainment, Stan's company, is Gill Champion. He is sitting in the backseat with his ear pressed to his cell phone talking away to the folks at ABC, giving them our estimated time of arrival. Stan is threatening to pull the car over and make him walk if he isn't quieter.)
SL: (*asks Gill*) Do you want the top up?

JM: He wants the window up.
SL: I thought I had put it up. I have to stop somewhere to put the top up. (*Gill is talking loudly into the phone so that the other person can hear over the noise of the traffic.*) Gill, you know there's a word in the English language, it's called "whisper." Can I make a right turn here?

JM: Your characters have evolved over time, once you've moved on to other things, and you've been very gracious when people ask you what you think of so-and-so's treatment of Spider-Man. For example, when

Todd MacFarlane gave the costume bigger eyes, you said, "It was interesting." How do you feel when other people take them over?
SL: I don't feel that these are my characters. I might feel that way if I owned them. I have no propriety right in them. Marvel Comics owns them lock, stock, and barrel, and whatever they want to do with them, they have the right to do it. I may think this way is better than that way, or that I like my version better than what they did, but what is the point of complaining about it? And every time a new artist takes over a script, that new artist is going to do it his way. See, I was a little different. When I was head editor I tried to insist that all the artists drew a script the way it had been drawn before, but, oh, for years now, it's like when an artist takes it over, it becomes his script, and he can make the characters taller, shorter. If you look at FF and Reed Richards, Johnny and Sue, you can hardly now recognize them. If you didn't see them in the context of the script you wouldn't know who they were.

JM: How do you feel about revisionist history then? Changing origins for example. The example that comes to mind is the miniseries called *Truth*, where the first Captain America's were in fact African Americans.
SL: Well, let me put it to you this way. When you have been publishing magazines for year after year after year, the problem is that you hope the reader doesn't get bored and say, "I've read this book before, it's the same old thing." Now you can either be clever enough and keep the origin intact and come up with new gimmicks all the time, or you can take an easier way out—change the origin, change the sex, change the birthplace, change everything. And if it were me, I would try to keep the origins intact, but again, I don't like to criticize that, because it's a business. They want to sell books, and if they honestly think that changing the origin will renew a reader's interest, then they have every right to do it.

JM: Surely an artist has to be confined to certain parameters. You can't make Peter Parker female, for example.
SL: I wouldn't think they could do that.

JM: So it's hard for an artist to put his or her own stamp on a series or character. Is there a sense that, just as you mention, you don't own it, Marvel owns it, they can do whatever they want? But now reading the paper today about the lawsuit you just won against Marvel . . .
SL: No, that won't affect it. I still won't own the characters.

JM: That has nothing to do with signing them over?

SL: Marvel owns them, has always owned them, and will always own them. The lawsuit just has to do with the contract saying that I'm to receive a certain share of the profits. That's all.

JM: Where this is leading is a question about intellectual property rights. I can come up with something, I can sign it over to Marvel or Marvel owns it, because I'm just an employee of the company . . .

SL: Well, it really depends on the initial agreement. When I started working for Marvel, the standard procedure was that the company owned what the artist and writer did. The artist and writer were employees—workers for hire. Some people, as the years went by, got smart and said, "Wait a minute, I'm willing to create a new character for you, but either I want to own it or own a part of it." So again it depends on the deal that you make.

JM: Do you think the latter situation is better in recognizing the creative talents of the person?

SL: I don't know. I worked under the former situation and so did all the guys I was with, and we were pretty creative, even though we didn't own the characters. I think if you are going to be creative, you're going to be creative, and you're not going to hold yourself back because you don't own the thing. It's still a job. You still want to be successful. But if you're smart and you're a creator today, you certainly try to get some rights to what you're doing. Now again, it's not always possible because the person you're selling to may not like what you're doing so much, and he says, "Look, I'm willing to do it and I'll own it, if not, goodbye, I don't need it," and you have to decide. Do I want to do it? It's like applying for a job—do you want to take it or not?

JM: You've been on both sides of the table. What sorts of rights or responsibilities do you think the individuals have? What rights do or should the creator have, versus the person paying your salary?

SL: Again it's hard to say, the person who is publishing the book is investing a lot of money. It costs a lot of money to publish. He is paying salaries, paying rents. And if the book doesn't sell, he's the one who loses the money, so he certainly has a lot of rights and should be listened to. And by the same token at the same time, it's an art form and the person . . . if the creator owns the script, he should certainly have the right to do it the way he wants. It's like anything else. You have to hope the creator and the publisher see eye to eye, and when you do, you have a good situation. When they don't, it's difficult.

JM: In the book I gave you [Thomas Inge's *Conversations with Charles Schulz*], there's a couple comments that came up in interviews regarding *Peanuts* and marketing. Schulz would get his back up when they would say, "You're selling too many products." And he says, "Look, I haven't changed the cartoon, everything else is sort of gravy." Do you feel the same way, that you should be able to capitalize as much as you can?

SL: Well, I think you certainly should have the right to capitalize on your creation. Now, there are a lot of people who feel that the minute you start making too much money on something, you are no longer an artist, you become commercial. I don't think there's anything wrong with that, so long as the art remains good and popular. And if people want to buy toys and games and dolls based on that, I think it's wonderful. They do it with Spider-Man. And it makes people very happy. I know our house-keeper, she has so many Spider-Man dolls and little Spider-Mans hanging from her automobile. She loves them. Why deny the public a chance to have representations of something they like?

JM: I read a newspaper interview or comment from 1972 that you were making one of your famous college appearances. The journalist wrote there was great rapport between you and the crowd. "To Lee it was an enjoyable business, to the freaks it was a sort of cosmic experience." To me that sounds rather negative.

SL: No, I think it's wonderful. By freaks he meant devoted fans, and he meant to them it was something so wonderful, it was like a cosmic experience, and that's very important to me as a business. Whatever you do to make money is a business. I'm sure when Michelangelo was doing the Sistine Chapel and getting paid for it, to him it was a business, but to the world later on it became one of the great works of art. When Charles Dickens was writing his stories, he was a commercial writer—there's nothing wrong with that.

JM: Is there a way we can promote more of the writers, artists, and editors of comics? In movies, fans can list off names of all the people involved.

SL: You do it the way I said, by listing credits, but beyond that what can you do?

JM: I'm speaking more of the fact that there are film classes, art classes, but not a lot of comic book classes.

SL: You can only do that if there's a demand. Believe me, if there's a demand they'd have that. There's a lot of colleges that teach courses on the comic. There's all these comic conventions across the country with regularity. There's a lot of that. Comic book stores, comic book people are always asked to speak at different schools and organizations. It's done pretty regularly now more than when I started out.

JM: But during the late sixties you were on tour constantly. What happened in these sessions that you gave?

SL: I would just talk about comics in a way that would make Marvel sound wonderful. My whole purpose was to promote Marvel. And if I promoted Marvel, I was also promoting comics in general. But I was really speaking as an ambassador for Marvel. That was my job, that was my crusade.

JM: How did you get to become the face of comic books?

SL: Because I was the one guy who spent years traveling all over the country, doing countless radio and newspaper interviews and later television interviews, and nobody else bothered. And nobody could do it that well. Sometimes people would do an interview . . . I'll never forget, Jack Kirby was one of the greatest guys I've ever known, but he was not good at public relations. Years ago when we were working on the *Fantastic Four*, we were just getting started, and there was this very well known radio talk show host called Barry Grey, and Barry Grey invited me onto his show to talk about comics and especially the *Fantastic Four*. I was thrilled. I said I'd like to bring Jack Kirby with me, because he's an integral part of this thing, and Barry said great. And so Jack and I went to the studio. Barry said, "Well, you people at Marvel of course are sort of the runner-up, DC is the big comic book company, but you guys are coming up pretty well, doing a good job." And Jack said: "We're bigger and better than DC! We're much better, we're bigger! We sell more books than they do!" And I was kicking him under the table trying to get him to shut up, because I liked the idea that we were thought of as this little company sniffing at the heels of the big company, because that's what gets people to root for you, and Jack didn't understand that, and he didn't understand why I didn't want him to say, "We're bigger, better than they are and sell more books!"

JM: Rooting for the underdog . . .

SL: Well, at that particular time it was better to be known that way.

JM: Now, it may have flipped around the other way starting in the seventies. Did that have a negative impact?

SL: Oh, well, they can't deny it. Marvel is the biggest. Whether it has a negative impact or not depends on . . . I'm not the spokesman really anymore. I don't know how they would handle it. I'd know how to handle it. I don't know who does the interviews now or if anyone does.

(We are passed by a fancy car.)

SL: Hey, is that the new Bentley coupe? I'd sure like to get a look at it. Maybe we'll get a look at it when it turns. Okay, go ahead.

JM: Are there any instances where someone you were working with, or under you when you were editor, where they had a significantly different social perspective on it than you? I know Ditko, for example, is an objectivist. Was there any of that going on?

SL: No, we didn't really talk about Objectivism or anything like that. Sometimes we would, and rarely, but we would disagree on story points.

JM: Nothing underlying any story point . . . ?

SL: Not that I was aware of.

JM: Just what would be the best thing for this character at this time.

SL: No, nothing I can recall.

JM: You used to stand on your desk and act out scenes? And you would say, "The character doesn't put the book down, he THUMPS it down!"

SL: Well, sometimes for the artist, they would be drawing and there wasn't enough action, it wasn't interesting enough, exciting enough, and the best way to illustrate what I wanted them to draw was to act out the scene, which I enjoyed doing because I'm a ham anyway.

JM: Speaking of being a ham, you have this persona that everyone knows, alliterations and the use of language in a very significant and methodical way. Did you just develop that? Putting words together in a certain way—did this come natural?

SL: I don't know how to answer that. It's just something I liked to do. I wasn't born putting words together, as I told you. When I read a lot as a kid, when I read the Bible or Shakespeare, I was really impressed. Even though I might not have understood a lot of what they said, I listened to the rhythm of the words and the way sentences were structured. Believe it or not I used to love reading poetry as a kid, and there were good ones and bad ones, and I hated the bad ones and loved the good ones. And the ones that I thought were good would be considered corny now, because I loved the ones with good rhymes and good meter, and the one thing I hated were the kinds of ones in the *New Yorker Magazine* where a) you didn't know what they were saying, b) they didn't rhyme, and c) there seemed no rhythm to them. Maybe I shouldn't say that because it sounds like I'm knocking the *New Yorker*, which I love. I never understood the poems in it. Free verse. I hated free verse.

JM: How can it be a poem if it doesn't rhyme? (*I laugh.*)
SL: To me.

JM: Okay, some "what if?" types of questions for you. If DC didn't come up with the *Justice League*, which was the reason for your wanting to come up with the *Fantastic Four* [to compete against DC], what would have happened?
SL: Your guess is as good as mine. I would have done something else, but Martin said to me, "Let's do a book, with four characters like the *Justice League*," but that's all. I didn't copy the *Justice League*. The *Fantastic Four* is completely different. It's just it was the first time I think he said to me, "Let's put a bunch of heroes together." That was the only influence that the Justice League had—it was a lot of heroes we put together.

JM: What if after that . . . was *Spider-Man* next? Or wait. It was the *Hulk*.
SL: The *Hulk*.

JM: It lasted six issues, right?
SL: Yup. The first run.

JM: Is that because he was grey?
SL: No, he was only grey in the first issue, he was green after. No, it's because Jack didn't have time to draw him, and we never thought it was that important, and we got involved in the *X-Men* and other things. In those days we didn't know what would be big and what wouldn't. But then later on, we went back to the *Hulk* because we got a lot of mail.

JM: So if *Spider-Man* then didn't succeed, you would just go on to something else?

SL: Oh sure, if *Spider-Man* hadn't sold, we'd have forgotten about it. To us they were just scripts. We were making them up, and we'd hope they'd sell, and some sold better than others, so those we kept.

JM: You've worked with so many people. I was going through a list of names of people like Bill Everett, Russ Heath, Joe Maneely . . . name after name after name. What did you walk away with from these folks? What did you learn from these people?

SL: I don't know . . . they were all guys at work. They were all incredibly talented. They were . . . each of them had a totally different personality. I enjoyed working with them. I didn't learn anything.

JM: No?

SL: Any more than you learn from everyone you know. I'm probably learning things from you about the human condition. I didn't go home at night and say, "Gee, I just learned so and so from Bill Everett."

JM: Any creative influences from them, however?

SL: Gee, I don't know how to answer that. Each one of them drew in a totally different style, and when I wrote for them, I would try to tailor what I was writing to what best suited their style. Like I guess if you are writing a screenplay for one actor, you'd write it a little differently than if it's for another actor.

JM: And that's the reason you moved to Ditko from Kirby on *Spider-Man*.

SL: Oh, Kirby did it all wrong. What he did was good, but it wasn't what I wanted.

JM: You mentioned how it was just a business and the need to put food on the table. During the fifties, there were so many different genres that you were writing in, but now it all seems to be superheroes.

SL: Nothing I can do about it.

JM: What was the change?

SL: It's very simple. The publishers found out that readers couldn't get enough of superheroes. It's like anything else. It's a business. When automobile manufacturers suddenly realized that everybody wanted to buy SUVs, suddenly a few years ago they became the biggest sellers. Now, if superheroes stop selling, then you'd find something else. It's always about what the public is buying.

JM: But during the time, you were writing *Millie the Model*, Westerns.
SL: They were selling very well at the time.

JM: Why were people so interested in different things, but now it's just one?
SL: You'd have to ask every one of the people in the world.

JM: Nothing changed?
SL: Trends would change. There would be a couple of years when Westerns were the big sellers, then suddenly everybody seemed to want the *Millie the Model* type, then horror stories, then romance books, then mystery, crime. I mean we just followed the trends and gave people what they wanted. For example, when I was a kid in New York, one day all the kids in the area would be on roller skates. It would be roller skate season. Then a couple weeks later, people were playing touch football. Now, why? There was no signal: "all right stop." And after a while they'd be playing marbles. I didn't know why, but people get bored.

JM: Wow, we're getting through a lot.
SL: Good, good, I'm glad you came down. See what I put up with, Gill? (*Stan is giving me a light-hearted ribbing.*) You think it's easy being an Icon?

JM: It isn't easy being an Icon.
SL: (*quietly and very reflectively*) It truly isn't.

JM: There's a lot put on your shoulders.
SL: And don't forget I have to act "iconish" all the time, so that the public isn't disappointed. (*quickly recovers and adds*) That's why every minute of the day I have to be totally magnificent. (*He chuckles.*)

JM: So the creative process . . . you're coming up with a character or a series. You know there's a trend out there or you want to capitalize on something . . . walk me through the process. Do you sit down and say, I'm going to have a male character who works at a bakery . . . ?
SL: You know, I think really the first thing you think to yourself is, what are they not publishing now? What kind of character doesn't exist now? And that's very hard. And Gill and I have the same problem now in the movies. We want to do a comedy or a mystery or whatever the hell. Well, what can we do that is different from what is out there, and yet is close enough to the ones that were successful so we know will appeal to the same audience? And it's just a matter of thinking, and some people

are better at it than others. And I'm pretty good at it. It's just like some
people playing piano better than others or whatever. It's hard work. You
have to sit by yourself and think, and you write something down and,
"Hell, that's no good," or "Oh, I think this . . . oh no, it's been done
before" . . . And finally you jot something down and say, "Hey, I don't
think it's been done before." So that's one thing—you want to make
sure it was never done before. And second, you yourself have to like it,
and then you have to say, will anyone else want to see it? And if you
feel it hasn't been done before and you like it and you think other
people will like it, then you got it. And I don't know any better way to
explain it.

JM: You sort of go through the litany of names or concepts?
SL: Sometimes I come up with something on the basis of a name. You
have a name that you think is great. You get the name, then you say,
"Oh, what can I write that would be applicable to the name." That's
happened to me a lot. Names are important. It has to be something that
grabs somebody.

JM: So you get the name and ask, what sort of thing would this person
do with that kind of name?
SL: Then you say, what trait will I give this character that will make him
interesting? You have friends, or you know a lot of people?

JM: I have friends. (*We all laugh.*)
SL: No, what I mean is, a friend is someone who will always interest you.
I mean there's some people that don't interest you. I mean if you are
stuck with people for dinner and you think, "Oh Christ, I have to be
with him." When you create characters for a story, you create a character that people are interested in, that they'd want to read about. He has
to have some kind of personality that will grab the reader, whether he's
very evil; he's very excitable; whether he's got a great sense of humor;
whether he's got a lot of problems and you want to know what caused
them and how he'll solve them; whether he is psychopathic; whether he
is schizophrenic; whether he is talkative; whether he is sullen . . . You
have to decide who is the character and is there something about him
interesting enough that somebody wants to read his story and not someone else's.

   (We turn down a dead end street while I'm turning over pages of
notes.)

SL: I like how you are turning all those pages over! (*He and Gill are figuring out which way to go.*) Hey, how about Mr. Silent over here!

JM: I'm keeping silent so you can figure out where you are going.
SL: Oh, I can talk and get lost at the same time. Why am I stopping when there's no stop sign? How do you get to Carnegie Hall?

JM: Okay.
SL: Go.

JM: A little bit of history here.
SL: Oh, I'm not good at that. I have no memory.

JM: What was the time like in the thirties in forties?
SL: I was in my teens!

JM: You are young and innocent . . . getting coffee for Joe Simon . . .
SL: That was 1939.

JM: It was known as the Golden Age.
SL: Oh, this shit about the Golden Age, the Silver. I don't know what is what. People give them names. I started out as an assistant. By assistant, I filled their ink wells; I went down and got the coffee. I also did proofreading for them, and I guess I was pretty good at it. It's all in my biography, you know all that.

JM: You were mentioning earlier about picking up relevant things and putting them in the books, like World War II.
SL: Well, you could hardly avoid it.

JM: Did you have the same thing in the fifties, sixties, and seventies?
SL: Oh, I don't know.

JM: I mean you had the Korean War, Vietnam War, social unrest.
SL: We mentioned them. Those things would crop up occasionally. Not much. Really mostly in the war stories. I don't remember what years, but there was a time I was doing a lot of war stories. We had *Combat Kelly*, *Combat Casey*, *Battlefield*, *Battleground*, and names like that. War stories, battle stories, a whole bunch of them.

JM: There was a lot of political unrest on campus.
SL: Uh huh.

JM: Did you do stories . . . ?

SL: Yeah, we did some stories that dealt with campus unrest, but we didn't go overboard.

JM: With all the legends you've worked with, can you pick out key traits and say that this guy was a great this, this guy was a great that . . .

SL: Russ Heath was a great ladies man. He had a lot of kids I remember. I loved his work in black and white.

Bill Everett was very imaginative, very creative. His work was very stylized.

Joe Maneely was probably the fastest artist I ever worked with, and one of the most versatile. It was just tragic that he died so young. I think he would have been one of the legends of comics. Who else is there?

JM: You did the *Spider-Man* strip with John Romita.

SL: Romita was wonderful. I could give him any script at all and he would do it magnificently. He was the greatest all around—excellent, dependable. He was one of the best artists in the business. He could do anything. He drew beautiful girls, as did Russ Heath.

JM: What about your brother?

SL: My brother [Larry Lieber] was very good. The only problem with him is that he was such a perfectionist that he drew slower than he should have. He didn't have to because he could draw fast, but he was never satisfied with what he did, so he did it over and over. He also wrote, but he spent most of his time drawing.

JM: John Severin?

SL: Oh, Severin was great! He had a style all his own. It was almost an old-fashioned style. His thing was accuracy. If he drew a man riding a horse, you could see every bit of leather on that saddle, and you could feel the spurs. He was just great. A wonderful inker and wonderful penciller. And great detail . . . a great pen and ink artist.

JM: Gene Colan?

SL: Gene drew like a movie director. He was very into motion pictures, and he loved posing every panel as if it were a scene in a movie. And he was also incredibly stylized. You couldn't mistake his artwork for anybody. Gene was one of the best. Very, very cinematic.

JM: Dick Ayers?

SL: Dick Ayers was a guy you could always call on when you were in a jam. He could draw anything, and he loved doing it. He loved what he did. He was an inker, a penciller, he could letter if he had to. He was just a joy to work with.

JM: Gil Kane?
SL: Gil Kane was also an incredibly talented guy. He had a style all his own. And no matter what script he drew, you knew it was Gil Kane's artwork. He was fast, and he was great at the superhero stuff.

JM: Marie Severin?
SL: Marie Severin was great. She was good at adventure stuff. I think she was even better at humor things. She was a wonderful cartoonist. And she was also a great colorist. She was a tremendous asset to the company.

JM: Syd Shores?
SL: Syd was a fabulous inker. He inked a lot of Jack Kirby's work in the beginning. And then he himself drew *Captain America*, and he drew a very powerful, beautiful *Captain America* script. His work was always just slightly stiffer than some of the others; Jack's was much looser and more explosive. But Syd drew a beautiful, clear, sharp script.

JM: Al Hartley?
SL: Al Hartley drew beautiful females. I gave him the *Patsy Walker* strip to do for a long time. And he did a great job. He even did a newspaper script for me, maybe *Mrs. Lyon Cub*, for a short time. I think he preferred teenage-type things. He was very good at it.

JM: The fifties with the *Seduction of the Innocent* . . . while you were "seducing the innocent," how did that affect you and the industry?
SL: Well, that book affected the whole business. It almost put EC out of business. They dropped all their horror books. It didn't affect us that much because the one thing the censorship board was against was sex and violence, and we didn't have much sex and violence in our books. But it affected the whole industry because this guy Dr. Wertham, who started it all, made the average person who didn't know anything about comics but who read his quotations, made the average person say, "I don't want my kids reading comics." Wertham was blaming them for everything from child pornography to murder. The industry was hurt.

JM: With great power . . .
SL: Comes great responsibility.

JM: Here's an example of someone trying to do good from his own perspective, but it has all these negative consequences.
SL: You're right. You're right.

Hey, one thing about Wertham that people don't know—he was a good writer. When I was fourteen, I had read a book of his. I don't remember the name now [It's *Dark Legend*], but it was a case history about a boy who murdered his mother. I don't know why I read it, where I got it from, but it was a good, well-written book, and I thought, gee, this guy is smart and a good writer, and he later became the fanatic who was ranting against comics. I almost felt hurt, disappointed that this guy that I had I respected would be the kind of guy he turned out to be.
JM: What ever happened to him?
SL: He died at some point. I have no idea.

JM: Sales plummeted?
SL: Yeah, but eventually they leveled off. The whole business has its ups and downs.

JM: In the sixties it's much more open. Older readers are really getting into *Dr. Strange* . . .
SL: Oh, I forgot about Dr. Strange.

JM: . . . And people ask how you came up with those incantations and why don't they work for them.
SL: You know those incantations were funny. I can't tell you how many college lectures I did when the kids would say, "We've been studying your incantations, and obviously you've based them on old druidic legends or Stonehenge." But I just made them up. I liked the sound of them.

JM: And then when did you move into the overseeing role? In the seventies?
SL: I became the publisher at some point, and that's when I started really traveling around. I wasn't doing much writing, and I don't remember what the hell I was doing. (*laughs*)

JM: How was the climate then? Fun?
SL: Oh, it was always fun, I enjoyed everything I did all the time. I enjoyed it when I was writing the books. I enjoyed it when I was editing them. I loved to travel in those days. I went all over the country, in fact all over the world. I went to Japan, Italy, I went to Scandinavia. Always talking about Marvel.

Stan and Gill run up to the offices at ABC and are back down in less than fifteen minutes after a successful meeting.

SL: I had to explain to them [the folks at ABC] that my voice was hoarse because of this Canadian. (*We all chuckle.*)

We get back into Stan's car and head back to Beverly Hills. I only have a couple of questions left from my long list.

JM: Are there any misunderstandings or misconceptions that you'd like to clear up, that people have written or said about you over the years?

SL: I would like to confuse the public by saying that everything that has ever been said about me is absolutely true. And since people have said different things, let them wonder, "What are we to make of that?"

JM: Last question. If you could ask yourself a question that no one has asked, what would it be?

SL: I wouldn't. I don't go around asking myself questions. It's bad enough having to answer other people's questions. No, seriously. There's nothing really I want anybody to know about me particularly. I don't really spend much time thinking about what others know about me. I do my work. I like people. I like being with them. And that's it. I don't know how any human being on earth could possibly have a bad thought about me, because I think I'm wonderful. I may have mentioned that I really am my biggest fan! (*laughing*) If only there were more of me, what a wonderful world it would be . . . You gotta say, "said with a laugh," because when I've said something jokingly, it comes out bad in print. I mean, when you read, "Stan Lee said he was his biggest fan," you wonder, "Who is this swelled-headed son of a bitch?" (*He says jokingly.*)

God Woke:
A Poem

STAN LEE

Written ca. 1970. Previously unpublished.
Printed by permission of Stan Lee.

God woke.
He stretched and yawned and looked around
Haunted by a thought unfound
A vagrant thought that would not die.

He rose and scanned the endless sky
He probed the is
He traced the was
He searched the yet to be.

And then He found the planet Earth
The half remembered planet Earth
Steeped in pain and tragedy.

And all at once He knew.

He saw the world that He had wrought
To suit His master plan.
And then He saw the changes brought
By the heedless hand of man.

Man,
So frail, so small
Yet lord of all.
Striving, writhing
Hustling, bustling
Sowing, growing
Ever going
Ever yearning
Ever learning
        Never knowing.

Less than righteous
Less than just
And in the end
Condemned to dust.

He heard the man sounds everywhere
The shots, the clangs, the roars, the bangs
The endless clammer, guns and hammer.
And then He found, to His despair
The haunting, hollow sound of
        Prayer.

A billion bodies ever bending
A billion voices never ending.
Give me, get me, grant me, let me, love me, free me, hear me, see me.

While He pondered, watched and waited
Endlessly they supplicated.
Chanting, ranting, moaning, groaning,
Sighing, crying, cheating, lying.
But towards what goal?
What grand direction, this pious tide of genuflection?
To please their Lord?
To please their God?
He raised His head and laughed
        Laughed hard.

See man, the enigma, calling for aid
Ever demanding, ever afraid.
Man, the enigma, bewailing his fate
Yet plagued by inaction 'til ever too late.
Paradoxical man, so fearful of death
Yet squandering life and lavishing breath
Wasting his hours
Diluting his days
Accomplishing nothing
While he prays and he prays.

Hypocritical man, pompous and preening
Mouthing his rote just from the throat
Words without feeling, sounds without meaning.

Such arrogance
Such gross conceit
To think oneself somehow elite
To demand each prayer be heard with care
While painfully, vainfully, all unaware
One's omnipotent, infinite, absolute Lord
        Is bored.

God frowned.
How dare they believe that the Way and the Light
Can be constantly badgered from morning till night?
By what senseless standard, by what senseless rule
Do they treat their Creator as if He's their tool?
While proclaiming His glory
Do they think Him a fool?

Who else but a fool
With a cosmos to savor
Would be bound just to Earth
Granting boon, granting favor?

Who else but a fool
With a cosmos unfolding
Would linger with man
Ever praising and scolding?

Who else but a fool
With a cosmos to stray in
Would conceive him an anthill
And like a prisoner stay in?

Who else but a fool
Would create mortal man
And then be expected to tend him
Mend him
Cry for him
Die for him
Over and over and over again?

God sighed.

I gave them minds as I recall
It was all so long ago.
I gave them minds that they might use
To choose, to think, to know.
For the hapless weak must need be wise
If they would prove their worth.
And then I gave them paradise
The fertile, verdant Earth.

At first I found the plan was sound
And somewhat entertaining.
But once begun, the deed now done,
My interest starting waning.

The seed thus sown
The twig now grown
I left them there
Alone.

Alone
Among the planets and the stars
And the endless, fathomless all
Alone
Bathed by light and clothed by dark,
'Midst the vague and the vast and the small.
Alone
Alone as I have ever been

As I shall ever be.
Why do they not accept it?
How else can they be free?
Why do they not accept it?
Why do they search
        For me?

Why?
When their own little lives are so barren and brief.
When all of their pleasures are tarnished by grief.
In the space of a heartbeat
Their present is past.
They cling to each moment
Though no moment can last.
When the end comes so quickly
And they soon are forgot
Why do they seek
For that which is not?

Like unto children lost in the night
They search for a God to guide them.
Like unto children huddled in fright
They must have their God beside them.
But what sort of children
From cradle to grave
Would grant Him obeisance
Yet make Him their slave?

They have conjured a heaven
And there He must stay.
Ever responsive, be it night, be it day.
He must love them
Forgive them
Comply when they pray
Ever attentive
Never to stray.

And
Like unto children
In their childish zeal
They worship their dream

Thinking fantasy real.
God pondered.

He
The Be All, the End All
The Will and the Way
The Power, the Glory
The Night and the Day
The Word and the Law
The Fount and the Plan.
Lord God Almighty
Was baffled by man.

He was puzzled by the paradox
The irony within.
If only He could show them
But where would He begin?
How to make them understand?
How to make them see?
How to make them recognize
Their own insanity?

They live for gain
And strive in vain
To circumvent their death.
But all their gold
And wealth untold
Won't buy an extra breath.

They bestow acclaim
And shower fame
On those who rise to power.
But those who care
Who love and share
Are forgot within the hour.

They're prone to fight
To use their might
For whatever flag they cherish.
But those who cry "To arms!" don't die.
Their young are sent to perish.

Yes,
All unsung
They kill their young
Who fall and die
And then they cry.
But why?

A different house of worship
A different color skin
A piece of land that's coveted
And the drums of war begin.

Only death can triumph
There's no place left to hide.
Yet, still the madmen ply their trade
Certain God is on their side.

Of all who live
Who crawl and creep
Who take and give
Who wake and sleep
Who run, who stand
Who dot the land
From shore to shore
Man, only man
None but man
    Wages war.

Only man
Eternally killing
Only man
Infernally willing
To concede himself grace
To bury his race.

Only man
Earnestly praying
And piously saying
As the battles increase
He does what he must
For his motives are just.
The mayhem, the carnage, the slaughter won't cease

But no need to worry, God's in his corner
He's killing for peace.

Man!
His greed, his hate, his crime, his war
The Lord our God could bear no more.

He looked His last at man so small
So lately risen, so soon to fall.

He looked His last and had to know
Whose fault this anguish, this mortal woe?

Had man failed maker, or maker man?
Who was the planner and whose the plan?

He looked his last, then turned aside.
He knew the answer.

That's why
    God cried.

Index

199; as playwright, 122; as president of Marvel, 152, 162; and problems of, 75; as publisher, 64, 65, 71, 157; responding to Kirby's charges, 91, 92, 93; sensing Marvel's success, 89, 90; speaking on colleges, 15, 28; as spokesperson, 208; and starting at Timely, 85, 86; supervising movies, 122; and those who take over his books, 99, 100; at Timely, 122, 123, 135, 137; what entertains him, 183; on why he stopped writing, 100; on why kids like comics, 48; and wife and daughter, 117; and winning writing contest, 85, 86; work on promoting television and movies, 64; and world travel, 217; on writing again, 150; writing at home, 143, 144; writing for believability, 172; and writing like poetry, 51; writing Spider-Man screenplay, 113; writing Spider-Man strips, 126–30; writings, 177; as young editor at Timely, 57, 58, 61
Lee, Stanley R., 111
Leiber, Larry, 127, 139, 140, 187, 215
Leiber, Stanley, 57, 179
Letters: from fans, 72, 73; from parents, 90; to Stan, 191
Lev Gleason Publications, 62
Liebowitz, Jack, 138, and Martin Goodman golf game, 137
Linda Carter, Student Nurse, 161
Linus, 43
List, The, 121
Literacy, 196, 197
Literary criticism, 198, 199
Little Lulu, 19
Loesch, Margaret, 100, 113
Loki, 64, 171
Lovecraft, H. P., 181, 182

Lucas, George, 108, 110
Luck, 79

MacFarlane, Todd, 205
Mad Magazine, 12, 32, 35, 61
Mail: and complaints, 23, 24; and politics, 24; from readers, 18, 19, 23, 24
Mandrake the Magician, 79
Maneely, Joe, 183, 211; Lee's admiration of, 183
Man-Thing, 156
Marvel, 62; beginnings, 134–65; bigger than DC, 208, 209; comics and age of readers, 9, 23, 24; comics similar to movies, 171; competition with DC, 176, 177; and competitors copying, 11, 12; creation of, 131; expansion into movies, 75; influence on movies, 107, 108, 116; and intended audience, 33, 34; lawsuit, 205, 206; and merchandise, 68; method, 123; in mid-sixties, 142–46; moral tone of, 123; as most significant event since 1950, 104; name change, 175, 176; and number of comics sold, 10, 11, 14; office in the sixties, 89; ownership of characters, 205, 206; and power over readers, 18; realism, 63; in seventies, 145–50; style, 138; surpassing DC in sales, 160; as underdog, 89, 177, 208, 209; universe, 171; Writer's Test, 144, 145
Marvel, by Les Daniels, 124
Marvel Age of Comics, 70, 83
Marvel Bullpen page, 67
Marvel Classics Comics animated show, 67
Marvel Girl, 170, 192
Marvel Monsters DVD, 200
Marvel Mystery Comics, 176